A DIVIDED LIFE

A DIVIDED LIFE

A Personal Portrait of the Spy Donald Maclean

ROBERT CECIL

Quill
William Morrow
New York

To Kate
whose memory helped
to unravel the tangle

Library of Congress Cataloging-in-Publication Data

Cecil, Robert, 1913–
A divided life: a personal portrait of the spy Donald Maclean / Robert Cecil.
p. cm.
Bibliography: p.
Includes index.
ISBN 0-688-09431-7
1. Maclean, Donald, 1913–   . 2. Spies—Great Britain—Biography,
3. Spies—Soviet Union—Biography. 4. Espionage, Russian—Great
Britain—History—20th century. I. Title.
UB271.R92M333 1989
327.1′2′0924—dc19   88-38794
                       CIP

Printed in the United States of America

First Quill Edition

1 2 3 4 5 6 7 8 9 10

Contents

List of Illustrations

Acknowledgment of Sources

The *Notes* show where printed sources have been used; thanks are here expressed to the authors and publishers concerned. The extracts from Documents of British Foreign Policy and from various documents held in the Public Record Office are reproduced with the permission of the Controller of Her Majesty's Stationery Office.

Most of those who kindly allowed themselves to be interviewed, or replied to written enquiries, are also listed in the notes. Certain people, for varying, but valid, reasons, did not wish to be named; their testimony is ascribed to 'private information'. In naming names I begin – and not solely out of courtesy – with the ladies. I am much in the debt of Miss Patrica M. Barnes, Head of the Library and Records Department of the Foreign and Commonwealth Office. I am greatly indebted to Mrs Philip Toynbee, who allowed me to read her late husband's Cairo diary. Miss Sheila Kerr (Mrs Mallard) generously gave me access to her careful researches in Washington. I am grateful for valuable help given by Lady Mary Dunn, Lady Grimond, Lady Luce and Lady Robertson. Miss Patricia Reynolds not only undertook typing, but also gave advice on copyright.

Chapter 1 (Gresham's) owes much to Colonel George Judd and Professor Brian Simon, who were Maclean's contemporaries.

Chapter 2 (Cambridge) put me heavily in debt to Mr Valentine Lawford. Mrs Hinton, Librarian at Trinity Hall, found new and interesting traces of Maclean's sojourn there. Insights into his undergraduate years were also provided by Professor Lionel Elvin and Mr Jack Roach.

Chapters 3 – 9 (diplomatic career) could not have been written without the kind cooperation of many former colleagues in diplomacy, among whom I wish specially to mention Sir Roderick Barclay, Mr Walter Bell, the late Sir Thomas Bromley, Mr George Carey-Foster,

Sir John Curle, Sir Frederick Everson, the late Mr David Footman, Mr Michael Hammond-Maude, the late Sir Geoffrey Jackson, Mr Valentine Lawford, Sir Fitzroy Maclean, Sir Frederick Mason, Sir Lees Mayall, Sir George Middleton, Sir Patrick Reilly, the late Sir David Scott-Fox and Sir Evelyn Shuckburgh. I derived benefit from discussion with Lord Sherfield, though I am aware that he disagrees with certain of my conclusions. Mr Robert Kee and Mr Ralph Izzard also proved very helpful. I had several talks with the late Professor Anthony Blunt. It cannot be easy to evaluate the evidence of a practised deceiver; I have taken him at his word where it fits the facts and/or is corroborated by another source.

In Chapters 10 and 11 (the Moscow years) I relied largely on the testimony of visitors and transients, such as the Reverend Robin Denniston, Mr Nigel Burgess, Mr Mark Frankland, Dr Dennis Ogden and Mr Sam Russell. The final pages owe a great deal to the Reverend Oscar Muspratt, Vicar of Penn.

To anyone who considers that his or her help has not been acknowledged I express my apologies.

Foreword

Donald Maclean was nearly four years older than I, which for a boy is a chasm; and when I went up to Cambridge it was already a year since he had gone down. I cannot recollect ever meeting him, but I probably did because at the age of five or six I used to be taken to children's parties at the Macleans'. Our great friends the Clives were almost their next door neighbours. That had its hazards. On one occasion Lady Maclean confided in Hilda Clive that her doctor had recommended her to gargle with port to relieve the tightness in her throat. What was she to do since her household was teetotal? 'Port?' said Hilda Clive, 'I'll fetch you some at once from our cellar.' Horace Clive was not pleased to learn that evening that Lady Maclean was swilling round her tonsils and expectorating the contents of a bottle of his prized Dow '08. But I'm sure the orange squash flowed at the children's parties.

The story of the Cambridge spies is still a lively footnote in the history of the inter-war generation. Why did these well-born young men become Soviet agents? Who recruited them, why did they so hate their class and despair of their country? The story turned into a long-running inquest upon the culture and morality of their generation that the coroner kept on adjourning as spy after spy fell out of his cupboard. Nor is this surprising. As each was exposed the explanations and excuses offered for their conduct became more and more ingenious; and perhaps it is worth while examining them.

That teetotal house provides the first clue to Donald Maclean's character. The high-minded often breed children who rebel against their parents' beliefs, but in their rebellion you can see the same character and temperament at work. Many Victorian free-thinkers were the children of devout evangelical parents; but though they rejected God, they were as strict as their elders in upholding the same

moral principles. Their children in turn rejected those moral
principles, the ethos of the patriarchal family and its sexual code; but
they retained the same hostility to worldliness and the same determination to find personal salvation in communion with a group of
intimate friends. In just such a way the sons of Liberal Party
dignitaries considered their fathers' politics to be a string of hypocritical equivocations. In what sense, they asked, were regurgitations
of the principles of free trade and the League of Nations relevant
to Hitler and unemployment? Yet Donald Maclean also inherited
the austerity, the puritanism, the anti-Establishment, non-conformist
conscience that governed his father in his youth. These attributes
drove him into the arms of the Communist Party. The party yes; but
why into the arms of the Comintern? Others brought up as Liberals,
like Stephen Spender, became communists for a few months and then
recoiled, appalled by their experience. Others, like Brian Simon,
remained attached to the party all their lives but they did not become
Soviet agents. There was nothing in Maclean's background to justify
his decision to become a spy; and it says something for the strength of
his upbringing that he was the only one of the six main spies who
found the actual practice of deception and concealment distasteful.

   The most common excuse for the spies is that they were victims of
the thirties and that they only went a stage further than the mass of
their intelligent contemporaries were willing to go. Victor Kiernan, a
veteran communist, has argued that the thirties justified any action.
The left were then fighting 'absolute evil'. How should the young
communists of those days not believe their cause was 'absolute good'
even if 'painful experience showed that the second of [these beliefs]
was in part illusion?' Loyalty to the dying past was as archaic as
drawing-room table manners. In fact, it was the unemployment of the
early thirties not Hitler that drove some of the young to communism.
The Jarrow Marchers were the symbol of the unemployed. For
though some areas such as the Midlands, or cities such as Leicester,
were hardly affected, those in the black areas who were out of work
lived on minimal relief, harshly administered. Europe had known
booms and slumps before now, but the collapse of currencies and
business across the Continent, and still more in the citadel of capitalist
America, demanded an explanation. The explanation was at hand. 'I
began,' wrote Koestler,

   'to read Marx, Engels and Lenin in earnest. By the time I had
   finished ... something had clicked in my brain which shook me

like a mental explosion. To say that one 'had seen the light' is a poor description of the mental rapture which only the convert knows . . . The new light seems to pour in all directions across the skull: the whole universe falls into pattern like the stray pieces of a jig-saw puzzle assembled by magic at one stroke. There is an answer to every question: doubts and conflicts are a matter of the tortured past.'

Marxism explained so much that outraged the young: imperialism, the class struggle. Like the priest of Nemi, it fulfilled the wish of every generation to kill its predecessor. Above all it explained the rise of Hitler and the fascist state; and it was in Spain in particular that the image of 'absolute good' fighting 'absolute evil' took its most poignant shape. The young intellectuals did not see that war as the culmination of a century and a half of civil strife. They ignored the mortal weakness of the Spanish government as the nation splintered and chunks of the left, as well as the right, fell away and rejected the government's authority. But no one can have a glimmering of the feelings of the intelligentsia who does not recognise how the Spanish Civil War obsessed them. As the plight of the Republic became more desperate they became convinced that Chamberlain's and Eden's indifference to German and Italian intervention were part of a plot to sell the pass in Europe as it had been sold in Ethiopia. Thus it came about that for the spell-binders of the Left – Laski, Kingsley Martin, Low, Michael Foot, Bevan – the wickedness of the British capitalist government was more to be feared than Hitler. Rearm and the arms would be used to shoot trade-unionists organising the great general strike that was to stop the Tories waging a war of aggression against the anti-fascist front. Even Orwell, disillusioned on his return from Spain, opposed rearmament. Looking back on his feelings as a school-boy Richard Wollheim defended his practice of holding at the time two conflicting principles – opposition to Hitler and opposition to rearmament. He explained that:

'Communism was an indispensable ally in the fight against fascism. It gave the fight authenticity. I did not think myself as prepared to join up until the German invasion forced Russia into the war. Then it gradually gained authenticity for me.'

Authenticity is a shady customer. For a state of affairs to be 'authentic' it must correspond to what life *ought* to be like. When reality did not match your picture book illustration of the world you withheld your approval. As a result the Popular Front sank deeper into self-deception because the alternative was, as Kiernan came to admit, 'too painful'. When Anthony Blunt excused himself on the grounds that 'almost all the intelligent and bright young under-graduates had become Marxist under the impact of Hitler coming into power', he wanted to assure his audience that no one of any merit could have thought differently from the way he did. In fact there were large numbers of intelligent and bright young men who refused to get themselves into the bind of arguing that Hitler must be resisted by force but on no account must Britain rearm. Nor did they believe in the Zinoviev trials and the grotesque confessions of the guilty. It struck them that Gide's repudiation of Stalin's regime was more convincing than the endorsement of it by Shaw and the Webbs. Nor did most intelligent students think Stalin's regime represented 'absolute good'. Still less did they consider transferring their allegiance to it as did the spies. The communists did all they could to discredit the Labour Party, but some of the intelligent believed Bevin and Dalton were right while others, however much they distrusted Chamberlain, did not doubt that the British worm would in the end turn.

The spies saw the thirties through the lens of ideology, not through experience. When Blunt was being interrogated by Peter Wright he told him that he did not understand the thirties. Wright replied that he understood them only too well. That was when his father, sacked from the Marconi Company, took his son away from school, unable to pay the fees, and took to the bottle. Wright did not think this gave him the justification to sign up with a foreign power and take orders from its agents.

The spies, said Kiernan, did what their consciences told them to do and they should be honoured. Such a primitive view of ethics could be used to justify almost any iniquity. The state of politics was dispiriting but not desperate. The euphoria of Munich was over in a day. After the rape of Czechoslovakia the young were convinced that war would come. The Nazi-Soviet Pact, the partition of Poland and the grovel-ling volte-face of communist parties throughout Europe removed the last remnant of an excuse for remaining an agent of the Comintern. Even if one stretches charity far and allows that an ardent young communist, convinced that Conservative governments would always kow-tow to fascism, could be excused for making the dramatic gesture of becoming a Comintern agent; and even if one understands how he might fall for the flattery that Stalin himself saw his reports and had him in mind, there was no reason in the summer of 1940 to lose faith in the government. None of Churchill's countrymen doubted his resolve to fight Hitler and Mussolini. The Nazi-Soviet Pact should have made all the spies reconsider their allegiance as Goronwy Rees did. For after the pact their reports could have been passed from the Soviets to their Nazi allies.

To be young is to be certain what is wrong with the world but to know one is powerless to change it. The Cambridge spies were not satisfied with marching in demos and proselytising. They wanted action. Among the generation before theirs at Cambridge there had been a number of outstanding scientists who were intrigued by the prospect of power and thought communism gave them their best chance to control and influence their fellow men. Gowland Hopkins wanted a body of scientists to sift scientific papers that gave clues to the solution of social problems; Ritchie Calder wanted the House of Lords replaced by a senate of scientists; Frederick Soddy wanted scientists to replace politicians; Julian Huxley wanted a central planning council to replace Parliament; Joseph Needham and C. H. Waddington predicted the next stage of evolution would be the collectivist state. Most influential of all was 'Sage' Bernal who declared that scientists must become the rulers of the world: but for that to happen a communist revolution was necessary. Nothing in Orwell's imagination matched the horror of Bernal's utopia. It was Bertrand Russell who said that the intellectuals of the Left became besotted by the idea of power and for that reason admired Soviet Russia where it was so conspicuously wielded.

There was, however, a more sophisticated defence of the spies and it was made by the most internationally famous novelist of their generation. Graham Greene was a virtuoso composer of variations on the theme of betrayal. He exonerated his old friend Philby by comparing him to one of those heroic Jesuit priests who returned from their seminary on the Continent to subvert the England of Elizabeth I. He went even further in a lecture he gave in Hamburg on 'The Virtue of Disloyalty' in which he regaled the students by attacking that bourgeois poet Shakespeare winging his way to a house and a coat of arms at Stratford, a Catholic apostate, the apologist of the existing order, out of tune with all those in his time and in ours who have stood up to protest against Authority. What a contrast Shakespeare was to his fellow poet, the Jesuit Southwell, who died in torment on the scaffold executed for 'disloyalty'! The writer, said Greene, must always stand for the victims and be ready to change sides at the drop of a hat. In our times the writer in the West must be disloyal to capitalism and the writer behind the Iron Curtain must be disloyal to communism.

Graham Greene's theory of disloyalty was developed by the new master of the spy story. John le Carré became the head executive of the corporation he took over from Buchan, Maugham and Dornford Yates. He realised that it was no longer possible to sell the old vehicle in which our men were heroes and their spies were villains. Sandy Arbuthnot, Ashenden and Jonah Mansel were as obsolete as drophead coupés or Hispano-Suizas. There was a souped-up model with a sexy Italian body built by Ian Fleming, but the only thing that designer cared about was knowing that martinis should be stirred not shaken. Le Carré's new model had every gadget: he was a master of the jargon – skip distances, Joes, Gees, nose-cones and burn boxes. How should he not be since he himself had once been a member of the Firm? He wanted his readers to brood on the psychology of the spycatcher, the spy-runner and the spy. All three betrayed each other day in day out as if they were in a circle of the inferno. What then was the moral difference between spying for the Soviets and spying for the West? In his novel le Carré's 'perfect spy', Magnus Pym, betrays everyone he loved. At school an upper-class boy who befriended him to the headmaster; a Czech refugee to the officer of the Firm who had recruited Pym; the officer and the Firm by becoming a spy; his wife and son by running out on them. The East may be worse than the West but not by much.

Brecht used to say, 'The East and the West are both whores. But my whore is pregnant.' In the eighties le Carré epitomised the despair of the intelligentsia about the future. He saw the Firm as the symbol of Britain's decline, a country where 'failed socialism is being replaced by failed capitalism'. The old ruling class that in its incompetence recruited the Cambridge spies and then bungled their arrest was finished; but what was the alternative? On the one hand a party whose leaders spent their time running away from the country's problems, abdicating power to pressure groups and knifing their two best men so that neither should lead the party. On the other a party with a spiv philosophy in which the consumption of goods and money, preferably gained by dubious means, were the ultimate values.

These arguments are not convincing. Graham Greene's pretty little trope about disloyalty rests on the premise that there was not a penny to choose between the culture of totalitarianism and the culture of western democracy. But how can one pretend that these differences do not exist? Somehow the image of Philby as the fearless Jesuit in Elizabethan times seems a bit shop-soiled. Unwise too. One does not have to be Macaulay or Froude or Kingsley to prefer Tudor rule to the gloomy repression of the Inquisition in Philip II's Spain. It was not as if there had once been a communist regime in England as there had been a Catholic church celebrating mass according to the Roman rite. And what is le Carré doing but playing the old philosophical game of claiming that what seems to be true is not true? He is arguing that if the confessions of the old Bolsheviks seemed improbable, all the more reason they were likely to be guilty.

The spies were also defended by those who relied on utilitarian ethics. One professor declared that Blunt's work on art history should be weighed against the 'minor and ultimately irrelevant part of his life'. He was in effect arguing that Blunt's contribution to scholarship and his academic career were so distinguished that their addition to the sum of human happiness was far greater than any diminution of that happiness which his spying could have brought about. But utilitarianism is not an infallible guide. Aristotle was right to perceive that ethics are grounded in character and human nature and derive from actual situations. That is the kind of knowledge which is more likely than calculations about the sum of human happiness to make us behave honourably. Honour was not a virtue that played much part in the moral discourse of the years between the wars. It was one of the words which Paul Fussell identified as debased by the language of the First World War where men died 'honourably' on the fields of Flanders when in fact they died drowning in mud or frothing at the lips, gassed in a crater. Honour was one of the words which Bentham removed from ethics because it threw no light on whether an action was one which would promote individual happiness or the greatest happiness of the greatest number. So the apologists for the spies quoted Sir John Harington's explanation why treason never prospers, 'For if it prosper, none dare call it treason.'

But did not Harington's great contemporary suggest in *Julius Caesar* that honour had to be considered before one betrays one's friends and the State? 'Well, honour is the subject of my story,' said Cassius when he set out to recruit Brutus. He knew that unless he could convince Brutus that it was honourable to kill Caesar he could not win him over. But Mark Antony's irony about the honourable men who killed Caesar rings true. All the conspirators, he said, did what they did in envy of great Caesar, save only Brutus; and Octavius ordered that Brutus' 'bones tonight shall lie,/ Most like a soldier, ordered honourably'. Was there a single one of the Cambridge spies who acted honourably?

Although technically the spies never committed treason as the Soviet Union was never at war with Britain, how do they compare with Roger Casement who did commit treason in the First World War when he ran arms to Ireland to use against the British? Like other Irish patriots, Casement lost faith in Britain's promise to grant Home Rule, and the die-hard defiance by Carson and his associates in the summer of 1914 gave him good cause to doubt it. As an Irish patriot he declared he owed allegiance to Ireland rather than to Britain – even though in international law Ireland then did not exist. Philby and the rest did not have Casement's justification. No part of the Soviet Union languished in British hands. Nor by 1940 could there any longer be doubt about what Stalin's regime was like. Were the iniquities in British life so acute that Philby had to do cruel deeds for Stalin's inhuman secret police?

Men do dishonourable acts but some are acquitted because their character is noble and resplendent. Stauffenberg, Trott and the July 1944 plotters felt their government had betrayed them by standing for hideous ideals and putting those ideals into practice; and therefore their honour demanded that they should break their oath of loyalty to the Reich. Did the Cambridge spies face such a conflict? They may have been as dedicated as the German plotters. But honourable?

Some excused Philby on the grounds that as a professional he could hardly be blamed for betraying would-be Soviet defectors. That was part of his business. Yet he not only sent Soviet defectors to their death but anyone in Europe who had worked for the British during the war against Hitler. The railwaymen in Hungary and Romania who had reported the train-loads of German troops on the move to Greece were marked down by Philby as capitalist agents and were liquidated after the war. Blunt too had blood on his hands. The don who excused his spying as a 'minor and irrelevant part of his life' had a curious standard of irrelevance. Blunt informed his Soviet control of the existence of a British agent in Moscow who provided M16 with Politburo documents. The man disappeared. And in the course of his surveillance of diplomatic bags Blunt passed on to the Soviet Union information about agents and other individuals hostile to communism.

Philby admitted no duties to his wives, his women or his colleagues. He regarded them as walk-on parts in the drama he was playing. After he fled to Moscow he took Melinda Maclean away from her husband; and then realising that advancement in the KGB would be more likely to come if he married a Soviet citizen, he ditched her. Donald Maclean brought sorrow to his friends, disaster to his family. Robert Cecil has wise words to say about another casualty in his breach of official life. He diminished that sense of total trust in each other that members of the Diplomatic Service used to have and which the Soviet Service, under surveillance by the KGB with its diplomats always in fear of denunciation, so markedly lacked. Today incredulous journalists pillory the naivety of the Foreign Office for not suspecting Maclean whose erratic conduct off-duty was disgraceful. In those days it was unthinkable that an Esterhazy could exist within the Service. No longer.

There was one last excuse that Blunt used when Goronwy Rees told him he was going to denounce Burgess to MI5. Blunt quoted E. M. Forster's aphorism that faced between a choice of betraying his country and betraying his friend he hoped he would have the guts to betray his country. Rees had replied that the antithesis was false – one's country was a dense network of individual and social relationships in which loyalty to one particular person formed only a single strand. It was a put-down both of Blunt and Forster. Justified too. Forster had gone on to say, 'Love and loyalty to an individual can run counter to the claims of the State. When they do – down with the State, say I, which means that the State would down me.' But what State? The State to which he had just given two cheers because it was a democracy? To the England, the countryside which he loved, to its ordinary, irreverent, independent citizens? Everyone who reads Forster's essay can see what he detested: States where the supporters of the regime wore brown, black or red shirts. But what of the States where they did not?

Maclean and Burgess, Philby and Blunt, were loyal to each other. Blunt cleared evidence incriminating Philby from Guy Burgess' flat. But what of his other friends? He and Burgess never stopped saying how much friendship meant to them and how devoted they were to their friends. Victor Rothschild said that when MI5 told him of Blunt's guilt he could hardly believe that someone he had admired as much for his moral principles as for his intellect had been a Soviet agent: 'You never get over a blow of that sort.' Ill-judged as Forster's aphorism was, it is clear what he meant. He prefaced it by writing:

'Personal relations are despised today . . . and we are urged to get rid of them and to dedicate ourselves to some movement or cause instead. I hate the idea of causes.'

The Cambridge spies betrayed their friends as effectively as their country. They believed in a cause. Love of one's country is not a cause.

Noel Annan

At last the secret is out, as it always must come in the end,
The delicious story is ripe to tell to the intimate friend;
Over the tea-cups and in the square the tongue has its desire;
Still waters run deep, my dear, there's never smoke without fire.

Behind the corpse in the reservoir, behind the ghost on the links,
Behind the lady who dances and the man who madly drinks,
Under the look of fatigue, the attack of migraine and the sigh
There is always another story, there is more than meets the eye.

W. H. Auden: *Collected Shorter Poems*
(1930–44), Faber, 1950

Prologue

On the evening of Tuesday, 29th May 1951 I was returning to London after taking a week's leave in France from my post as assistant in the American Department of the Foreign Office. I had been staying in Barbizon with an American friend who drove me to Orly Airport. On the approach roads, cars were being stopped by the French police who were making a quick check of the travellers' identities. Little did I guess that one of the men for whom the French police, at the request of Scotland Yard, were searching was the head of my Department, Donald Maclean. The other absconder was Guy Burgess, who had recently returned to London under a cloud from the British Embassy in Washington. The two men had left the shores of England for good on the night of Friday, 25th May and were soon behind the Iron Curtain; but this was suspected at first only by the few officials in the Foreign Office, the Security Service (MI5) and the Secret Intelligence Service (MI6), who had seen the evidence that Maclean had been working for Soviet Intelligence (then known as the NKVD) ever since he had entered the Diplomatic Service in 1935.

I was not one of those privy to this secret. When I appeared at my desk next morning I was greatly surprised to be greeted with the exclamation 'Thank God you've turned up anyway!' It was explained to me that on Monday, Donald's American-born wife, Melinda, had telephoned to enquire whether her husband was at work, since he had gone to Paris for the weekend with a friend and had not reappeared. Silence about his disappearance was enforced on everyone. When I learned the friend had been Burgess, a heavy drinker and notorious homosexual, I assumed that the pair had gone off on a drunken spree, had perhaps accosted a burly French sailor and had been dumped unceremoniously in the Seine, where their bodies would no doubt be fished out in time. The case, unfortunately, was to prove a good deal more complex; it was to shake the Foreign Office and the intelligence community to their foundations and cast a long shadow over Anglo-American relations. It is because of these important repercussions that the story, which has been related more than once by those who played no part in it, deserves to be retold by one who knew most of the participants and himself had a share in some of the events narrated.

After the news of Maclean's disappearance had become public knowledge, I received at the Foreign Office a visit from Señor Leguizamon, the Argentine Minister-Counsellor, who explained, with slight embarrassment, that on the afternoon of 25th May – the day of the flight – he had called on Maclean and made an oral communication concerning the current Anglo-Argentine trade negotiations; he wanted to know whether the substance of his government's communication had been duly noted. After he had gone, I sent for the file. Sure enough, there in Maclean's sloping script, with one or two of the irregularities that latterly had crept into minutes recorded after a late lunch, was a full and accurate account of what Señor Leguizamon had told him on the afternoon of the day on which, after a lunch celebrating his thirty-eighth birthday, he had left the Foreign Office for good, abandoning both his overt career and his covert work for the Kremlin.

At that time I did not know for sure that Maclean would never return, though I suspected it. Later, thinking over this episode, it seemed to me that it threw a shaft of light on the character of the missing man. His commitment to Marxism, as we shall see, reflected in certain respects the troubled period in which he grew up and influences exerted on him; but how are we to understand his commitment to his legitimate duties, his service to the country that he betrayed? For he was a spy who, in his own way, gave good service to both his employers. A partial explanation is that, in doing so, he maintained his 'cover' and made sure that the Foreign Office would give him assignments in which the highest grade of intelligence would be accessible to him. This is certainly true; but on the afternoon of 25th May the die was cast; the net was closing and he knew it. Plans had already been laid for him to quit that night, never to return. He had finally closed the option to become 'Sir Donald', like his father. His careful notation on the file could neither redeem his reputation, nor throw the hounds off the scent. No, he made it because he had been trained to do so and his good habits were as ineradicable as his bad. His action, in short, was that of a man whose personality was divided into two compartments; the split had begun early and the duality of his strange career had accentuated it. His whole life reflected the division; after thirty-eight years rooted in Britain, he had gone to spend the last thirty-one years in the USSR. It is this divided life that we shall explore in the pages that follow.

It is to a great extent the complexity of his character that justifies devoting a book to the story of his life. There is no such creature as a stereotyped spy, except, perhaps, in the ranks of the Soviet KGB (as the NKVD is now called). I knew Burgess, Blunt and Philby, as well as Maclean; all were different, not only in personality, but also in the motivation that led them into lives of deceit and betrayal. Donald Maclean, however, was the one I knew best and it is his career that has continued to haunt me.

In August 1969, I recorded in my diary:

'I had a dream the other night about the Embassy in Washington in the late 1940s. There was no reconstruction of the scene in my mind, but I was consorting, within some institutional framework, with Jock Balfour and Donald Maclean, so Washington it must have been. The atmosphere, as in all my Foreign Service dreams, was oppressive, in the sense that there was a load that I was trying to sustain ... In my dream I was discussing with Donald what one hoped for from life. I said I hoped for reasonable contentment and to give satisfaction in my work. What more?

'"Oh!" he said, "I want happiness and success."'

This reply, when I awoke, struck me as absurd, conforming to the theory that in dreams reality is reversed, like writing held up to a mirror; for the career of a spy can hardly lead to happiness and even success tends to be precarious and mostly short-lived.

On second thoughts, I realised that it all depends on what one understands by happiness and success. For ordinary mortals, these words have mainly subjective meanings; thus happiness is a state of mind, often linked with physical well-being and harmonious partnership with another person. But for a serious Marxist – and Maclean was never less than that – it must be otherwise, because ideology keeps interfering, like a film director with a crowd scene, who is less concerned with the individual figures than with the mass effect. For the uncorrupted Marxist, happiness cannot be a subjective state; it must be related to the well-being of the community, understood in materialist terms. For this reason those who pursue the *ignis fatuus* of ideology will often neglect domestic happiness, where it lies ready to hand, in order to engage in desperate schemes for the betterment of mankind. For them, similarly, success must be measured by the degree to which their efforts serve to promote collective happiness, even if their own subjective happiness suffers.

It is this train of thought that has given to Marxism and other millennial creeds their recurrent trend towards puritanism, as ideologues, from Robespierre to Lenin, strove to bring to birth the 'new man', who would sacrifice everything for an abstraction – the vision of an idealised humanity. It is a vision that has brought a special kind of unhappiness to idealists who, in a world of inter-national and ideological confusion and conflict, have tried to pursue their ideal in devious and even despicable ways. Among such men must be numbered some of the ideological spies, like Maclean, who misguidedly believed that the dirt on their hands was cleansed by the innocence of their long-term objective. Another spy, who shared with Maclean much of the illusion and the unhappiness, was Leopold Trepper, the *maestro* of the 'Red Orchestra' who, after his unremit-ting efforts for the USSR in the wartime underworld, was later rewarded with nearly ten years in Soviet prisons and anti-Semitic persecution in post-war Poland. Maclean never fared as badly as that; but he would have read Trepper's lament with a touch of fellow feeling:

> 'I belong to a generation that has been sacrificed by history. The men and women who came to communism in the glow of October, carried along by the great momentum of the rising revolution, certainly did not imagine that fifty years later nothing would be left of Lenin but the body embalmed in Red Square. The revolution has degenerated and we have gone down with it . . . . We wanted to change man, and we have failed. This century has brought forth two monsters, fascism and Stalinism, and our ideal has been engulfed in this apocalypse.'[1]

Maclean was not exposed, either as spy or as exile, to the extremes of harassment and ill-usage that dogged Trepper's steps; but, looking back on his life, he would have recognised a similar struggle to face reality, whilst fending off the cynicism and opportunism that take over when idealism lies in ruins.

Alain Besançon, who teaches Russian history at the Ecole des Hautes Etudes in Paris, has described Soviet ideology in terms that throw light on Maclean's predicament:

'Russian communism in its puristic form is an austere creed; it is against pleasure; it frowns upon desire; it thinks highly of martyrdom and suffering.'[2]

Maclean with his ambivalent attitude towards his stern father and his Presbyterian upbringing, was both repelled and attracted by the discipline implicit in such a creed. Attainment of his ideals required discipline; but he also had bodily needs, connected with sex and alcohol, which were in conflict. This tension exacerbated the split in his personality, of which he had become aware at Cambridge, before the NKVD had come into his life. Soon afterwards, in a spirit of sacrifice and stimulated by the risks involved, he accepted the NKVD's order to go underground. This imposed a severe discipline on him, but his unregenerate nature kept breaking out, putting everything in jeopardy.

There are other reasons for drawing a portrait of Donald Maclean; as an ideological spy, he belongs to a vanishing era. Today, when the USSR is a military superpower but has a third-world domestic economy, it has largely lost the capacity to seduce young men who, because of discontent with their parents, their prospects or some other aspect of their environment, are tempted to believe that one quick dose of revolution will cure all ills and that the Marxist millennium is just round the corner. Today's spies are much more likely to be victims of blackmail or their own greed. It was not so in the 1930s, when Maclean and I were at Cambridge. I was not myself converted to communism, but I could read the minds of those who were impatient with Baldwin's lethargy in the face of the imperative need to tackle unemployment and rearmament. Russia, by contrast, was *terra incognita*, land of mystery and, for some, infinite promise, where dreams would come true and the evils of contemporary society be corrected. If old men insisted that the dawn in the East was a false dawn, that made it all the more likely that young men would run to meet it.

Kim Philby died in Moscow in May 1988 and all the members of the Cambridge Comintern are now dead (George Blake was never a true ideological spy). Since we cannot study this dying breed either in captivity or 'in the wild', the next best course is for the student to put himself in the hands of someone, like the present author, who is a product of the same class and educational system and a former inhabitant of the same diplomatic jungle. If I had been more perceptive, or more suspicious, I should have more to tell and might even have been the cause of shortening Maclean's career in espionage. In that event, however, I should have been less typical of the Service to which, like him, I belonged. Forty years ago an Embassy was the Ambassador's house-party; it was unthinkable that one of the guests could be spying on the others. Ideology, in any case, was only a modish synonym for misplaced zeal; security was a tedious insistence on administrative detail. It was Burgess and Maclean who changed all that. Those who have entangled the story in a web of conspiracy theory have displayed a failure of historical sense; they have simply failed to understand the period and the people. There were shrewder observers than I in positions of greater authority, who were equally slow to grasp what Maclean was at.

Was his wife Melinda, one of those who, until his flight in 1951, remained in ignorance? We do not know and Melinda, who is living in the USA, keeps her secret. Only one writer, who knew her, has tried to tell her story and he was able to take it no further than 1953, when she went to join her husband in Moscow.[3] It has been my aim to fill this gap, for gap it is; there can be no doubt about her importance in Maclean's life, especially during the Cairo–London period (1950–51), irrespective of what she may have known about his 'silent war' (to use Philby's phrase). There is a sense in which her life has been more of a tragedy than his; Donald was sustained to the end by his political beliefs and hopes, while Melinda shared them, if at all, only in a superficial way – she was always a creature of the here and now.

In Moscow Maclean, the betrayer, suffered his own betrayals. His wife betrayed him with Philby and others. But worse, life in the USSR was in itself a betrayal of his ideals, for which he had sacrificed happiness and success. The long stagnation of the Brezhnev era was a challenge to the beliefs that had severed him from his own country and friends. His adopted country, where queues lengthened and labour camps remained full, was rejected by his three children, as they made their homes in the West. In the wider world peace through international negotiations seemed to come no nearer. Because he was no blind fanatic, but a man of intellect, his response to these disappointments was to make contact with dissident elements, who were working in conditions of great difficulty not to overthrow the system, but to reform it. When he died in March 1983, however, nothing had apparently been accomplished. Brezhnev's successor, Andropov, was bearing down on the dissidents harder than ever. What, he must have wondered as he lay dying, had happened to the mythical country of his boyhood, the socialist paradise that had so dazzled him?

When I was a boy, I read an old-fashioned story with the title: *The House with the Golden Windows*. The boy in the story goes for a walk and strays beyond the neighbourhood with which he is familiar. As evening comes on, he emerges from a wood on the edge of a broad valley. Behind him the sun is declining and its rays pick out on the opposite hill-side a splendid mansion, the windows of which gleam like pure gold. 'One day soon', he says to himself, 'I'll go and take a closer look.' He turns back into the wood and heads for home. Years pass; the boy is sent away to school; his parents move house. The day comes, however, when he finds himself in the right part of the country; he has never forgotten the house with the golden windows. This time he emerges from the wood on the crest where the house stands. It seems untenanted, the garden neglected; some of the panes that once shone so brightly lie shattered. It is as if the house that had lived in his memory had never existed.

Is it a true picture to see Donald Maclean standing amidst broken glass and abandoned flower-beds and looking in disillusionment at the once resplendent mansion of his imagination? Probably not; both hope and pride make all of us tenacious of our dreams. There is compelling evidence that he had tried, cautiously but insistently, to mend the damaged window-frames and weed the flower-beds. As he patiently explained to his students the complexity of Western policies, teaching them, or at least some of them, to discard the old rhetoric about 'fascist hyenas' and think in less emotive terms, he may well have nurtured seeds that since his death have blossomed as *glasnost*. We do not yet know how durable *glasnost* may prove to be; some of the flowers may not be hardy perennials; but Maclean would have given them a welcome, believing that he had done what he could to prepare the soil.

1

The Early Years

Cyril Connolly wrote of Maclean and Burgess in the year after their disappearance: 'Politics begin in the nursery . . . . Before we can hurt the fatherland, we must hate the father.'[1] It is a dubious thesis; in any case, as applied to Maclean, it goes much too far; there is no evidence that he hated his distinguished father, Sir Donald Maclean. On the other hand, there can be no doubt that the relationship had an important bearing on the son's development and thus in his conversion to communism and recruitment into Soviet espionage. We must therefore begin, not just in the nursery, but with the father and his background.

According to the psychological writer, Hans Toch, a conditioned person is one who

> 'has learned to impose the beliefs of his parents on his encounters with the world. These beliefs provide structure where there frequently is none, offer certainty where there is ambiguity and predict events which are indeterminable.'[2]

This conditioning effect is all the more powerful where the parent is successful and authoritative, as Sir Donald unquestionably was. Young Donald acquired, as a child, his father's structure of belief and retained his believer's posture after rejecting almost the entire content of what his liberal-minded, Christian parents had held sacred. In his world, which was gravely disordered in comparison with that in which his parents had grown up, he substituted the figure of Karl Marx both for God the father and for his own father, Sir Donald, but at all times he remained at heart a true believer and persisted in this attitude, though with some modifications, even after being exposed for over thirty years to the reality of communism in the USSR. Eric Hoffer has discussed the claim of mass movements that 'the ultimate and absolute truth ... is embodied in their doctrines and that there is no truth nor certitude outside it. The facts on which the true believer bases his conclusions must not be derived from experience or observation but from holy writ.'[3]

For Sir Donald, holy writ was the Bible; for young Donald it became the Communist Manifesto. For him, and for some of his contemporaries at Gresham's School, Holt, there were only books and pamphlets; none of them had direct experience of how, in practice, communism was developing under Stalin. Their belief was grounded in a different soil from that of the Ukraine, where the *kulaks* and their families would soon starve, in order that communism, as conceived by Stalin, should live. Their state of mind is well expressed in a letter written by Michael Straight to his mother, after he had become a communist at Cambridge: 'My actions are based upon my personal needs ... I want to believe.'[4] These needs and this want must be further examined; but first we must sketch in Sir Donald's career.

He may be said to have incorporated most of the middle-class values of his time, which his son so emphatically repudiated. When Sir Donald died in 1932, Stanley Baldwin was one of those who paid eloquent tribute in Parliament to his qualities: 'In Donald Maclean I see a soul as clean as the West wind that blows over Tiree, where he was born.'[5] His hearers were no doubt impressed; not so the biographer, since Sir Donald was not born in Argyllshire, but in Farnworth, near Bolton, in 1864. It was his father, John Maclean, who was born in Tiree and, like so many Scots, came south to seek his fortune. Failing to achieve this in Lancashire, he travelled further and settled first in Haverfordwest and then in Carmarthen, where he manufactured boots and shoes. He did well enough to envisage training his sons, Donald, the elder, and Ewen, as professional men, after they had shown themselves good scholars at Queen Elizabeth Grammar School at Carmarthen. Donald first studied as a solicitor at Llanishen and was then articled to Rowland Brown, a Carmarthen solicitor. For Ewen a medical career was envisaged; he completed his education at Edinburgh University and was so successful as a gynaecologist and obstetrician that he was knighted in 1923 and five years later became President of the British Medical Association.

Donald began to practise law in Cardiff in 1888 and before long formed a partnership with another solicitor, named Handcock. As a Presbyterian, he felt an affinity with Welsh nonconformists, who were anxious to see disestablishment of the Anglican Church in Wales and looked to the Liberal Party to support them. Donald was also an ardent backer of the temperance movement, at a time when reform of the licensing laws was on the Liberals' programme. He was very active in political and commercial life and became secretary of the Cardiff Chamber of Commerce and a staunch Free Trader. His advocacy of all these Liberal causes brought him to the notice of Asquith, who in 1905 was expected by some Liberals to become the next Prime Minister. When in January of the following year the Liberals triumphed at the polls, it was Campbell-Bannerman who formed the government, but Asquith was his Home Secretary and right-hand man. To this rising star Maclean hitched his political wagon.

The election of 1906 brought Maclean into Parliament; he and the historian, G. P. Gooch, displaced two Conservatives in the Bath constituency. Both men were in the forefront of Liberal plans to remodel the universe, to which G. B. Shaw disparagingly applied the German word *Weltverbesserung* (zeal to improve the world). Gooch's chief interest was in foreign affairs, as he campaigned against Turkish oppression of Christians and Armenians in Asia Minor, and opposed importation of indentured Chinese labour into South African mines. Maclean agreed with him, but concentrated more on domestic issues, such as labour exchanges, old-age pensions and National Insurance. His talents were also employed to sustain the party's finances and he was put in charge of funds set aside to keep control over two organs of the press, the *Westminster* and the *Birmingham Gazettes*.

Major changes in his life occurred in 1907. In order to carry out his new parliamentary duties, he took up residence in Seymour Place, near Marylebone Road, and soon became a regular worshipper at the neighbouring Presbyterian Church. He also became a partner in the law firm, Church Rackham & Co. of Lincolns Inn Fields. He kept his Cardiff practice going. It was not until 1911 that payment of Members of Parliament was introduced (a meagre £400 a year), and he needed more money, because he intended to get married. The bride, whom he married in the same year, was Gwendolen Margaret, daughter of Andrew Devitt, a Surrey magistrate living at Oxted. She was his junior by sixteen years. They made a handsome couple: he had a florid complexion and since his late twenties his hair had been white. She was a fine-looking woman with a lively manner; some twelve years later, when Asquith invited them to dinner to meet the Prince of Wales, he described her as 'young and quite good-looking ... with glowing cheeks and glittering eyes'.[6] The evening was a great success.

Maclean's political career had mixed fortunes in 1910, when two elections took place. In the first, he and Gooch were ousted by Conservatives from their seats at Bath. Maclean then moved north to safer Liberal pastures in Scotland, and in the second election won Peebles and Selkirk, a constituency in the heart of the Tennant country, where Margot Asquith was raised; he held the seat till the end of the Great War. He enjoyed reviving his Scottish roots and paid several visits to his fellow Liberal MP, Walter Runciman, on the island of Eigg. In August 1912 he received a summons from the chief of his clan, Colonel Sir Fitzroy Maclean, to attend a gathering at Duart Castle, Isle of Mull. This reminder of his ancestry prompted him in the following year to christen his third son Donald Duart. His diary records on 25th May 1913: 'Baby arrived 2.30 pm.'[7] He soon acquired the nickname 'Teento', a corruption of 'teeny don'. His elder brothers were Ian and Andrew.

In the House of Commons Donald *père* was not regarded as a great orator, but by 1911 had earned repute as a man of sound, objective judgment and a good administrator. In that year he became deputy chairman of committees and continued in that capacity till the end of the war. On the outbreak of war he was made chairman of the Aliens Internment Committee and two years later, when conscription was introduced, chairman of the Appeals Tribunal. In the June Honours of 1917 he was knighted (KBE). This may be regarded as a conciliatory gesture towards one of Asquith's old friends on the part of the new Prime Minister, David Lloyd George, who had taken office in the preceding December. It was not until the famous 'Maurice debate' of May 1918, when Asquith challenged Lloyd George on the issue of Haig's reinforcements, that relations between the two men became irreparable. This personal antagonism led to a split in the Liberal Party in the 'coupon election' of December 1918, in which the Lloyd George Liberals owed their seats in many cases to Conservative tolerance; the 'Wee Free' Liberals, who opposed the coalition, went into the wilderness without their leader, Asquith, who lost his seat. Sir Donald managed to hold his (Peebles and South Midlothian) and became chairman of the parliamentary party. Lord Riddell recorded in April 1919 a conversation between Lloyd George and the leading Conservative, Bonar Law, about the Liberal challenge to the former's leadership. When the Prime Minister remarked that the 'Wee Frees' were 'trying to work up enthusiasm for Donald Maclean', Bonar Law commented, 'He won't fill the bill.'[8] When the coalition dissolved in October 1922, Sir Donald lost his seat in the subsequent election.

During these years the Maclean family had increased; Nancy was born in 1918 and four years later the fourth son, Alan. They had moved to a larger house in Southwick Place on the west side of the Edgware Road. In July 1921 Sir Donald made his will, which was witnessed by his friend Walter Runciman; everything was to go to his wife for her lifetime in trust; she and the testator's brother, Ewen Maclean, were the trustees. There was no independent provision for the children. Sir Donald had no intention of abandoning his political career; reverting to South Wales, he began cultivating the Cardiff East constituency. He was actively, if frustratingly, involved in negotiations designed to give the 'Wee Frees' access to the political fund that Lloyd George had amassed – in the main from the sale of honours. No solution to this problem had been reached before 1924, when Ramsay MacDonald's first Labour government resigned, precipitating an election. Sir Donald, failing to win Cardiff East, looked wistfully across the Bristol Channel to the traditional Liberal heartland of Cornwall. In 1925 he was adopted by the constituency party of North Cornwall and from that time the family began to enjoy holidays at Newquay. He did not re-enter Parliament until 1929.

Seven years in the political wilderness gave him the chance to concentrate on his legal practice and his children's education. One aspect of the Liberal reformism, with which he had identified himself at the turn of the century, had concerned the educational system. It was not only that, as a nonconformist, he had joined in the criticism of Balfour's Education Act of 1902, which had provided finance for Anglican schools; as one of the rising middle-class Liberals, he also had misgivings about the traditional public schools, which had seemed sacrosanct to the party's old-fashioned Whiggish element. To the younger generation of Liberals the legacy of Eton, Harrow and Arnold's Rugby was seriously flawed. The continued emphasis on the classical languages was, in the eyes of the modernists, out of keeping with the times. The elevation of team games to a cult had given rise in traditional schools to a self-constituted aristocracy of athletes, which struck unprejudiced observers as unhealthy. Above all, these observers had their doubts about prevailing moral standards, despite the prevalence of the Anglican clergy on the staff of the public schools.

One of the schools that had avoided these errors was Gresham's School at Holt near the coast of north-east Norfolk. It had been endowed in the mid-sixteenth century as a free grammar school for deserving boys of the locality under the trusteeship of the Fishmongers' Livery Company of the City of London. Because it was so remote from London in an area of no great prosperity, it was slow to

1   Sir Donald Maclean, KBE

2   Canvassing in Cornwall: Lady Maclean on right of picture

3   Headmaster's House, Gresham's: Maclean on headmaster's left

develop into a school taking fee-paying boarders and it was only after the rebuilding of 1860 that it began to take shape as a modern school. Accelerated development started in 1900 with the appointment as headmaster of G. W. S. Howson; his science master was J. R. Eccles, who in due course succeeded him and was headmaster when Sir Donald decided to enrol there his three older boys, first in the junior house and then in the senior house, Woodlands, which was run by Eccles himself. The line of thought that led Sir Donald to this decision influenced some of his Liberal friends; among those who sent their sons to Gresham's were C. P. Scott of the *Manchester Guardian*, Walter Layton (later Lord Layton) of the *Economist* and Ernest Simon, the Lancashire industrialist and economist, who became Lord Simon of Wythenshawe. Eccles was delighted to have at Woodlands these sons of distinguished fathers, certain that they would help to form a real aristocracy of merit and give a lead to the whole school which, by 1928, the year in which young Donald became a prefect, numbered 260 boys, of whom 230 were boarders.

Although by that date Gresham's ranked as a modern public school, there were certain features that set it apart from those rooted in the nineteenth-century tradition. Sports were encouraged, but not to the extent of selecting teams to compete with other schools; Gresham's was accordingly largely spared that polarisation into athletes versus aesthetes, which characterised most public schools in the 1920s. Eccles was able to bring up boys with a more balanced concept of what maturity would mean; he was not in favour of ruling over 'fuzzy-wuzzies'; even if he had been, he would not have believed that success in the rugger field was a prerequisite. As it happened, young Donald was a keen rugger player, playing in the scrum, but he saw no inconsistency in pursuing his studies with equal enthusiasm.

Another distinguishing mark was that Gresham's was little more than half the size of the more prestigious schools of that period. This was the result of a deliberate decision on the part of Eccles, who held that only in a school of modest proportions, in which he could know all boys individually, could he apply the unique 'honour system', by which he set so much store. As some have strongly condemned this system, fairness to Eccles requires us to examine it first in his terms. We are able to do this because in 1928 he addressed the annual conference of the Parents' National Educational Union and subsequently had his address privately printed. He described how he used to see each boy soon after his arrival in the school:

'I speak to him of truth, and frankness, and honour; of purity in thought, and word, and deed; of the value and importance of hard work and honest work.'[9]

The boy, on assignment to a house, was asked to promise his housemaster that he would scrupulously avoid 'indecency, bad language and smoking ... If he fails to keep his promise, the understanding is that he tells his housemaster.'

Eccles claimed for his system that 'the moral problem, which is such a disturbing one to many schoolmasters ... can be dealt with very effectively on these lines.' He was enabled to reduce punishment to a minimum, especially corporal punishment, which was inflicted 'very rarely indeed'. He conceded, however, that his system would be unlikely to work as well in a larger school.

For the view of one who was on the receiving end we can turn to an essay by W. H. Auden, written in 1934. He began by finding much to praise in the school's surroundings, 'watching a snowstorm come up from the sea over the marshes at Salthouse and walking in a June dawn ... by Hempstead Mill'. He respected, too, the good sense of the school authorities, who 'set virtually no bounds, a liberty I believe rarely abused'.

After this, one is surprised to read the often quoted sentence: 'The best reason I have for opposing fascism is that at school I have lived in a fascist state.'[10] One shudders to think what invective he would have used if he had been at Marlborough, Charterhouse or Wellington. It soon transpires that what Auden execrated was the 'honour system', which he condemned as a means of turning boys into 'neurotic innocents'. He evidently saw in it a form of thought-control, as imposed in totalitarian states, and exploiting for this purpose the emotion of loyalty and honour, which he names as 'the only emotion that is fully developed in a boy of fourteen'. It was certainly an emotion that Himmler's SS knew how to exploit; even their belt-buckles carried the motto: '*Meine Ehre heisst Treue*' (I name my honour loyalty).

Auden's outburst must seem exaggerated until one comes to a specific point that Eccles, for obvious reasons, touched on only in passing. Auden, after relating the obligation to confess to the housemaster any breaches of these promises, added: 'If you saw anyone else break them, you should endeavour to persuade him to report and if he refused you should report him yourself.'

All that Eccles admitted is: 'I like every boy to feel that he is pledged to allow nothing to go on in the School, if he can help it, which reflects upon the good name of the School.'

The phrasing is evasive, but the intention is clear: behind the mask of honour a system of delation has been set up. Read in this light, Eccles' whole address takes on a much less agreeable character. For example, he scored off rival headmasters by writing:

'I passed a public school the other day in which the windows were barred from the basement to the highest floor. Bars are unknown on our windows ...'

What he fails to reveal is that all Gresham's boys had their trouser-pockets sewn up: some might regard this as even more degrading than barring windows.

We must now consider what psychological effect this form of conditioning might be expected to have had on young Donald. In the short term the system worked well enough; he had a successful school career, both as scholar and games player. Though he did not become head boy, like his brother, Ian, he was a prefect in the headmaster's house and impressed contemporaries as having a natural capacity to exercise authority. What is more, he left school with an unblemished moral reputation. He had been a big fish in a small pond and found that he liked to make a splash; this is sufficiently shown by the splash that he made in the much larger Cambridge pond, when restraints had been removed. Wanting to exert power as a prefect at a school where conformity to a strict code was required, he paid lip-service to it, whilst thinking his own subversive thoughts. Throughout his life he had unshakable confidence in the validity of his judgments, coupled with arrogance in rejecting those of others. Outward conformity with their values thus became a stalking-horse, behind which he could more easily pursue the alternative course that he had mapped out. He did not act in this way because he particularly relished playing a part; it is significant that he never appeared in any of the plays that were a feature of the cultural life of the school. He practised duplicity as the most effective means of going his own way without sacrificing the substance of power. It was a bonus point that, in doing so, he was mocking those higher authorities whose ethos he despised. The parallel between such an attitude towards school superiors and, at a later date, towards superiors in the Diplomatic Service pursuing misguided policies, scarcely needs to be emphasised.

There remains the question where Donald acquired the alternative

ethos that he substituted for that which prevailed both at school and at
home; in short, how he became a communist. For there is no doubt
that the foundation of his belief was well and truly laid at Gresham's.
This is not meant to imply that there was any deliberate attempt to
politicise pupils; the prevailing ethos was Christian and bourgeois.
However there was certainly a rejection of 'jingo' patriotism, such as
had long marked older public schools and is reflected in Kipling's
Stalky & Co. Among thoughtful parents, like many who sent their
sons to Gresham's, the Boer War had undermined imperial convictions and India's insistent demand for self-government had further
shaken faith in Empire. Above all, the slaughter of the First World
War had superannuated the military virtues. Gresham's boys still contemplated careers in the army and the school, like others, had its
Officers Training Corps (OTC). Indeed Donald was a member of it
and rose to the rank of Lance-Corporal; but emphasis was laid on the
defensive nature of armaments and the need to rely on the League of
Nations to keep the peace. In short, the tone of the school was
reformist and socialist ideals were more acceptable than they would
have been at the older schools. During the brief reign of Ramsay
MacDonald and his first Labour government, his Minister of Education, Sir Charles Trevelyan, was invited to Holt to present the prizes
on Speech Day. The Master of Magdalene, Cambridge, A. C.
Benson, himself the son of a public school headmaster, heard
Trevelyan's speech and did not like what he heard:

> 'He made a vulgar attack on the old Public Schools – and rejoiced
> that the blue-blooded land-owning aristocratic product was down in
> the market ... He spoke idealistically and with some passion and
> impressed the boys ...'[11]

Donald was only eleven, but we can safely assume that he was one of
the boys who was impressed.

So much attention has been paid to communism at Oxbridge in the
late 1920s and early 1930s that it is easy to overlook how many
undergraduates reached university ripe for recruitment; the same,
incidentally, was true in the radical 1960s; schools may be isolated
communities, but they are not immune from political epidemics.
Maurice Dobb, the Trinity economics lecturer, who in May 1932 in
the Cambridge Union carried the motion that 'This House has more
hope in Moscow than in Detroit', had first become interested in
Marxism at Charterhouse. Tom Driberg joined the Communist Party

of Great Britain (CPGB) whilst a boy at Lancing. Esmond Romilly, nephew of Winston Churchill, who ran away from Wellington in 1934, provoked the newspaper headline: 'Red Gold in English Public School'. He was soon joined at the communist bookshop in Red Lion Square by Philip Toynbee, who had run away from Rugby. None of these schools, however, had a recent radical heritage as distinguished as that of Gresham's. There was the laureate of the decay of capitalism, W. H. Auden, who had seen disaster approaching:

> 'All this time was anxiety at night,
> Shooting and barricade in street.
> Walking home late I listened to a friend
> Talking excitedly of final war
> Of proletariat against police – '[12]

There was also the man of action, Tom Wintringham, who visited Moscow as early as 1920 and four years later became editor of the *Workers' Weekly*. In 1925 he was gaoled with other members of the CPGB for inciting soliders to mutiny. A decade later he was an outstanding figure in the International Brigade in the Spanish Civil War.

Neither of these torch-bearers was Donald Maclean's contemporary. The one who was, and exerted great influence on his thinking, was James Klugmann, born on 27th February 1912 and thus a little more than one year older. He came of a prosperous Jewish family, living in Hampstead. He had not been admitted to Woodlands, the prestigious house, but made away with most of the school prizes. Many years later he claimed to have become a communist in order to annoy the school authorities. However that may be, he took naturally to Marxism and proved a formidable exponent of the creed; until his death in 1977 he continued to exert great influence on young people coming into the movement. In school holidays 'Kluggers' was a frequent visitor at the Macleans' house in London. Others of his generation at Gresham's, who later became communists, included Roger and Brian Simon, sons of Lord Simon of Wythenshawe, and Bernard Floud, who at Oxford was an active member of the October Club. They cannot be said to have formed a communist cell at school, though all except Klugmann were in the same house; but they certainly constituted a group of high intellectual calibre.

It is probable that Maclean's tendency to lead a double life, almost as a matter of routine, would have been less marked if confined solely to school life; but it persisted to some extent also in his home life.

He had a loving relationship with his mother, but as his interest in politics increased and his views diverged more and more from those of his father, some tension was inescapable. His eldest brother, Ian, was more easy-going than Donald and less politically orientated, but even he found his father self-righteous and intolerant of disagreement. Regular church- or chapel-going, family prayers and bans on Sunday games, and on alcohol and tobacco on all days, had been familiar features of life in nonconformist households before 1914. Such restrictions in the freer atmosphere of the 1920s, however, were less easily tolerated by the younger generation. In the recollection of the youngest son, Alan, his father became more relaxed in his sixties; family prayers were gradually abandoned and at Penn, where the Macleans had a country retreat called Elm Cottage, they would sometimes attend the Anglican church, instead of the local Methodist church. After Sir Donald's death, Alan did not follow his brothers to Holt, but was sent to Stowe, a modern public school but one cast in the traditional mould; it had the advantage of being in the same county as Penn.

A father who is a busy public figure is liable to have a problem communicating with his children, especially if there is a large age gap. Sir Donald was a very busy man; he had his law firms in London and Cardiff and had to nurse his Cornish constituency. In November 1930 he spent a weekend at Holt and gave an address on the League of Nations; it was only his second visit in over four years in an era when no schoolboy ever went home in term-time, unless he was sick. It was Donald's last year before going to university; the age gap between him and his father was forty-nine years. Sir Donald at sixty-six was no longer the same crusading young Liberal who had entered Parliament in the great days of Campbell-Bannerman. When in May 1926 the General Strike occurred and Lloyd George was inclined to sympathise with the TUC, Asquith took the opposite view and, as always, Maclean was with him. Ian and Andrew, following their father's lead, took minor strike-breaking jobs, one as railway porter, the other as delivery boy: Donald did not. He was beginning to show in small ways that he was thinking for himself. In the winter of 1929 he and his younger brother, Alan, were confined to the house, recovering from influenza; both were bored and Donald, to cheer up his seven-year-old brother, played soldiers with him. Alan was proud of his kilted Highlanders, who were ranked against turbaned sepoys; when he played alone, the Highlanders always won. When Donald played, it was the sepoys who triumphed; as he explained, 'It's their country. Why should the British always come out on top?'

The Gresham's connection was becoming attenuated. In October 1927 Ian left to read law at Emmanuel, Cambridge; he was destined, without any enthusiasm on his part, for one of his father's law firms. Andrew was backward and, when Donald began to overtake him, he was withdrawn from the school. Donald was recognised as having an aptitude for languages and his father sent him in summer holidays to France and Germany. He met in Munich Lady Mary St-Clair Erskine, daughter of the Earl of Rosslyn, who was 'finishing' there. They went sight-seeing and played tennis together. Donald was six-foot tall and still growing; he impressed her as grown-up for his age.[13] With his fair hair, blue eyes and striking good looks, he was approached by a Nazi and asked, much to his disgust, if he would pose for a photograph, depicting 'the perfect Aryan'. In the German elections of September 1930 the Nazi Party astonished observers by rising at a single leap to become the second largest party in the *Reichstag*; the writing was on the wall.

Before the paralysis of the Wall Street crash of September 1929 had begun to cross the Atlantic, an election had taken place in Britain, bringing Ramsay MacDonald's second Labour government into power. Although Lloyd George had at last poured out his fund in a belated attempt to save his party, only fifty-nine Liberals were elected. Maclean, though he had scorned assistance from the fund, was one of the survivors. As the unemployment figure soared, dole queues lengthened and gold reserves drained away. Free trade, which was virtually the only doctrinal cement holding the shattered Liberal Party together, came increasingly under attack. Maclean held to the dogma of his youth; but he was critical of the government's reluctance to impose drastic economies. In February 1931 he moved an amendment to a Conservative motion, which forced MacDonald to set up a committee to advise where the axe should fall. By August the time for committees was past; MacDonald resigned and then accepted the King's invitation to head a coalition government. Only four of his former colleagues stayed with him and, to avert complete reliance on the Conservatives, efforts were made to bring in Liberals, even including those, like Maclean, who still clung, at least in theory, to free trade. His family were spending the summer holiday at Newquay, where young Donald devoured the newspapers each day and complained bitterly of the betrayal of the Labour rank and file through the perfidy of their leader. On 25th August a telegram arrived from Sir

Donald, who had remained in London, announcing that he was to be made President of the Board of Education with a seat in the cabinet. He held his constituency in the election that followed and so, after a career of a quarter of a century in politics, achieved ministerial rank for the first time. He was not destined to enjoy it for long. Meanwhile the fruits of the National government's deflationary policy were turning bitter. In September at Invergordon sailors of the Atlantic fleet, whose pay had been cut, mutinied, allegedly under communist influence. One of those condemned for having suborned the sailors from their allegiance was Len Wincott, who was dubbed 'A hero of the Soviet Union' and invited to the USSR. Donald, whose sympathies were with the mutineers, was to meet Wincott many years later in Moscow.

For young Donald, too, a new vista was opening with new challenges. He had left school behind him and in the autumn of 1931 was going to Trinity Hall, Cambridge, where he had won an exhibition (minor scholarship) in modern languages. In later years he must have looked back wistfully to those relatively tranquil years spent on the Norfolk coast. The turmoil of the great ideological divide was only just beginning to trouble him; the schism that was to mark his life was barely visible. The demon drink was still locked away in the cupboard and the sexual conflicts that were later to beset him were still dormant; in this respect he was a late developer. Gresham's was, in the jargon of the time, 'a pure school', meaning that there was little active homosexuality. No doubt there were sentimental friendships between older and younger boys; but there were no scandals ending in expulsions, such as occurred in those days at larger schools. At Gresham's one attractive sixteen-year-old, who was taking the part of Portia in the school play, was discreetly warned by Eccles that he might be propositioned; the boy was completely mystified. A couple of years later on a visit to Cambridge he was lured into the back of a car by Donald, who made an abortive assault on his virtue.[14] It was at university, not at school, that he began his first tentative experiments in sex.

Sir Donald had less than ten months before him, in which to build on his long-deferred success. In so short a period he could not register any striking achievement; if he had lived another three months, he would probably have resigned from the government with Sir Herbert Samuel on the tariff issue. Nonetheless his inclusion in the National government was the culmination of a political career of which his family could be proud. Young Donald showed his pride in his first

Cambridge year. His supervisor in French was Jack Roach, who was keen to reform the educational system. After several discussions about this, Donald offered to bring directly to his father's notice a paper Roach had written. During the vacation Roach received a letter from Donald, confirming that he had duly laid the paper, beside the usual copy of *The Times*, on his father's austere breakfast tray of tea, toast and marmalade.[15]

As the son of a successful father, Donald was affected in two contradictory ways. Being himself ambitious to succeed in life, his first need was to emerge from the shadow of his father and assert his own individuality. A common way in which a son does this is by taking up a stance markedly different from that of his father, instead of trying to outdo the latter on his own ground. As Sir Donald moved to the right, his son gravitated naturally to the left. Young Donald, however, had sufficient respect for his father's achievement to have absorbed, consciously or unconsciously, character strengths that had contributed to it. Like the father, the son was attentive to detail and conscientious in completing his tasks. He believed, like his father, that if you reasoned with people, you could bring them round to your point of view. Like his father, he was convinced that he was right and, despite setbacks, remained faithful to his creed. He inherited, too, his father's Presbyterian conscience, so that, after every moral lapse from grace – and they were many – he was torn by remorse. As he grew older and his life became more complex and more dissipated, these inherent virtues became partially submerged; but to the end of his life they would re-emerge, like islands of solid earth above the turbulent flood waters.

2

Cambridge and the Comintern

Trinity Hall is not the oldest, largest or most prestigious of Cambridge colleges; but its admirable situation compensates for whatever it may lack in other dimensions. Wedged between Trinity and Clare, it commands a section of the Cam with access to the footbridge that carries Garret Hostel Lane across the river. The buildings are harmonious and college gardeners have traditionally cultivated deep borders of hollyhocks and delphiniums. In the high panelled hall former Masters, founders and benefactors, many of them lawyers, look down from their frames on the academic community, the dons on their dais and the undergraduates in their gowns lining the long tables; all stand, as the Latin grace before meat is read. Donald was by no means a man of ceremony and tradition, but the appeal of the college could not have failed to impress him, arriving as a freshman in October 1931. As an exhibitioner, he could count on a room in college and not until his third and final year did he leave Latham Court and look for 'digs' in the town.

As a young man of spirit and ambition, he would have found the University both a stimulant and a challenge. At Holt he had become prominent in the confined environment of a relatively small school; it had whetted his appetite. In the wider and freer surroundings of Cambridge he began to deploy his talents and flex his muscles. His contemporaries were struck by his good looks, easy wit and debonair manner. Whilst he was still finding his feet, these charms masked his intellectual arrogance and his opinionated adherence to convictions once formed. Of these the most powerful were his belief that he was destined to excel and his faith in Marxist analysis not only for the political problems of the day, but for interpreting the whole gamut of economic, social and even artistic activity. Even before the end of his first year he began to throw off parental restraints and engage openly in communist 'agitprop'. He joined a demonstration of the un-employed, which clashed with police *en route* to Hyde Park; helmets rolled and Donald, conspicuous by his height and fair hair among shorter men in cloth caps, was one of those led away to the nearest police station. A telephone call was there made to Lady Maclean, who duly claimed her son.[1] Police in those days were deferential towards Cabinet Ministers and no further action was taken. He came home chastened and relieved to find his father absent, probably busy in the House of Commons.

It was not long before he was finally delivered of paternal control. At the beginning of June 1932 his father suffered a severe heart-attack; he did not go into hospital, but took to his bed in Southwick Place, where he was nursed by his wife. On 15th June, at the age of sixty-eight, he died. There were tributes from all sides; the King sent a telegram to Lady Maclean. In the House of Commons all shades of political opinion from Baldwin to Maxton of the Independent Labour Party united in his praise. Sir James Barrie mourned him: 'I esteemed him beyond most men, perhaps more than any man I have known of recent years.'[2] Barrie also described him as 'an elder of the church', meaning the Presbyterian Church; but in death the Anglican estab-lishment took him over. In any case Lady Maclean had never had much enthusiasm for the Presbyterians or for the Methodist Church in the village of Penn, where her husband had sometimes put in an appearance. The well-attended memorial service was held in St Margaret's, Westminster, and the funeral at Trinity church, Penn, where a Celtic cross was erected over the grave. Over fifty years later the ashes of his errant son, Donald, were buried under cover of darkness in the same plot. Once the period of mourning was over, there was a marked relaxation of parental authority; sons coming to supper in flannels, after playing tennis, were no longer sent upstairs to change. Donald was able to air his political views before a domestic audience that included his admiring, if sometimes puzzled, mother.

In his first year he had made only casual contact with the vigorous communist group in neighbouring Trinity; but on his own home ground in Trinity Hall he had already encountered active supporters of the party-line. Three of his seniors had made names for themselves. The oldest, who graduated in law in 1932, was H. L. E. Dreschfield, who had helped to organise the Society for Cultural Relations with the USSR; in May 1933 one of its meetings was disrupted by student toughs. Others, who graduated in 1933, were the scientist, Alan Nunn May from King Edward's School, Birmingham, and Fred Pateman from a Leicester grammar school, who spoke earnestly in the Union in support of resolutions such as that 'Class War is inevitable'. Maclean never spoke in the Union; he had a contempt for rhetoric and preferred to argue his cause in smaller discussion groups. It is probable that he would have agreed with what the young Stephen Spender wrote in his diary: 'Doubtless my own contempt for my father's public speeches is what undermines my faith in political arguments.'[3] Like Spender, however, Maclean, as we shall shortly see, was prepared to exploit the persuasiveness of the written word.

Much has been written about the hard core of communists in Trinity, who first re-animated the Cambridge University Socialist Society (CUSS) and soon became the driving force in it, so that before the end of the decade it had nearly 1,000 members in an undergraduate community of about 7,000. In the rapidly changing student population this expansion could not have been achieved without the continuity provided by lecturers, Fellows and postgraduates, among whom two leading figures were Maurice Dobb and Roy Pascal. At one time they shared a house, where the League Against Imperialism used to meet for discussion. Another influential couple, bound by emotional as well as political ties, comprised Anthony Blunt and Guy Burgess. Blunt, a Fellow of Trinity, had come up from Marlborough in 1926 to read mathematics, but in the 1930s was concentrating on his artistic interests; he took a stand against cubism, surrealism and other excesses which, in his view, alienated the proletariat from art. He preferred the 'socialist realism' of Soviet artists and the 'new realism' of the Mexican masters, Rivera and Orozco.

Burgess had come up to Trinity to read history in 1930 and had been introduced by Blunt into the Apostles, an exclusive intellectual group, which had been founded in the mid-nineteenth century. In the past decade its co-opted membership had moved Left and it contained an inner cabal of homosexuals, to which Blunt and Burgess belonged. Whilst Blunt measured the world about him with a cool eye, Burgess, an Old Etonian and sparkling conversationalist, was altogether more flamboyant; he seemed equally at home among the 'horsey' men of the Pitt Club and the 'green-room queers' of the Footlights, whose annual revue was the delight of the 'fast' set. The association of Blunt and Burgess was sufficiently familiar for their contemporary, Valentine Lawford, to write in a book published in 1963 (i.e. before Blunt's treachery had been disclosed) how he had stood 'in a window overlooking Trinity and threw a banana at the people emerging after luncheon through the Great Gate, not caring in the least which of three possible human targets it hit: the broad one who looked like a rowing blue, the short one whom I knew as Guy Burgess, or the long, thin one who was Anthony Blunt.'[4]

Although Maclean never formed a trio with these Renaissance men, there is no doubt that they were responsible for initiating him into homosexual practices in a way that Gresham's had not done. As Lord Annan has written, Burgess 'regarded it as his duty to liberate as many of his own class as possible from the thrall of bourgeois sexual inhibitions'.[5] Burgess and Blunt were committed communists, but they took to communism much as Christopher Marlowe took to atheism; it added to life the spice of danger. Neither of them ever set out to change the world; they were enjoying it too much for that. Maclean, with his ex-Presbyterian conscience, was different; he had more in common with the hard men among the conspirators, most of whom were heterosexual. Here the leading figures were David Haden Guest, John Cornford and Kim Philby. Haden Guest had been briefly gaoled in Geräny in 1931 after taking part in a communist demonstration; he died in Spain. So did Cornford, whose friend, Margot Heinemann, then at Newnham, has remained true to the faith with which he had imbued her. Philby was another who was not content to talk Marxism over a glass of sherry; when he went down in 1933, he went to 'Red' Vienna, where the forces of reaction were at work, eliminating the socialists and communists. In that year the Trinity cell gained a powerful adherent in Maclean's friend James Klugmann, a future historian of the party, whose sister married Maurice Cornforth, a graduate student of philosophy, who also enhanced the intellectual distinction of the group. Another from Holt, who came into residence in 1933, was Brian Simon, who was to become President of the National Union of Students; Maclean lost no time in calling on him and urging him to join the party, as he did in the following year.

The ideological commitment and self-confidence of the Cambridge communists did not lead them into the illusion that they could succeed, as commissars, without the backing of the rank and file of the Cambridge University Socialist Society. Similarly, at national level, the CPGB was busy trying to hitch its outboard motor to the slow-moving barge of the Labour Party. Such tactics have come commonplace today, but were relatively novel in the period before the Second World War. It was in the year after Hitler came to power in January

1933 that Popular Front tactics were gradually introduced and formally adopted at the Seventh Congress of the Comintern of 1934. In the British trade union movement, however, this process of 'boring from within' had been in operation for a long time and was familiar to those brought up in a family environment of trade unionism. One such was Lionel Elvin, a graduate of Trinity Hall, who had been President of the Union in 1927; he had remained in Cambridge as a lecturer and had rooms in the same court as Maclean about whom he had certain suspicions:

'We recognised that such people from a comparatively affluent background might be moved by a genuine social conscience, but as someone from a trade union background I felt that they knew very little about the working class that figured so largely in their talk. I rather resented the publicity that made out people like Auden as the voice of the young Left.'[6]

Many years later, when Elvin was working in Paris with UNESCO and heard of Maclean's disappearance, he at once arrived at the correct explanation of it and was surprised that friends in the British Embassy were so slow to come to the same conclusion.

I first met Donald towards the end of 1932, when we were fellow guests at a tea-party given by a wealthy, middle-aged spinster in her large house on the outskirts of Cambridge. It stood amidst well-kept lawns and shrubberies and tea was served by maids in starched cap and apron. It was an unlikely setting in which to meet a communist for the first time, though I did not then know that Donald was a member of the party and in such surroundings he attempted no propaganda. His face is the only one that I still recall from that gathering, apart from that of my sister, who was at Newnham. It was a handsome face, the fair hair swept back in Rupert Brooke style from a high forehead. In those days he was slimly built and this exaggerated his height, which was nearly six foot four inches; height apart, he had the air of looking down on the company and, though softly spoken, he could give his voice an edge if he chose. My sister was reading English and it was she, I recall, who mentioned John Milton, about whom I then made some disparaging remark. Donald would have none of it and I was firmly put in my place; after all Milton had been a republican. After tea we got on our bicycles and rode most of the way together, he to Trinity Hall, I to neighbouring Gonville and Caius.

Maclean had considerable pretensions to being an intellectual. The

Modern Languages tripos, which he was reading, concentrated on literature; he also read extensively in contemporary English fiction. In the winter of 1933–4 he wrote a book review for *Cambridge Left*, to which other leading communists contributed, such as Cornford, Charles Madge and the Irish scientist, J. D. Bernal. Donald reviewed *Contemporary Literature and Social Revolution* by J. D. Charques, praising the book in slightly patronising terms for its readiness 'to hint at a Marxist conception of literature'.[7] He found hopeful traces in D. H. Lawrence's *Sons and Lovers* and E. M. Forster's *Passage to India*; but roundly condemned in a single, sweeping paragraph Walpole, Galsworthy, Huxley, Eliot, Waugh, Joyce and Virginia Woolf. He did not mention his father's friend, Barrie, who was presumably beneath contempt.

If when Donald went up to Cambridge he had been under the impression that claims to being an intellectual would give him status in the party, he would soon have been disillusioned by the old-timers; status could derive only from a proletarian background. Just as all Britons, because of the British Empire, must have a bad conscience vis-à-vis innocent Russians, so undergraduates, supported by their parents' inherited wealth, must redouble their efforts to make amends to the workers, from whom that wealth had been stolen. As Koestler has written, 'Intellectuals of middle-class origin were in the Party on suffrance, not by right; this was constantly rubbed into us.'[8] The lesson was rammed home by the relative affluence of Gown in Cambridge, as contrasted with Town, and was summed up in the phrase: 'No revolutionary theory without revolutionary practice'. In pursuit of Marxist 'praxis', Burgess was put to work fomenting a bus strike in Cambridge; Cornford frequented a building site, not to earn money, but to benefit by contact with the workers. In the same cause, others spent a week of their vacation in the homes of Welsh miners. Pressure on the bourgeois to earn his passage made it easier for the party to keep him standing in the rain, selling the *Daily Worker*. It was this pressure that led some to their death in Spain; others, as we shall see, were singled out for the equally dangerous, but less creditable, role of spy.

By the end of Donald's second year he had come to have a distinctive profile not just in his own college, but in the University as a whole. In the Michaelmas term, 1933, the magazine *Granta* began to feature a series of interviews with students, who were in differing ways representative, under the rubric: 'The Undergraduate in the Box'. Donald was interviewed fourth in this series, but his interview did not follow the recognised question-and-answer pattern; instead, it has all the marks of having been written by Donald himself. The interviewer begins in an orthodox way by stating that it is his 'job to examine the undergraduate's personality'. 'But which one?' Donald enquires, and proceeds to outline three, none of which has anything in common with the others. The first is 'Cecil', who is the caricature of an aesthete, 'slipping into my velvet trousers', talking about Picasso and F. R. Leavis. The second is 'Jack' who, when asked how he spends his time, replies (in the jargon of the period):

'Oh I just crack around, you know. Buy a few club-ties here and smash up a flick there. Bloody marvellous.'

When 'Jack' is dismissed, by being told 'you'd better go and oil your rugger boots,' one recalls that all through the winter of 1932–3 Donald had, in fact, played rugger for his college. Finally, 'Fred', the hard-working one, is paraded and boasts that he belongs to eleven societies and has read to one of them 'a paper on Lessing's *Laokoon* (in German, of course)'. 'Fred' concludes that he hopes to get a first-class degree, an achievement registered by Donald in the next year. Asked which of these personalities he prefers, he replies:

'I like them all equally. I see no standard against which to set them, no hierarchy in which to put them – they are all of the same value to me.'[9]

There is a surprising shade of self-deprecation about this last answer, which can perhaps be explained by the omission throughout the interview of any reference to his political aims and ideals. Although the tone is light-hearted, the interview reveals awareness of a divided nature and the problem of reconciling discordant elements. There can be no doubt that communism and alcohol, though drugs of very different kinds, both offered means of effecting unification of a split personality.

A few days after this interview was published there occurred what the *Granta* described, without exaggeration, as 'The Armistice Day Riots'. Since the First World War the tradition had grown up of turning 11th November into a 'rag', which provided harmless entertainment for most students and rather fewer members of the public, who were expected to fill collecting-boxes for the benefit of the British Legion. Some older people, who had lost close friends and relatives in the war, disliked this way of commemorating the dead; but trouble only began when the event was politicised. There was a Student Anti-War Council with Dobb as secretary, which the *Granta* described as 'a body generally suspected to be flavoured (or tainted) with Communism'.[10] In the week before Armistice Day the Tivoli, a local cinema, had shown the film *Our Fighting Navy*, which was so much disrupted by organised demonstrators that the management were forced to withdraw it. This irritated some members of boat clubs and rugger clubs and, when it became known that the pacifists intended to march on 11th November to the War Memorial, it was decided to break up the procession. As it advanced across Parker's Piece with shouts of 'Against War and Imperialism', it was attacked and police had to draw their batons in order to restore order. Julian Bell and Guy Burgess were prominent in the running battles, in which Maclean also took part.

Maclean took this event, which created some scandal, as his theme in the Lent term, 1934, issue of the *Silver Crescent*, the Trinity Hall students' magazine, of which he had become editor. He launched his attacks in verse as well as in prose.

DARE DOGGEREL. NOV.11

Rugger toughs and boat club guys
In little brown coats and old school ties.
Tempers be up and fore-arms bared
Down in the gutter with those who've dared.
Dared to think war-causes out,
Dared to know what they're shouting about,
Dared to leave a herd they hate,
Dared to question the church and state;
Dared to ask what poppies are for,
Dared to say we'll fight no more,
Unless it be for a cause we know
And not for the sake of *status quo*.
Not for the sake of Armstrong Vickers,
Not for the sake of khaki knickers,
But for the sake of the class which bled,
But for the sake of daily bread.
Rugger toughs and boat club guys
Panic-herd with frightened eyes,
Sodden straws on a rising tide,
They know they've chosen the losing side.

Donald's editorial was equally forthright, laying great stress on the decline in world trade, coupled with massive rearmament and traffic in arms. In a separate article in the same issue he insisted:

> 'England is in the throes of a capitalist crisis ... If the analysis in the Editorial is correct, there is an excellent reason why everyone of military age should start thinking about politics ...'

Not all contributors took the high ground of politics; one reverted to the familiar style of undergraduate journalism, flippant and facetious:

> 'After the bloody revolution of March 13th the colleges have been renamed and re-appropriated. Magdalene is a clinic, King's a delousing station, and Marx, Engels and Lenin Hall has already launched a new boat – the USSR. The tomb of Donald Maclenin in red bakelite in Market Square is used by thousands.'[11]

College magazines did not have a wide circulation; but in his final year Maclean had become a campus figure and most of us knew that he was a communist. My own enlightenment occurred one morning, when I dropped into his 'digs' in Bridge Street. He had a commodious room on the first floor, furnished with at least one good leather armchair. He proffered me one of his expensive Balkan cigarettes, adding that I must not stay long, as his whole morning had already been wasted by an argumentative Buchmanite, trying to convert him to Moral Rearmament. 'Why so much effort?' I wanted to know. 'I'd be a feather in their cap,' he replied, 'because I'm a communist.' I made no comment, but inwardly registered that this elegant young man in his leather armchair was not my idea of a communist. It was an error into which many people, wiser than I, would fall before Maclean's nefarious career came to an end.

I did not charge him with insincerity, however, because a week or so earlier I had seen him in action on a cold, wet afternoon in Royston. Another of the 'front' organisations, in which the communists mobilised a wide range of non-ideological supporters, was the Cambridge University Solidarity Committee, of which Cornforth was secretary. It was linked with similar committees along the route to be taken by hunger-marchers (the famous Jarrow March was by no means an isolated event), who were coming south to attend a Congress of Action at Bermondsey Town Hall in the last week of February 1934. As the marchers would pass no nearer to Cambridge than Royston, local organisers provided buses to take students to a point from which they could accompany the unemployed men for a few miles, before being returned to their colleges. Originally I had no plans to go, but a Newnham girl, whose favours I was seeking, asked me to go with her and I fell for a pretty face, where broader human sympathies had not moved me. We duly joined the march and, clutching the arm of my girl friend, I looked ahead and saw the tall figure of Donald, striding purposefully along, arm in arm with some genuine proletarian. His face wore a look of dedication that I could not hope to emulate.

'Hope to emulate' – the words are used advisedly; there were many of us who admired the men of commitment. We believed that if we, too, could lose ourselves in dedication to a cause, this would solve our personal problems, to say nothing of the problems of the world around us. Commitment, we thought, like falling in love, would lift our hearts and minds above the complexities and frustrations of day-to-day existence. Not to be animated in this way seemed a source of self-reproach. Unfamiliar, as we then were, with the false trails of ideology, we failed to see that, if the urge to set the world to rights grew to unwieldy proportions in the heart of a young man of high ideals, it carried with it the danger of exploitation by unscrupulous men. Nietzsche wrote:

'A living thing can only be healthy, strong and productive within a certain horizon; if it is incapable of drawing one round itself . . . it will come to an untimely end.'[12]

Donald's horizons at this period were expanding far beyond the Cambridge fens; his mind was reaching out to the impoverished millions in India, whose sufferings he equated with British Imperialism. His opposed horizon was that of the Russian steppes, where happy Soviet peasants, freed at last from the centennial yoke of Tsarism, were growing unprecedented harvests to nourish the infant republics of the USSR. If he had fulfilled his original intention of visiting the USSR, it is conceivable that, like Malcolm Muggeridge, he might have gleaned some fragment of the truth, namely that the violent collectivisation of agriculture was being resisted and *kulaks* were pitilessly sacrificed on the altar of ideology. Such accounts of famine as reached the London press were at once dismissed by Maclean and his friends as the wicked distortions of the press barons. The fine print of reality was ignored, in order to focus on the lying slogans splashed in white paint on the walls of slum tenements and railway sidings. Yes, there was suffering behind those walls. Yes, something could have been done, but too many do-gooders ignored the wisdom of William Blake: 'He who would do good to another must do it in minute particulars; general good is the plea of the scoundrel, hypocrite and flatterer.' The lesson that Maclean failed to learn was that it is through our better nature that ideology seduces us, turning the fresh stream of idealism into poison. It is a strange paradox that sympathy with suffering humanity helped to make him a spy.

Before broaching the question of Maclean's recruitment by the NKVD, one more example of his promotion of left-wing causes deserves to be mentioned, since it shows him in a more rational, even prescient, role. This was his advocacy of changes in student rights and university reform, some of which were adopted in the 1960s. As already stressed, his Marxism took in public life in all its aspects and, looking about him, he saw many flaws in university administration, which he ascribed in a letter to the *Granta* to 'the capitalist, dictatorial character of the University'. His main demand was for a Students' Council, 'democratically elected on a college and faculty basis', which should be able to 'put through its demands against any opposition from the authorities.' Full equality for women students was demanded, together with the right of students to use university and college premises for political meetings. Maclean's anti-imperialism came to the surface in his insistence on abolition of 'official supervision of Colonial students'.[13] Indian grievances were kept alive in Cambridge by visitors to the Union, such as Krishna Menon and Palme Dutt, as well as by resident speakers, such as Lakshmi Ja of Trinity and Pieter Keuneman of Pembroke. The Indian Society, the Majlis, was deeply penetrated by communists, partly through the exertions of the Canadian, Herbert Norman. Because of the supervision of Indian students, none was issued with a party card. Maclean's emphasis on these reforms, like his serious approach to student journalism, marks him off from most of his contemporaries, who tended to regard these years as an agreeable interlude between the rigours of school and the competitive world, in which they would have to earn their living. Some would have said to him, as to Malvolio: 'Thinkest thou because thou art virtuous there shall be no more cakes and ale?'

If there is little difficulty in understanding why Maclean became a communist, it is harder to grasp why he took the drastic and irrevocable decision to become an agent of the NKVD. Part of the explanation is that, to a sincere communist in 1934, it seemed a less drastic decision than it turned out to have been a dozen years later, when it was clear in the West that capitalism was again on the march. In the last years before the Second World War communists like Maclean were much affected by what was called 'the sinking ship psychology'. Even today there are a few converts to communism of those days of political and economic crisis, who still seem puzzled that the capitalist world failed to collapse, as Marx and Lenin had predicted. In this context one must remember not only the economic disasters in Europe but also the isolationism and depression in which the USA was sunk; few in Britain in 1934 could have foreseen that the New Deal would succeed, that Roosevelt would be three times elected and that he would lead the USA into a war, from which she would emerge in thriving prosperity. Donald and his friends unquestionably believed that it was only a matter of time before communism was everywhere calling the tune; it was the 'sodden straws' of the class system who, as he had written in his doggerel, had 'chosen the losing side'.

I never had a chance to discuss with Donald how he came to make his fatal commitment to work for the USSR, but I did have such a discussion with Anthony Blunt a couple of years before his death. I suggested to him that even in the mid-1930s the dominant figure of Stalin should have been sufficiently repellent to inhibit a young idealist from working for him. Blunt corrected me: 'We did not think of ourselves as working for Russia,' he said. 'We were working for the Comintern.' The Comintern, or Communist International, which was established in 1919, was misleadingly described by the Soviet Foreign Minister, Litvinov, as 'a collegium of Communist Parties who shared common objectives'. Young people with a superficial understanding of politics and ideology continued to be deceived by this façade long after the Comintern had become no more than an alternative channel for the pursuit of Soviet aims. It was a necessary channel, whilst many countries refused to enter into diplomatic relations with the USSR, and it had its own espionage network. This developed whilst Lenin cherished the belief that revolution would soon spread to Germany and then to the rest of Europe. During the power struggle between Stalin and Trotsky, which ended with the latter's exile in 1929, Stalin coined the slogan 'Socialism in one country' and ceased to regard the Comintern, which contained a high proportion of Trotskyists, as a major instrument of policy. This change was not immediately apparent, however, especially as the NKVD, which lacked staff with knowledge of Europe and its languages, needed time to exert control over Comintern agents, who performed invaluable work both in the field of propaganda and in that of espionage.

The final stage of Stalin's path to unchallenged ascendancy was marked by the first Moscow show trial in the summer of 1936 of the 'Old Bolsheviks', one of whom was Grigori Zinoviev, the first chairman of the Comintern. From that time many non-Russians, working abroad for the Comintern, NKVD and GRU (Soviet military intelligence), began to realise that for them, too, the writing was on the wall. It would have been too much to expect, however, that Oxbridge undergraduates, intoxicated by the rhetoric of international proletarian revolution, could have recognised how these ideals had been degraded to serve Stalinist policies. They preferred to discount what they read as the perversions and exaggerations of the capitalist press. Meantime the rhetoric had grown more imperative, as Hitler rose to power in Germany, threatening the very survival of the Soviet fatherland.

To those young people who, like Maclean, feared the threat of fascism and longed to oppose it, nothing was more frustrating than the confused and divided attitude of the Left towards the dilemma of British rearmament. Towards the end of the year 1933, when Hitler had left the League of Nations and Japan was defying the League of Nations in Manchuria, it was becoming clear to thinking Marxists that pacifism, as practised by George Lansbury, who in 1931–2 had led the Labour Party, was no adequate answer to the rise of fascism. It was, however, deeply rooted in the party. Gavin Ewart, who had been a communist at Cambridge, wrote in his *Election Song 1935*:

> 'If you enjoy the running blood,
> The boring trenches and the flashing sabre,
> The young man trampled in the mud,
> Then don't vote Labour.'[14]

The objections of the Left were not confined to being trampled in the mud; they also objected strongly to putting money in the pockets of arms manufacturers and dealers, 'the merchants of death'. Moreover, rearmament would lead logically to conscription, which would expose young men to brutal discipline and patriotic indoctrination. Yet without some organised mobilisation of resources, fascism could not be resisted. Labour, which continued up to the outbreak of war to oppose conscription, never solved this conundrum.

The student Left was not pacifist at heart, as it showed by volunteering to fight in Spain; what it rejected was to be mustered as the foot-soldiers of capitalism. The more robust posture of the CPGB had great appeal, as did the argument that the Red Army was the stoutest bulwark against Hitler's Wehrmacht. Student communists were not at first faced with the crude proposition that they should work for the USSR: they were told that their services were being enlisted by the Comintern. By working for the Comintern, they would be helping their brother communists in countries such as Germany and Italy, where the party had been outlawed. The headquarters of the Comintern were in Moscow, because there the party was in power and could undertake central direction of the efforts that, in the long run, would bring peace and freedom to all. Meanwhile the Comintern representatives in the various countries knew best how individual contributions to the common cause could be co-ordinated. It was, of course, flattering for a young man to learn that he had been under observation and was regarded as peculiarly fitted for a difficult and even dangerous task. Maclean, who had a good opinion of his own abilities, would have been gratified to hear that he was not expected to be a humble day-labourer, trying to organise strikes of college servants, or become a hack-writer for news-sheets that nobody would read. To go underground, to become a 'mole' (though the term was not used at that date), appealed to the elitist in him. He was not one of those who had gone to stay with coal-miners in his vacations; by entering a profession, such as diplomacy, he would have the satisfaction of serving the cause without abandoning the fleshpots of the society he was aiming to destroy.

The agent who recruited Maclean was an 'illegal', that is to say an agent who had to live by his wits and did not enjoy 'cover' as a member of a Soviet Mission. Theodore Maly, known as 'Teddy', had a romantic story well calculated to appeal to a young man with ideological motivations. Elisabeth Poretsky, wife of another of the notorious 'illegals', has described him as 'a handsome, tall Hungarian with blue eyes and the charming smile of the naturally shy' – a fair description of Maclean himself.[15] 'Teddy' was a man of culture, who had trained as a priest; his younger brother was a gifted concert pianist. Serving as a chaplain in the Austrian army in the First World War, he had become a prisoner of the Tsarist army, which was already riddled with Bolshevist propaganda. He had been converted to communism in prison camp, as was to happen many years later in the Korean War in the case of George Blake. When the revolution came,

'Teddy' joined the *Cheka*, the forerunner of the OGPU and NKVD, but applied to be sent abroad, as he could not stand the growing brutality that marked the *Cheka*'s expansion.

Ivan Maisky, who knew Britain well and became Soviet Ambassador in London in 1932, is sometimes credited with the idea of recruiting young men of good family, who showed ideological commitment. The first implication of this tactic was to have 'talent scouts' in universities, who could gauge the degree of commitment and aptitude for the double life. The best known of the Cambridge talent scouts was Anthony Blunt, though in the case of Maclean he never admitted having had a hand in his recruitment. When in 1937 Blunt recruited the American, Michael Straight, who was studying economics at Trinity College, he told him, 'It will be necessary for you to cut all political ties.'[16] Straight was then given his instructions, which meant returning to work for the cause in his own country. Maclean's instructions were that, after giving up political activity, he should enter the Diplomatic Service, where at the right moment he would best be able to serve the cause. This long-term strategy fitted in well with the sensitive handling practised by an agent such as 'Teddy': it also meant less pressure to produce immediate results. Where routine NKVD agents were accustomed to shackle a new recruit by insisting that he at once accept money or gifts, an ideological spy, like Maclean, was allowed to show his idealism by declining to do so. This helped him to keep his self-respect.

Although the transformation of undergraduate into spy might be a long-term process, certain decisions had to be taken promptly. One was abandonment of Maclean's project to go to the USSR as soon as he left Cambridge and teach English there. He gave up, too, the idea of applying for a Fellowship: his thesis was to have been a study of Jean Calvin and the rise of the bourgeoisie. Instead, he would have to turn his mind to subjects such as modern history and economics, which were obligatory in the highly competitive examination for the Diplomatic Service. In order to compete in August 1935, he had to attend a preliminary interview one year in advance; the intervening period would have to be spent at one of the London cramming establishments, which specialised in Civil Service examinations. As this meant another year of financial dependence on his mother, Lady Maclean had to be told. She was delighted to hear that Donald wanted to become a diplomat and was sure Sir Donald, too, would have approved. But what about his communist beliefs? He passed off her enquiry with a light touch, 'You must think I turn like a weathercock;

but the fact is I've rather gone off all that lately.'[17] Lady Maclean heaved a sigh of relief.

The next step was to concentrate on the final part of his tripos and this preoccupation would have been taken as explaining his withdrawal from political activity; at no point did he make any explicit renunciation. For a few weeks he put aside everything except the revision that blighted the May term for students in their final year. They had no time to listen to the madrigals sung under King's bridge, or take a boat up the river to Grantchester. Instead there was the last-minute flutter through the set texts, culminating in the ordeal in the vast, bare interior of the Corn Exchange, where the examination took place. Trestle tables, each with a candidate's name on it, stood on the concrete floor; sunlight filtered through the glass expanse of the roof. There Donald wrote steadily, in his slanting hand, for successive stretches of three hours. When it was all over, he pushed back his folding wooden chair, well satisfied with what he had done: it was a familiar sensation. In June came the verdict: he had earned his BA degree with first-class honours.

Early in June a taxi drew up outside his 'digs' in Bridge Street and his trunks were loaded into it. He looked out as the taxi passed the Union, where he had applauded communist speakers, and after passing Parker's Piece, turned into Station Road by the War Memorial, scene of one of the open conflicts he had now forsworn. His three years at Cambridge had been a period of lost innocence and mounting excitement: now it was all over. He would have looked back, if at all, without nostalgia. Like the youngest son in the fairy-tale, he was embarking on a life of adventure; before him lay the dark forest, through which he must find his way, if he was to encounter and slay the dragons of capitalism and imperialism. It would be a more tortuous path than he expected and some of the dragons would not be quite as the nursery tales of Karl Marx had depicted them.

3

The Citadel Betrayed

The best view of the Foreign Office was – and still is – from the footbridge that crosses the lake in St James's Park. In summer and early autumn tall trees break the regularity of the façade, but do not diminish the massive tower that rises from the flank of Horseguards Parade. From that strategic corner site the spacious rooms accommodating the Foreign Secretary and his Permanent Under-Secretary have for many decades looked out across the Park and, as dusk slowly enfolds it, successive generations of statesmen have watched the ducks returning to roost and the lights beginning to glow. Some of them will have watched with the sombre reflection that lights were going out all over Europe and chickens coming home to roost. Such might well have been the thoughts of Sir Samuel Hoare, involved (as Maclean was to write more than thirty years later) in a 'foreign policy catastrophe . . . driven from office' by a hostile wave of opinion.[1] What Hoare had been trying to achieve towards the end of 1935, when Maclean first entered the Foreign Office, had been to avert the formation of the Berlin-Rome axis by conspiring with Pierre Laval to satisfy Mussolini with part of Ethiopia before he could take it all. Public opinion in Britain and France would not stand for it and Maclean applauded the wave of hostility; but this did not alter the fact that the precarious Stresa front against Hitler had fallen apart and war had come one step nearer.

Foreign Secretaries might come and go, but in 1935 it still seemed that the Foreign Office stood foursquare as a symbol of Britain's enduring authority in a crumbling world. Behind the Foreign Office in the direction of Whitehall were the Dominions Office and the Colonial Office; flanking these was the India Office. This cluster of buildings, all in the same style and of the same solidity, constituted the controlling mechanism of British overseas power. The dynamo that drove the engine, however, was running down; trade was stagnant; the wealth and industrial vigour that should have produced ships, tanks and aircraft were no longer adequate to defend the country's scattered possessions. It was an uneasy time for a young man to enter upon his inheritance, unless, of course, it was not his intention to sustain it. If that young man was Donald Maclean, he was more likely to share H. G. Wells' vision of a future in which the social system, and the great country house that symbolised it, were equally doomed. 'It is like an early day in a fine October. The hand of change rests on it all, unfelt, unseen; resting for a while, as it were half reluctantly, before it grips and ends the thing for ever.'[2] As Maclean mounted the worn steps of the Foreign Office in October 1935, he can have had little doubt that the hand of change was about to grip that complex of buildings and that he himself would be one of the agents of change. He had no intention of announcing what he meant to do; his influence would be unfelt, unseen; but it would be effective, because history was on his side, as it was on the side of Marxists everywhere.

In August of that year he had overcome the final obstacle; he had been examined by the Civil Service Commission and duly admitted to the Diplomatic Service. He had achieved his aim after months of intensive cramming at 'Scoones', one of the two main establishments in London that existed for the purpose. 'Scoones' was located on the upper floors of an old house near the British Museum, which was the domain of Monsieur Turquet. He was stout, with a florid complexion, and his white hair and overhanging moustache gave him a resemblance to Clemenceau, which was enhanced by simulated outbursts of rage, provoked usually by an error of French syntax. The chief subjects taught, in addition to French and German, were Modern History and Economics. The only teacher for whom Maclean felt political affinity was the brilliant young economics tutor, David Glass (the late Professor D. V. Glass), who was only two years older than he was. Glass had graduated in 1931 from the London School of Economics, which was, if anything, orientated even further to the Left than Cambridge. He supplemented his small income by tutoring, whilst he worked as a research assistant to Sir William Beveridge. In those days he expounded the frailties of the capitalist system in a way that tended to convince his hearers that it was doomed.

Maclean did not choose his friends among his fellow students for their politics; two of the friends he made at this time were sons of ambassadors with no radical leanings; both had been at Oxford and were distinguished by a certain *panache*. One was Tony Rumbold (the late Sir Anthony), whose father was a baronet and had lately retired from the Diplomatic Service. The other was Robin Campbell, whose father went to Belgrade as Ambassador in August 1935; a few years later Maclean served briefly under him in Paris. Robin Campbell failed the examination, much to his father's chagrin. Rumbold passed and soon began to court Felicity Bailey, whom Maclean had known at Cambridge; when Rumbold married her at St Margaret's, Westminster, in June 1937, Maclean was his best man. He was finding it no problem to take on the protective colouring of those among whom he would be working.

On the opening day of the examination the candidates made their way in some trepidation to Burlington Gardens. Valentine Lawford, a successful candidate in the previous year, has described his uneasy sensation, as he sat

'in a shadowy hangar (smelling of varnish and rubber and freshly poured ink) with unsightly pipes as its sole decoration, and windows, on its south side, towards audible but invisible Piccadilly.'[3]

The only part of the ordeal that need concern us is the interview, which in so highly competitive a contest was 'make or break' for many. The chairman of the interviewing board was Tony Rumbold's father, Sir Horace, who, as Ambassador in Berlin when Hitler came to power, had shown himself a resolute anti-Nazi. On his right sat the only female board-member, Lady Violet Bonham-Carter, step-daughter of Margot Asquith and a good friend of Sir Donald Maclean. From young Donald's point of view the auspices could hardly have been more favourable. His prominence at Cambridge made it inevitable that he would be asked about his political opinions. He rejected the idea of denying political involvement, which would have cast doubt on his integrity, and opted instead for the role of a man of compassion, whose head was just beginning to take command from his heart. Yes, he conceded, he had had strong political sympathies, adding, 'And I haven't entirely shaken them off.' The deceptive candour of this reply is made all the more impressive by the testimony given by Macmillan to the House of Commons in 1955: 'His college authorities gave him an exceptionally good report in which no mention was made of left-wing views.'[4]

In taking this line, Maclean was acting more sagaciously than his fellow conspirators, Burgess and Philby, both of whom switched sides ostentatiously and attached themselves to Germanophile societies. In doing so they incurred the risk that the security authorities would regard such a turn-about as indicating instability, if nothing worse. Such a conclusion would have been especially plausible in the case of Philby, whose father, H. St. John Philby, was a known fascist and was actually imprisoned on the outbreak of war. Maclean's manoeuvre was more subtle and proved successful. In retrospect, it is easy to convict his interviewers of lack of insight, as if they had too readily succumbed to their own social prejudices. It is as well to remember, however, that civilised society is precariously balanced on the need, at any given moment, to give the other person the benefit of the doubt. It is the fact that secret services exist outside civilised society that makes them dominant in totalitarian states and unloved in democratic ones.

To accuse Maclean's interviewers of naiveté is also to show want of historical sense. Today we have a sad familiarity with the poison of ideology and the evils of mind-conditioning; the 1930s, by comparison, was an age of innocence. Among candidates the shrewdness of Lady Violet's questions was a byword: she was not an easy dupe. But her sons and daughters had virtually grown up with Maclean and liked him. How was she to believe that he had put himself forward to join the Diplomatic Service for the express purpose of betraying its secrets? Laura Bonham-Carter (Lady Grimond), recalling this period, has written:

> 'What was to me always unconvincing was his explanation of his defection (ie from communism): "I've joined the other side." Since a few minutes argument revealed that intellectually at least this was hardly the case, it did occur to me to wonder why he should have chosen the diplomatic service as his career.'[5]

This judgment suggests that the interviewing board may have abandoned the argument too soon; if so, the curtailment was to prove costly.

Maclean's camouflage was greatly enhanced by the fact that he blended so well into the social milieu in which he would be least suspect; he adopted what his friend Philip Toynbee called his 'society Bolshy role'. Attired in white-tie and tails and sometimes flaunting a cloak, Maclean was a very acceptable escort in the London season for 'the Liberal girls'; daughters of leading Liberals, such as the Bonham-Carters and Sir Archibald Sinclair. They danced to 'Body and Soul' and 'Smoke Gets in Your Eyes', and there was not much political talk. If there was, Maclean baffled his questioners with a mixture of flippancy and illusory frankness, as when he observed 'my future lies with the oppressors rather than the oppressed.'[6] He first met Toynbee at a ball in the summer of 1936 on the eve of the outbreak of the Spanish Civil War. Afterwards they went to a 'Negro night-club', ending up with a dip in the Serpentine 'as the sun rose over the park'. Toynbee wrote many years later:

> 'When he heard that I was a communist . . . he told me that he used to be one as well, that he was still a Marxist, but that his interests now lay with the ruling classes. I was shocked and fascinated by this ingenious monster, but charmed, above all, by his lazy wit and sophisticated good humour.'[7]

Toynbee, who was to play a major role at a critical moment in Maclean's life, had become, like his new friend, a communist sympathiser at school. He had run away from Rugby and with his fellow communist, Esmond Romilly, had taken part in demonstrations against Sir Oswald Moseley's Black Shirts. Later he had become the first communist President of the Oxford Union; but neither his political activities, nor his disordered love life, brought happiness. Reviewing this period of his life at a later date, he provided an explanation of a kind for the tendency of so many of his contemporaries to invest their hopes in the USSR: 'Looking around us at our own hells we *had* to invent an earthly paradise somewhere else.'[8] Meanwhile, neither Donald nor Philip felt any need to be debarred from enjoying the social pleasures of capitalism during the interim before the Soviet paradise took over.

For Maclean to have entered the Diplomatic Service at the first attempt was an achievement; on average, only six or seven were selected each year from the cream of Oxbridge graduates. He must have felt a glow of pride, as on that morning in October 1935 he walked up Downing Street and, after glancing across at No. 10, turned left under the cavernous archway into the cobbled courtyard of the Foreign Office. In those days of innocence, no passes of admission were required; after the first day the porters, like those at London clubs, were expected to recognise the regulars. Maclean, as he entered, would have been confronted by a full-length portrait of the Marquis of Salisbury in the regalia of the Order of the Garter. He would have been directed to walk the tessellated paving until he reached the antiquated lift; but he would probably have taken the broad stone staircase, since the prestigious Department that he was to join was on one of the lower floors. This was the League of Nations and Western Department, which dealt with the Netherlands, Spain, Portugal and Switzerland, as well as the League. It was to be the chief field of his activity for nearly three years and his first task was to adapt himself to it. If his superiors concluded that he was unlikely to adapt, he would be offered a transfer to a Home Department. This was the offer made in 1938 to John Cairncross, who two years earlier had passed first into the Diplomatic. He was not transferred because at Cambridge Anthony Blunt had recruited him for the NKVD, but because the Foreign Office, which knew only that he had secured a first-class degree at Cambridge, formed the opinion that he would not fit in.

Maclean faced no such problem; he adapted with little apparent effort. He was accepted into the circle of the elect and they soon closed ranks around him. His friend, Tony Rumbold, had joined the Central Department, which handled France, Germany and Belgium. They both put down their names for the Travellers' Club and would walk there together across the corner of the park and take their lunch under the benevolent eyes of their seniors. Beneath the unruffled surface, however, disturbing forces were at work. Few young men, finding themselves near the levers of power, could have felt much confidence in their country's foreign and defence policies. It certainly seemed to Maclean that those formulating these policies were at best irresolute in their opposition to fascism and at worst were preparing to negotiate some compromise along similar lines to the abortive Hoare-Laval pact. Britain was neither giving firm backing to the League of Nations, nor spending enough to equip the nation's armed forces. By way of contrast, the foreign policy of the USSR, directed by Litvinov, seemed full of promise, as in 1934 the USSR joined the League and in the following year concluded defensive treaties with France and Czechoslovakia. Such a policy appealed to Maclean as showing 'proletarian internationalism'.

Although few of the younger members of the Foreign Office would have given much unqualified backing to Soviet policies, most were strongly francophile and also favoured a programme of rearmament that would enable Britain to take a more vigorous stand. They were prepared to overlook Vansittart's role in the Hoare-Laval negotiations and placed on him their bets for firm resistance to Hitler's demands. The leading figure among these 'Young Turks' was Ralph Wigram, the head of the Central Department, who had been enraged by the insistence of the Admiralty on concluding with Hitler the naval agreement of June 1935, which relieved the Reich of the naval restrictions imposed by the Treaty of Versailles. Wigram fully shared the exasperation of the Quai d'Orsay, believing that maximum Anglo-French solidarity was necessary in order to deter Hitler. Ten years earlier he had been crippled by polio; but this had not prevented his becoming an active head of Chancery at the Paris Embassy. Back in the Foreign Office, he not only kept up his Paris contacts, but with the tacit approval of Sir Orme Sargent, the Under-Secretary in charge of his Department, he discreetly fed facts and figures about German rearmament to Winston Churchill, who was playing the gadfly on the lethargic flank of the Conservative Party. This well-intentioned leakage would have fixed itself in Maclean's mind. Many years later in Moscow, Burgess tried to convince Stephen Spender that he had not been a spy, but only a discreet purveyor of information:

> '"Everyone gives away information," said Burgess. "When Churchill was in opposition he used to give away confidential information about what the government was thinking to Maisky, then Russian Ambassador." He seemed to think that Maclean and he were in much the same position as Churchill.'[9]

Valentine Lawford, who had joined the Central Department in 1934, has recorded another significant instance of Wigram's independence. In 1935, when a French delegation was due in London to discuss the German menace, Wigram sent his wife on a special shopping expedition to Paris with instructions to tell French friends how best to deal with the British government in the impending discussions.[10] There can be little doubt that Maclean, either through Lawford or Rumbold, would have learnt of this tactic. If he did, he would have reassured himself that his own covert communications to 'Teddy' were only one step further out of line.

The 1930s were years of confusion and readjustment inside the Foreign Office. After the First World War it had been necessary to adjust to the new internationalism represented by the League; as fascist powers, including Japan, gathered strength, it became clear that weak links in the international chain meant that it would not hold back the resurgent forces, vitalised by uncouth ideologies, which in Whitehall were underestimated and, indeed, barely comprehended. As opinions shifted and orthodoxies crumbled, the Foreign Office made little effort to impose new dogmas; a substantial degree of heresy was tolerated, on the understanding that the basic belief

4   Maclean at Cambridge

5 The Foreign Office from St James's Park

6 Lord Halifax (centre front) and senior staff of the British Embassy, Washington, 1945: Maclean in back row with the author on his left

in upholding British interests was accepted. Gladwyn Jebb (Lord Gladwyn), who in 1937 became private secretary to Vansittart, has described the situation in these terms:

> 'What did distinguish the Office at that time was an intellectual liveliness and complete liberty, inside the machine, to say what you thought and press your own point of view, provided that outside you were reasonably discreet about the official line ....'[11]

In this atmosphere Donald's continued expression of Leftist views would not have struck his friends as providing grounds for suspicion of disloyalty.

In July 1936 an event occurred that had an impact on young minds that cannot be overestimated – the outbreak of the Spanish Civil War. The only comparable episode in more recent times, in terms of its radicalising effect, has been the war in Vietnam. In October 1967 the Foreign Secretary, George Brown (the late Lord George-Brown), flanked by Lord Chalfont and other Ministers, held a meeting of senior staff in the Foreign Office. Current antagonism to the war in Vietnam was touched on lightly, tending to the conclusion that it was generating no real anguish, except among those whose views were in any case hostile to the USA. As I was about to leave the Foreign Office to embark on a academic career, I expressed doubt whether this rather complacent attitude took into account the militancy of the students. Lord Chalfont then commented that young people often held extreme opinions, but later discarded them. My unspoken thought was that this was exactly what had been thought thirty years earlier about Donald and the group of young men to whom the designation 'Cambridge Comintern' has been applied.

The importance of Franco's rising, in giving a new impulse to opinion, lay in the appreciation that it was resistible and that, if it was not effectively resisted, the last chance to hold back fascism in Europe would have gone. In Italy and Germany nothing could be done; but in Spain history was being made under our eyes. If in this crisis of democracy nothing was attempted, the younger generation in Europe might have to live for decades with the evil consequences. Yet it was at this moment that Baldwin's government exerted pressure on the Popular Front government of Léon Blum to deter France from active support for Republican Spain. Instead, a Non-Intervention Committee was set up in London under the chairmanship of the Earl of Plymouth, the Parliamentary Under-Secretary of the Foreign Office, to draw a decent veil over the activities of those powers, chiefly Germany, Italy and the USSR, which were trying to determine the outcome of the war. Maclean was closely involved in the work of this Committee and it is impossible to imagine anything better calculated to confirm his view that, in agreeing to further Soviet policy, regardless of that of his own government, he had made a justifiable decision.

His assumption that the Committee represented nothing more than a hypocritical washing of hands, whilst Spain was crucified, was not, of course, a fair verdict on the policy adopted by his superiors. Sargent, who also supervised Maclean's Department, was a sincere anti-fascist, as we have seen. He had been raised in the belief that Britain must maintain a balance of power in Europe, in order to preserve the peace and independence of all. In August 1936 he wrote:

'If the principle of non-intervention in the affairs of Spain breaks down . . . it may well be that the first step will have been taken in dividing Europe into two *blocs*, each based on a rival ideology . . . horrible development.'[12]

It was indeed a horrible development and we have been living under its shadow since the end of the Second World War. But to Maclean such a development was not so much horrible as inevitable, as capitalism and communism battled on the world stage. Twenty years later, in the aftermath of Soviet intervention in Hungary, he wrote from Moscow to a friend in England, who disapproved of it:

'We were all united in wishing the French and Soviet governments *would* intervene to save the Spanish government from Franco and the fascists . . .'

In his eyes, Soviet tanks had been equally necessary in 1956 to save Hungary from Nagy and the Americans. The scene had changed, but not the scenario.

Maclean was distressed not only about non-intervention, but also about the massive influx into France of refugees from Spain, who were crowded into unhygienic and comfortless camps. His colleague of those days, Evelyn Shuckburgh (Sir Evelyn), who was secretary of the Non-Intervention Committee, recalls that Maclean was 'often very nervy . . . his ashtray always piled high with cigarette-ends'. He scarcely concealed his pro-Republican feelings and it may have been for this reason that in November 1936 he was assigned, as a corrective, the task of compiling a summary of Soviet infringements of the Non-Intervention agreement. It would have been useful for Ambassador Maisky to learn, before the next Committee meeting, that Lord Plymouth had decided not to put forward 'further complaints at this stage'.[13]

In May 1937 Neville Chamberlain became Prime Minister and lost no time in asserting his own foreign policy, which in due course acquired the dishonoured name of appeasement. As Chamberlain gathered around himself his own advisers, such as Sir Horace Wilson and Sir Frederick Leith-Ross, tensions grew both between the Foreign Office and Downing Street and within the Foreign Office. Wigram was dead; at the end of 1937 Vansittart was removed from the key post of Permanent Under-Secretary to a relative sinecure as Chief Diplomatic Adviser; the 'Young Turks' were left leaderless. Everywhere the sky was growing darker. John Cornford, whom Maclean had known well at Cambridge, wrote:

> 'Black over Europe falls the night,
> The darkness of our long retreat,
> And winter closes with a silent grip . . .'[14]

By the time the poem appeared in John Lehmann's *Penguin New Writing*, the poet had died in Spain, as the International Brigade of half-trained volunteers was butchered. Soon only the laments of the poets would be left to remind the politicians of the road they had not taken. In Auden's poem *Spain 1937* the phrase 'But today the struggle' recurs like a warning bell. The poem ends:

> 'We are left alone with our day, and the time is short and
> History to the defeated
> May say Alas but cannot help or pardon.'[15]

In February 1938 Eden and his Parliamentary Under-Secretary, Lord Cranborne, resigned. It seemed to Maclean that there was no longer any barrier to the policy that he condemned in his book, written in Moscow over thirty years later, as Chamberlain's attempt 'to use Germany as a military counterforce to the Soviet Union'.[16] Maclean's verdict is a manifest misjudgment of Chamberlain; nonetheless there was little enough in the policy of appeasement to tempt him back into allegiance to his own country. This was his misfortune; up to this

point his services to the NKVD cannot have involved him very deeply;
he had been learning his trade. Moreover there was around this time a
hiatus in Soviet control that might have facilitated escape. 'Teddy' had
gone to Paris in the summer of 1937 and was there anxiously debating
his future with other non-Russian 'illegals', such as Krivitsky and
Poretsky (Ignace Reiss); all knew they were gravely menaced by
Stalin's purge, which was gaining momentum. Elisabeth Poretsky has
related how she tried to dissuade 'Teddy' from going to Moscow:

'You know what is in store for you, they will shoot you!'
'Yes, I know . . . They will kill me there and they will kill me here.
Better to die there.'[17]

'Teddy' went to Moscow: no more was heard of him.

If Maclean had left the Foreign Office at that time and adopted
another career, it is just possible that he would have been left in peace;
the fact that he had worked without payment would have been in his
favour. But the time had not come for rethinking his commitment; the
critical moment would come in August 1939 with the conclusion of the
Hitler-Stalin pact, which made the USSR an auxiliary of Britain's
enemy. By then he was one year deeper into the mire and working in
Paris for a new 'control'. In any case it was no part of his nature to
change his convictions; all who knew him were struck by his self-
assurance; it would scarcely have been possible for him to admit that
he had been wrong. In Cambridge, where his opinions had been
formed, he had had other true believers beside him; in the Foreign
Office he had none, but he was not going to allow that to weaken his
resolution. Just as certain religious fundamentalists thrive on the
indifference or hostility that surrounds them, so Maclean in a
community of careerists and conformists clung even more obstinately
to his beliefs, which in his eyes set him apart from, and above, his
fellows. Outwardly, however, he would conform; he was learning to
play his role, an essential part of his apprenticeship as a spy. The
technique was that of splitting his mind into two compartments in the
manner described by Klaus Fuchs:

'One compartment in which I allowed myself to make friendships,
to have personal relationships . . . I could be free and easy and
happy with other people without fear of disclosing myself because I
knew that the other compartment of my mind would step in if I
approached the danger point.'[18]

Nevertheless there could still be pitfalls. One of those who had met Maclean at a debutante's ball in 1934, when he was still claiming to be a communist, was Fitzroy Maclean (Sir Fitzroy), who had since served in the British Embassy in Moscow and had no illusions about communism. Encountering Donald by chance in the corridors of the Foreign Office, he asked him, 'for want of anything better to say', if he was still a party member. Maclean, who would have had no difficulty in finding a bantering answer, if asked the question in a night-club, was evidently embarrassed; he dismissed his former allegiance as 'simply a childish aberration'.[19]

There can be no convincing reply to the query whether Maclean, at this stage of his covert career, rendered major service to the NKVD. One reason why it is hard to arrive at an estimate is that the NKVD, unlike Western intelligence services, has an insatiable appetite for gossip. When in 1931 Arthur Koestler joined the Communist Party (KPD) in Germany, one of the first tasks assigned to him was to cultivate a young man of good family, whose father was an ex-ambassador and 'entertained . . . members of the German general staff and of the diplomatic corps'.[20] Maclean's father could no longer play this useful, if unconscious, role but Donald would certainly have been encouraged to make contacts among high officials and report everything he heard and saw. Soviet long-term planning requires meticulous examination of target personalities, their social background and character defects. Information that would seem to be of slight value is eagerly absorbed, such as the relationship between politicians and their permanent officials, which must necessarily remain opaque to an observer raised in a totalitarian system. Maclean was unusually well-equipped to elucidate such mysteries.

In general, however, his reports must have chiefly concerned what he saw as the inexorable drift of British policy towards an accommodation with Hitler that would leave Stalin to face the fascists alone, whilst Britain and France held the ring. It was to avoid such a calamity that Stalin was beginning to withdraw his confidence in Litvinov, who was Jewish, and to replace him with Molotov, who would be able to do business with the Aryan Ribbentrop. We must give Maclean credit for not having known that it was Stalin who was preparing to reach an accommodation with Hitler; but we must regret that he knew so little of the courage and determination of Churchill. There was nothing in the background or experience of Stalin and Molotov that fitted them to understand that the British people cherished a resolute hatred of fascism and had a leader, waiting in the wings, who would help them to prove it, when the drums began to roll.

4

Paris and World War

In the autumn of 1938 Maclean had nearly completed three years as a junior member of the League of Nations and Western Department of the Foreign Office and he was overdue for transfer to his first foreign post. His long initial spell in London under the scrutiny of his seniors need not imply lack of confidence in his future; if there had been doubt, he would not have been sent to so testing and prestigious a post as Paris. It is clear that he had employed his talent to deceive to good effect and had begun to construct a legitimate career, under cover of which he could pursue the nefarious trade of a spy, to which he was also committed. He had accomplished this partly by applying his considerable natural abilities and partly by exercising a high degree of discretion and restraint. He had not only curbed his continuing left-wing sympathies but had also conformed in other ways to the well-delineated 'Foreign Office type'. In the process he had largely abandoned the Bohemian habits that had marked his Cambridge career. His adaptation suggests an analogy with the behaviour of a group of insects known as predacious mimics. These creatures adopt the appearance and habits of the less gifted and less venomous insects upon which they prey; they move with immunity among their innocent victims, picking off one or two, as occasion offers.

·Appearances are important, because if these conform to expectations, the observer is unlikely to look below the surface. There is a story from mediaeval Andalusia of a lesson taught by a Sufi to a local ruler, who believed that it was safe to judge by appearances and take everything at face value. The Sufi arranged for his dervishes to file down a narrow street lined on one side by courtiers and on the other side by knights. The ruler was astonished to learn afterwards from his courtiers that the dervishes had worn brown robes, whilst his knights insisted that the robes had been blue; neither group of observers was prepared for the possibility that the dervishes would wear robes brown on one side and blue on the other.[1] Foreign Office observers, likewise, were unprepared for the turncoat syndrome; consorting with Maclean, it never occurred to them that they might be betrayed. Like them he wore a white collar, usually starched, with a sober tie: it was not an Old Etonian tie, but it passed muster. Sponge-bag trousers and a black Homburg hat with the curled-up brim, popularised by Anthony Eden, completed the traditional picture. Outside the Foreign Office it had been *de rigueur* to carry a tightly-rolled umbrella; but some of the younger men had abandoned this practice after 1938, when the umbrella became a symbol of Neville Chamberlain and appeasement. So closely did Maclean conform, that he became known in the typing pool as 'Fancy-Pants' Maclean (as distinct from Fitzroy Maclean, who was 'Fitz-Whiskers').[2]

It was on 24th September 1938 that Donald took up his post as Third Secretary at HM Embassy, Paris. As was customary, he was met at the Gare du Nord by a Chancery servant, who helped to clear his heavy luggage through Customs and escorted him to the waiting car. He was taken to the hotel, where he would stay until he could find rented accommodation within the amount of his rent allowance. On the next day he walked for the first time under the high, stone archway leading to the famous Embassy in the rue du Faubourg St Honoré which had once been the home of Pauline Borghese. The gateway was flanked by a porter's lodge, from which he was narrowly, if discreetly, observed by the porter. The Ambassador's residence took pride of place and the adjacent Chancery, where Maclean was to work, was crowded into what had been the stables of the Borghese house in the previous century. He found that he was to share a small room with a fellow bachelor, Valentine Lawford, who was relieved to be able to discharge into a second green tin tray some of the mass of incoming paper that had to be processed and redirected either upwards, towards the head of Chancery, Harold Mack (the late Sir Harold), or laterally towards the Service, Press or Commercial Attachés.

Before the morning was out, Maclean was presented to the Ambassador, Sir Eric Phipps, a short, dapper figure with an eye-glass, who had been transferred from Berlin to Paris some eighteen months previously. He was married to the sister of Vansittart's second wife. He was not on good terms with his brother-in-law; but it had been assumed, when Phipps sent back from Berlin a stream of despatches, etching Nazi leaders in acid terms, that he shared Vansittart's mistrust of all things German. Soon after his arrival in Paris, however, he had sensed the marked reluctance of the French people, and in particular the influential and wealthy *deux cents familles*, to stand up to Hitler and face the hardships and privations of another war. To the distress of anti-appeasement elements in the Foreign Office, Phipps' despatches from Paris took on an increasingly pessimistic tone. One of those so distressed was Oliver Harvey, private secretary to Lord Halifax, the Foreign Secretary. Harvey, who was much less of a Tory than most of his colleagues, confided in his diary towards the end of September 1938: 'I have never read anything like the defeatist stuff which Phipps is now sending us . . .'[3]

France, as Maclean already suspected, was unequally split between a minority of *les durs*, who were prepared to resist Hitler, cost what it might, and a majority of *les mous*, who yearned for peace and were inclined to regard Hitler as a bulwark against bolshevism. Many years later he wrote:

'Without going back as far as the *Comité des Forges*, one may recall that from the early summer of 1940 until the end of the war, all but a small fraction of the French big *bourgeoisie* went over from alliance with Britain to alliance with Germany.'[4]

Maclean's arrival in Paris coincided with the critical days of the Munich conference, at which Chamberlain and Daladier demonstrated that they were prepared to entrust Czechoslovakia to Hitler's mercy rather than form a common front against him with Stalin. So much the Soviet dictator could observe for himself; but it was certainly of great advantage to him, as he conducted his 'agonising reappraisal' of Soviet foreign relations, to have a source in the Paris Embassy well placed to report that in France the will to fight was conspicuously lacking. Lawford recalls how on that September evening, when Daladier returned from Munich, Maclean and Lawford leant out of a Chancery window to watch the slow progress of the French leader through cheering crowds, as he made his way up the rue du Faubourg St Honoré towards the Elysée palace. Lawford was horrified by what had happened, yet relieved that the immediate threat of war had been lifted.[5] If Maclean's thoughts were different, he kept them to himself. It was not for him to emulate the courageous action of two of his contemporaries, Con O'Neill and Colville Barclay, who resigned from the Diplomatic Service after Munich to show their disapproval. It was a gesture that Maclean appreciated; many years later in Moscow, when Lady Rumbold (Felicity) asked him if there were any of his former colleagues whom he would like to see again, Sir Con O'Neill (as he had then become) was one of only three names that he mentioned.[6] But in 1938 the course of open, honourable opposition was no longer accessible to him; for better or for worse, he had chosen the dishonoured jungle-path of espionage.

I had arrived in Paris with my wife at almost the same time as Maclean. At first I did not see much of him, as the Consulate-General, where I worked, was at some distance from the Embassy. I soon found that he, too, was keeping his distance. The amalgamation of the Diplomatic and Consular Services still lay nearly six years in the future; meantime some members of the senior branch maintained something approximating to a class distinction between the two. I assumed that Maclean had adopted this distinction in the process of assimilation among his new colleagues. It did not occur to me that he was prudently putting space between all those who were familiar with his Cambridge past. It was around this time, as I learnt much later, that he found himself in the same railway carriage with his old friend James Klugmann. To the distress of the latter, Maclean buried himself in *The Times* and killed conversation with a few curt answers. This was not the only change that I remarked: it struck me that he was no longer the self-confident, Mandarin figure that I had known; on the contrary he seemed uneasy and hesitant. I ascribed this change to the heavy pressure of work, oppressing us all, and to his evident distaste for the party-going that formed an inescapable part of diplomatic life. He went through the motions, but in the social round seldom gave the impression that he was enjoying himself.

As a bachelor Third Secretary, he was not expected to do much entertaining; nor with his lack of private means – at that date still exceptional in the Service – would he have been able to branch out. He found for himself a large, rather gloomy apartment in the rue de Bellechasse, near the Invalides. It was sparsely furnished and guests sat around, as Lawford remembers, 'on collapsing sofas or orange-crates ...' A book-shelf held a few of his Marxist texts, some Tauchnitz paperbacks and the orange jackets of editions from Victor Gollancz's Left Book Club. On the occasions when Maclean entertained his friends, 'The food was primitive,' one of them recorded; 'the wine was French, red, but definitely *ordinaire*.'[7] On one occasion the guests were Robin Campbell and his first wife, the Hon. Mary Ormsby-Gore; each had a bottle of claret at his or her elbow. So rough and ready was the bedroom accommodation that, when Lady Maclean first visited her son, she was housed by Jack Crawshay, an honorary

Attaché, who had married a daughter of Lord Tyrrell, one of Sir Eric Phipps' predecessors in Paris.

Maclean had no difficulty in making friends where he wanted to; some of these should be introduced, as we shall meet them again. The Minister, Ronnie Campbell (the late Sir Ronald), was a bachelor, who took an avuncular interest in younger colleagues, especially if these, like Maclean, shared his Scottish background. Campbell was to have a crucial influence on Maclean's career. The senior First Secretary was Michael (the late Sir Michael) Wright, who was an avid worker and appreciated Maclean's drafting skills. His room-mate in Chancery, Lawford, relished the fact that 'he was always willing to take over the more boring jobs. He never frowned if I had an engagement to keep and wanted to leave early.' Lawford was also glad to discover that they could share jokes together. There was indeed a lighter side to Maclean's character, though it could lead on to violence if he drank to excess. Around Christmas 1938 at a party organised by the Naval Attaché, Capt. 'Hooky' Holland (who later had the painful duty of sinking French battleships at Mers-el-Kebir), charades were played and it was thought necessary to illustrate some word by forming a chorus-line. Donald and I in drag showed our paces high-kicking. At other times the mood was sombre. I recall an evening when my wife and I took him to the cinema to see Jean Gabin in *La Bête Humaine* based on Zola's story of drink and degradation. We tried to cheer Donald afterwards by offering to take him home for a night-cap; but he slouched off into the darkness, scarcely pausing to say good-night.

He soon had good reason both for reticence and for depression. In the spring of 1939 Stalin made discreet overtures to Hitler and, when later an Anglo-French mission arrived in Moscow to negotiate a pact, progress was distressingly slow. Because of the participation of France in the Moscow negotiations, the telegrams passing between the Embassy there and the Foreign Office were being repeated to the Paris Embassy, where Maclean certainly saw them. He was thus able to advise the Russians of the British response, as Stalin raised the stakes and drew closer to Hitler; indeed information attributed to secret British sources was carefully doctored in such a way as to make a Nazi-Soviet pact all the more necessary to Hitler.[8] Unknown to Maclean, the Russians had another agent in the Foreign Office, whom 'Teddy' had recruited in the heyday of his success as an 'illegal' in London. This agent was Captain J. H. King of the Communications Department, whose position gave him even quicker access to Foreign Office telegrams than was possible for Maclean in Paris.

King was not an ideological spy; he was driven to do what he did by the parsimony of his employers and his own need to support a mistress as well as the wife from whom he was separated. In September 1939 he met the fate that all spies dread: his treachery was revealed by a defector. Samuel Ginsberg, alias Walter Krivitsky, had been a senior officer in the GRU, who had later transferred to the NKVD. He had been a friend and colleague of 'Teddy', but in the autumn of 1937 had taken a different decision; instead of returning to Moscow to meet his fate, he had defected in France and succeeded in escaping the clutches of the NKVD and reaching the USA. Neither the FBI nor the Foreign Office showed much interest in him and in 1939, with the help of an American journalist, Isaac Don Levine, he began to publish his story in the *Saturday Evening Post*. When Levine told the British Embassy in Washington that Krivitsky knew about spies in the Foreign Office, the British at last decided to investigate and before the end of September 1939 King had confessed. In the following month he was tried *in camera* and given a ten-year sentence. Under wartime regulations the government were able to suppress this fact; but in April 1940, after Krivitsky had been brought to London for further interrogation, a secret memorandum based on his disclosures was circulated in the Foreign Office and would have been seen by Maclean, when he returned from Paris to resume work in London. As we shall shortly see, this memorandum would have greatly alarmed him.

Meantime the Moscow negotiations had taken their fateful course. The two dictators concluded that both could profit by the destruction of Anglo-French power and in late August 1939 the infamous Hitler-Stalin pact was signed and war became inevitable. Lawford, hurriedly recalled from leave in England, was 'appalled by German and Russian hypocrisy, duplicity and cynicism'. He assumed that Maclean shared his feelings and, in order to lighten the gloom, 'declared that the only course left for decent people like us was to join the Polish or Hungarian cavalry, and die fighting against hopeless odds ... he professed to agree and laughed uproariously.' All too soon the Polish cavalry were indeed dying under the weight of German tanks; Britain was at war and it was no laughing matter – least of all for Maclean. Hitherto he had been able to argue that Britain and the USSR shared a common anti-fascist aim, even if they pursued it by divergent methods. Now Stalin was giving aid to Britain's sworn enemy. There could be only one word for what Maclean was doing – treason.

We do not know who was Maclean's 'control' in Paris. If it was another 'illegal', a likely candidate would have been 'Teddy's' brother-in-law, Isourin, who worked for the NKVD. If it was a 'legal', it might well have been Kislov, the deputy NKVD 'Resident', who had charge of Philby during his career as a war correspondent first in Spain and, after the end of the Civil War, with the British Expeditionary Force in France.[9] It would have been too risky, however, for Maclean to have met at all frequently with a member of the Soviet Embassy and a cut-out would certainly have been used. Maclean's known literary interests would have made it plausible to select an intermediary from among the left-wing habitués of the cafés along the Boulevard St Michel. One of the dominant figures in these circles was the German communist, Willi Muenzenberg, a luminary of the 'League of Proletarian Revolutionary Writers', who since Hitler came to power had been the leading cultural representative of the Comintern in Paris and had sponsored the famous 'Brown Books' of Nazi terror. His right-hand man was Otto Katz, described by Arthur Koestler as 'a smooth and slick operator . . . dark and handsome, with a somewhat seedy charm'.[10] In November 1936, when Maclean had been in London, dealing with Non-Intervention in Spain, Katz had been instrumental in setting up a British committee to agitate against this policy. As a result, he had been refused readmission to Britain; but this did not sever his British links, which were strong in the universities. He co-operated with James Klugmann at Cambridge and Bernard Floud at Oxford in founding the World Student Committee against War and Fascism, and the latter recruited for liaison a personable young woman from one of the Oxford women's colleges. She came to Paris around the time of Maclean's arrival there and was a good deal closer to Katz than his wife, Ilse, would have wished.

In 1938 Muenzenberg and Katz launched in Paris a polemical magazine for the intelligentsia, *Die Zukunft* (The Future), which attracted such English contributors as Harold Nicolson, Norman Angell and E. M. Forster; its editorial office would have been for Maclean both a congenial and a convenient meeting place, as he began, with increasing self-confidence, to revert to his favoured 'Bohemia'. The ambience was intellectually stimulating, but Maclean, who had fine antennae, must also have caught the smell of fear. Stalin was busy purging the Comintern, as the NKVD took over its agents' functions. It was in 1938 that Muenzenberg received his summons to Moscow and decided to ignore it; this led to an uneasy relationship between him and Katz, who had sought safety in conformity with Stalinism. When war broke out, Muenzenberg was interned, but was released with other German refugees as the Wehrmacht approached Paris. He went south with two men posing as refugees and was found hanged in a forest near Grenoble. Katz and his wife escaped first to the USA and then to Mexico, but his date with destiny was only deferred; he was executed in 1952 in Czechoslovakia, during the Stalinist purge there.

Maclean would not have been human if he had not at this period had thoughts of escape. It would, of course, have meant throwing himself on the mercy of MI5 and abandoning his diplomatic career; to someone as proud and egotistical as he this would have been a high price to pay for peace of mind. The key question, however, was whether he could have slept safe at nights; there was plenty of evidence available to him that the NKVD had a long arm. Two years would elapse before Krivitsky was found dead in a hotel in Washington; but in 1938 there were two mysterious deaths in Paris which could scarcely have escaped Maclean's notice. Trotsky's son, Leon Sedov, entered a clinic supposedly staffed by White Russian *émigrés*: his condition was not serious, but soon became so and he never left the clinic alive. A few months later the headless body of his friend, Rudolf Klement, was dredged up in the Seine. As the NKVD became more ruthless, Maclean could have been under no illusion that the fatal decision that he had made in Cambridge was reversible. His veiled hostility to Stalin dates from this period.

The question arises what could have been the value of the reports he made to his 'control' in the first bitterly cold winter of the 'phoney' war. The Embassy was a small, closely-knit body and the two Third Secretaries saw virtually everything – not only the telegrams and formal despatches, but even the Ambassador's personal letters to Sir Alexander Cadogan (who had succeeded Vansittart as Permanent Under-Secretary) and Sir Orme Sargent. Relations between the Chancery and the Service Attachés were close and Maclean would have been well aware of the Maginot mentality that kept the Allied armies immobilised in their bunkers and obliged the RAF to drop leaflets, rather than bombs, on the Ruhr. He would have known, too, how near the Allies came to intervening on the side of Finland in her 'winter war' against the USSR, and how plans were laid in Paris staff talks to stem the flow of Russian oil into the German war machine by attacking Baku. All such information would have confirmed Stalin's belief that he had made the right choice and should stick to it, ignoring the provocations that were beginning as Hitler's power and audacity grew. The French Communist Party continued to oppose the war.

At this difficult and anxious juncture in his life he began to benefit from the distraction and stimulus of his first real love affair. As we saw in the preceding chapter, he had flirted with 'the Liberal girls', but he had not become seriously involved. One evening in December 1939, when he was prowling around the cafés of the *rive gauche* with an American friend, Bob McAlmon, they came in out of the snow and, entering the Café Flore, saw through the steam and smoke the waif-like face and trim figure of Melinda Marling. McAlmon knew her and made the introduction, so unwittingly terminating the relatively carefree existence that she had hitherto led. She was the eldest daughter of Francis H. Marling, Advertising Manager of the Pure Oil Co. of Chicago, where she had been born on 25th July 1916. Marling's father came of a Gloucestershire family and had been taken to the USA as a child. His wife, Melinda's mother, had been born Melinda Goodletts of a Huguenot family long established in the USA; her home life had been broken up by the divorce of her parents, when she was a child, and at the age of twenty she had eloped with Marling. The marriage broke up in 1928 and in the following year Mrs Marling took her three daughters, Melinda, Catherine and Harriet, to Switzerland and sent them to a school at Vevey, run by an Englishwoman. Many years later this teacher, after reading in a newspaper that Melinda was in trouble, wrote to her mother: 'I always remember her as a most loving character.'[11] The girls went to this school first as day-girls, then as boarders, when their mother returned to the USA to secure a divorce from Marling and marry Hal Dunbar, who was a wealthy New Yorker with property at South Egremont, Massachusetts. In July 1931 Mrs Dunbar, as she had become, collected her children from Vevey and settled them in New York. Melinda's pleasant memories of her two years in Switzerland explain why she went to live there after the disappearance of Donald.

Back in New York, Melinda was sent to the Spence School, one of the prestigious schools of the city, but she was never a keen student and it was clear that a university education would be wasted on her. When school days were over, she took a secretarial course and for a couple of months worked in Macy's book department; but earning a living also lacked appeal. In 1938, when she was nearly twenty-two, this aimless existence began to pall; she found she was even beginning to forget the French she had learned at Vevey. She therefore took a decision to go to Paris and take a course at the Sorbonne. She had a little money of her own and the rate of exchange was very favourable, so she could live cheaply in the student community around St

Germain des Prés and, if anyone had warned her that Europe was a powder-keg, she would not have paid much attention. It was not that she was in any way stupid; it was just that she found politics and economics boring. As for ideology, the word did not feature in her vocabulary. It was interaction with people that brought the colour into her pale cheeks and made her eyes shine. When she was animated, she was a very attractive young woman. She was *petite* and there was about her an air of helplessness which, even if it was somewhat misleading, had a considerable appeal to protective males.

Before long she settled down in the Hotel Montana, next door to the Café Flore, where the sages, most of them left-wing, used to hold forth. She was not much interested in their discourse, but she liked the bustle and the loud, confident voices of the students. Her own voice – and it was one of her attractions – had faint New England intonations, but a softness that is usually associated with the American South. In keeping with her supposed status as a student, she often carried an armful of books; but her actual reading consisted chiefly of magazines. The only habit that distinguished her from most of the other American girls was a liking for cigars. In the summer of 1939 she was joined by her youngest sister, Harriet, aged nineteen, who was studying French at Smith College and was due to take a course at the Sorbonne with a party of girls from the same college. The party cancelled its visit at the last moment, but by that time Harriet was already in Paris. Oblivious of impending hostilities, Melinda and Harriet hired a car, drove through the Loire Valley and got as far south as Carcassonne before turning back. War had been declared and the American Embassy was advising nationals to go to St Malo to await shipping. The sisters complied with some reluctance, but finding the ship delayed and accommodation much inferior to that of the Hotel Montana, soon returned to Paris. Not until November did Harriet finally sail, after being urged by Mrs Dunbar to come home to complete her education. Melinda stayed on; it was a decision that in its own way was as fatal as Donald's decision to work for the Comintern.

Melinda wrote regularly to her mother and it is significant that she mentioned Donald in one of her letters soon after meeting him, though she was careful to add: 'but I am not really in the least bit interested in him'. She protested too much. Her feelings, like his, were force-fed by the tensions of wartime. Six months after she had first met him she sent to her mother this pen portrait:

'He is six foot tall, blonde with beautiful blue eyes, altogether a beautiful man. He has all the qualities for a husband (at least, I think). He is the soul of honour, responsible, a sense of humour, intelligent, imagination, cultured, broadminded (and sweet), etc. Of course he has faults but somehow they don't clash with mine – except that he is stubborn and strong willed. I needed that as I was drifting along getting nowhere.'[12]

That was written just before she finally married him; she had not made up her mind without a struggle. Early in 1940 she had decided to put distance between herself and her problems and left for the South of France. From there she wrote him a letter which showed that she was already aware of one of his faults:

'If you do feel an urge to have a drinking orgy, why don't you have it at home – so at least you will be able to get safely to bed? Anyway, do try to keep young P. from completely demolishing your apartment.'[13]

We shall hear more of 'young P.', alias Philip Toynbee, who was honeymooning in Paris and encountered Donald and Melinda at the Café Flore.

Maclean had been unable to accompany her on her journey south because of pressure of work and changes of staff. In November 1939 Phipps had retired and been replaced by Sir Ronald (H.) Campbell, the only one of Maclean's Ambassadors who failed to record a favourable opinion of him; this verdict is the more surprising in that his son, Robin Campbell, had formed a friendship with him. Confusion in the Embassy had been averted by moving the Minister, Ronnie Campbell (later Sir Ronald [I.] Campbell). He was replaced by Oliver Harvey. In February 1940 Michael Wright was replaced by Roddie Barclay (later Sir Roderick). Maclean had lost his congenial roommate, Lawford, whose seat was filled by the Hon. Henry Hankey, younger son of Lord Hankey. Maclean missed Lawford's sense of humour and wrote to him that he could not have shared with his successor the wry joke about having to join the Polish or Hungarian cavalry.

All too soon it was May 1940 and it was not the Poles who were being overwhelmed by the tanks of the Wehrmacht. The Embassy looked on with horror, as the British army retreated on Dieppe and Dunkerque and the French armies disintegrated. Defeat in the field

precipitated the collapse of civilian morale: *les mous* were in the
ascendant and Marshal Pétain raised his grizzled head. Among the
Embassy staff there was little time for regrets or gloomy prognostica-
tions; telegrams from the Foreign Office streamed in, some of them
prefixed DEDIP, which meant that these could not be left to the
trained cypher officers but had to be decrypted by diplomatic staff.
Maclean took his share of this arduous work, which was usually the
prelude to translating the message into French. As the threat
of French capitulation increased, there were urgent appeals from
Churchill to Paul Reynaud, which had to be delivered at any hour of
the day or night. One night Maclean had to hand in such a note at the
French Prime Minister's private apartment and was received by his
mistress, Madame La Porte, in *négligé*.

Oliver Harvey wrote in his diary: 'such glorious weather – never did
the trees in the Champs-Elysées look so lovely.'[14] It would be five
years before a British diplomat would see the trees in leaf again. The
front line was moving daily nearer; the burning of archives had begun
and everyone kept a suitcase ready packed. On 16th May the British
Embassy sent home all wives and female staff and the American
Embassy urged all Americans to leave. It was at this juncture that
Donald proposed to Melinda. She wanted more time and replied that
she would like to return to the USA and think it over. In that case, he
insisted, they would not see one another again until the war was over –
perhaps never. On 25th May they celebrated his birthday in sombre
mood; she was continuing to demur. Finally, on Saturday, 8th June
she made up her mind; the fact that she was pregnant was no doubt
the decisive factor. On the following day she wrote to her mother:

> 'Please don't feel hurt that I haven't let you know before about my
> decision to marry Donald. But honestly I didn't know whether to or
> not. We decided very suddenly because it seemed to be the only
> chance as the Embassy is liable to leave Paris for some Godforsaken
> little place in the country ... I am sorry I haven't given you more
> details about Donald and I know you must be very worried and also
> probably disappointed at my marrying an Englishman.'[15]

Mrs Dunbar was to experience many more disappointments before
Donald ceased from disrupting her life.

It was a time of decision, too, for the British Ambassador and his
staff. Harvey recorded in his diary: 'French Government have now
decided to move away all but essential services. We are doing likewise

. . .'[16] Accommodation had been reserved in a *château* near Tours and on 10th June Campbell and his adjutants set out. They had been astonished by Maclean's announcement that he had chosen such a moment to get married; they left him to his own devices, after expressing doubt whether he would find a *Mairie* to undertake the ceremony. John Malet, Campbell's social secretary, who no longer had official duties, agreed to stay and act as witness and best man. By late afternoon they found that the *Mairie* of the Palais Bourbon was still open and Donald and Melinda became man and wife. Their troubles were only beginning; all Paris was on the move by bus, car, bicycle and even horse and cart. The long, slow procession ground to a halt whenever there was an air-raid or a car ran out of petrol. Queues formed wherever a shop was open and food could be bought. The Vice-Consul, who had taken my place some months before, was left behind in a bread queue and never caught up with the convoy; he reappeared in Marseilles some weeks later, having travelled most of the way on foot.

Donald and Melinda did not suffer that misfortune, but that first night of their marriage they got no further than Chartres. By the second night they had reached the outskirts of Tours, but could find no accommodation and had to spend the night in the car; it was a night punctuated by air-raids. Few marriages can have begun in greater turmoil. On 13th June the Military Attaché gave warning that, if the Embassy party did not at once cross the Loire, they might be cut off. The British Ambassador to Belgium, Sir Lancelot Oliphant, was already in German hands; Campbell decided to push on to Bordeaux, where the French government in tremulous uncertainty was assembling. That night Campbell and his entourage settled into the Hotel Montré in Bordeaux and there on the next day Donald and Melinda caught up with them. Barclay gave up his room to them and moved in with other grass-widowers.[17]

The curtain was rising on the last act; Reynaud's government was falling apart. The fate of France was about to be entrusted to the First World War heroes, Weygand and Pétain – not to fight it out, but to sue for peace. The estuary was filled with shipping and in Bordeaux food was running short. On 16th June, the Embassy staff, who were becoming less and less popular with local people, had a picnic lunch by the quayside with RAF rations, washed down with a couple of bottles of champagne. On the following day the Macleans embarked for England. Campbell and Harvey remained for a few more days, as prospects continued to deteriorate. On 22nd June the latter wrote in his diary: 'Armistice signed at 6 p.m. The French Government did not even bother to tell us.'[18]

If the Macleans had hoped to sail all the way home in a British sloop, they were soon disappointed; at sea they were transferred with other civilians to a tramp steamer, which had delivered a cargo of British coal to South America. At night Melinda shared a cabin with three women, whilst Donald slept in the corridor with the men. Food was sparse and by day the Macleans sat on deck, recalling succulent lunches and dinners eaten in Paris less than three weeks ago. The ship constantly zig-zagged and the voyage lasted ten days. The English Channel was clear of the last of the British troops, who had been evacuated leaving most of their equipment behind. As the Macleans disembarked, England was bracing herself to face the invasion that seemed bound to come, once Churchill had summarily rejected the German peace offer of 17th July. In Berlin, however, Hitler had not made up his mind. There was an alternative to risking an amphibious operation: he might instead invade the USSR.

The Macleans could hardly have begun their married life in London under more difficult conditions. They had no home and no furniture or household goods. For the first couple of weeks they stayed with Lady Maclean at Penn, and one weekend Lawford, whose family lived about ten miles away, came over on horseback to see them. Petrol rationing made travel by car a rare luxury; in any case Maclean's car had been left in Bordeaux. Clothes rationing also created difficulties: they had had to leave much of their clothing behind and coupons were needed even to buy handkerchiefs. They decided to move into a hotel and chose the Mount Royal near Marble Arch. They were still there in the late summer, when the Luftwaffe began its attacks on London, and a near-miss on the hotel forced them to find furnished accommodation elsewhere. They moved to Mecklenburg Square off the Gray's Inn Road. It was not a fashionable area; but Maclean, working in the Foreign Office, drew no rent or entertainment allowance and could afford nothing better. At night the bombs rained down; the Whitehall contingent of the Home Guard, Maclean among them, was kept busy pushing incendiaries off the roofs of government buildings. One morning, as we walked up Whitehall, passing the still smoking ruins of a part of the Treasury, we saw chalked on a smooth fragment of masonry the defiant tag: *Nec aspera terrent* (Nor does savagery affright us). As the Blitz continued and Melinda's pregnancy grew more advanced, they decided that she should go to the USA for the birth. Three days before Christmas 1940 she was delivered of a boy in the Harkness Hospital, New York, but he lived only a few days. Not until the autumn of 1941 did she return to London; by that time the Luftwaffe was fully occupied on the Eastern Front.

It was in 1940, after the fall of France, that Maclean had two meetings with Philby, their first encounter since the mid-1930s. There was nothing very risky about these meetings; Philby was about to sever his connection with *The Times* and was already in touch with Section D of SIS, in which Burgess was serving. Section D had been set up shortly before the war in order to handle sabotage, subversion and 'black' propaganda. In late July 1940 it was absorbed into a new organisation, the Special Operations Executive (SOE), and shed Burgess in the process; Philby was retained as a propaganda expert. As a result of his evacuation from Arras with the British Expeditionary Force, he had lost touch with his Soviet 'control', who had remained in Paris; he approached Maclean in order to re-establish contact. Maclean reacted cautiously and at their first meeting did no more than arrange to meet again; at the second meeting he gave Philby the necessary instruction.[19] It is interesting to note that Philby approached Maclean, whom he scarcely knew, rather than Burgess, whom he had himself recommended to the NKVD as a suitable recruit.

Back in the Foreign Office, Maclean would have learnt how close he had come to being unmasked by Krivitsky's disclosures. One writer has suggested that his distress at having so nearly been identified led the NKVD to redouble its efforts to dispose of the defector.[20] However, that may be, the fact remains that Krivitsky's mysterious death, which his relatives and friends never regarded as suicide, occurred early in 1941. The unnamed suspect, on whom he had laid the finger, was described as 'a Scotsman of good family', educated at Eton and Oxford, and an idealist who worked for the Russians without payment; he had had access to documents of the Committee of Imperial Defence, he 'occasionally wore a cape and dabbled in artistic circles.'[21] Krivitsky was interviewed not only by MI5 but also by Gladwyn Jebb (Lord Gladwyn), who had been private secretary to the Permanent Under-Secretary and thus the link-man between the Foreign Office and the secret organisations. In those days the Foreign Office had no Security Department and it was not until February 1940, when the debriefing of Krivitsky was over, that an unpaid adviser on security, William Codrington, was appointed, but with no staff to assist him. There is no evidence that Maclean came under scrutiny; the fact that he had neither been at Eton nor Oxford would probably have exempted him. On the other hand, some of the clues fitted – including the cape; after Cambridge he had certainly moved on the fringe of 'Bloomsbury'. The reference to the Committee of Imperial Defence would have suggested a more senior figure but, on closer examination, may be conclusive. We have seen that, before Maclean left the Foreign Office to go to Paris, he had been dealing with the Spanish Civil War, the disturbing appearance of Italian submarines in the Mediterranean, and the torpedoing of British merchant shipping. The situation was monitored by a sub-committee of the Chiefs of Staff, who reported to the CID. It is very probable that liaison with this sub-committee gave Maclean access to CID papers.

The alarm and anxiety that marked his return to London was aggravated by the failure of the Foreign Office to assign him to one of the prestigious political Departments. The division of France into occupied and unoccupied zones, the upsurge of de Gaulle and his Free French and the resultant conflict in the crumbling French Empire necessitated setting up a separate French Department. It was headed by Hal Mack, supported by nearly all the members of the Paris Chancery, except for Maclean; his former Ambassador was understood to have reported unfavourably on his untimely marriage and consequent failure to share the work of evacuation. Maclean felt his exclusion keenly, though he said little, and his routine promotion to Second Secretary in October 1940 was not affected. He was placed in the newly created General Department, which dealt mainly with the wartime Ministries of Shipping, Supply and Economic Warfare. This was not a field in which diplomats of those days claimed much expertise. I was myself working in the Foreign Office at that time and I recall overhearing two of my seniors complaining about a three-hour meeting that had been discussing how to deny wolfram to the Germans. 'What,' said one testily, '*is* wolfram anyway?' The General Department, aside from its head and Maclean, was largely staffed by outside experts. One of these was Aubrey Wolton, who respected his abilities, but regarded him as 'by nature a rather withdrawn and lonely individual'. Donald and Melinda never asked him home, though they spent several evenings together, going from pub to pub. Wolton recalls: 'I became quite attached to them both, but failed to make any close contact. They seemed so young and so lost.'[22]

Maclean had to adjust not only to a new Department, but also to a new 'control' in the person of Anatoli Gromov, who took up the post of Attaché at the Soviet Embassy in London in the late autumn of 1940 and in August 1941 was promoted to Second Secretary. He had travelled via Alaska and New York, where he had probably left his wife, Zinaida Mikhailovna, since she was not with him in London. He was a new-style NKVD officer, carefully trained in the procedures of *conspiratsia*, and insistent on copies of documents, wherever possible. In the days before the common use of the photocopier and Minox camera, such insistence increased the labour and danger of espionage. Gromov, who was code-named 'Henry', also took over control of Blunt, who had found a niche in MI5. In later life Blunt referred to 'Henry' as 'flat-footed' and a change for the worse after the more flexible control of the 'illegals'.[23] In the end Maclean must have come to terms with 'Henry', who followed him to the USA in 1944. Some seven years later 'Henry' having resumed his real name, Gorsky, was closely involved in the terminal phase of Maclean's career in espionage; he was deputy head of the First Directorate of the NKVD in Moscow, dealing with Britain and the USA, when the appeal came from London for asylum to be granted to Donald Maclean and Guy Burgess.

'Henry' appears to have tolerated close association between Philby, Blunt and Burgess, which offended against strict NKVD practice; the two latter, for example, were living in the flat in Bentinck Street belonging to Victor Rothschild (Lord Rothschild), who was then an officer in MI5. Maclean, however, was prudently kept apart; there is no sound evidence for the belief that he, too, was an *habitué* of the Bentinck Street ménage. It is necessary to stress this point, because a remarkable story has been put in circulation by Robert J. Lamphere, formerly of the FBI. According to this writer,

'to keep Maclean in line, Burgess got him drunk and photographed him nude in another man's arms, then blackmailed him so that Maclean would remain in Soviet employ.'[24]

These stirring events are supposed to have taken place in October 1941 or soon after; yet Burgess had been able to collect evidence with which to blackmail his friend since 1935; he had no need to expend film on him or arrange an orgy. Mr Lamphere might also like to explain what hold he thinks Burgess had over Maclean that Maclean did not have over Burgess. There would have been no need to make Burgess drunk in order to find him nude in another man's arms. Not every item that glistens in the FBI archives is pure gold.

Some months before this fictive episode is thought to have occurred, a reversal of alliances had taken place that gave new heart to the

'Cambridge Comintern'. Hitler's invasion of the USSR in June 1941, though it threatened the very survival of the Soviet state, must have come as a great relief to Maclean and the others. They could comfort themselves that both their legitimate right hand and their illegitimate left were serving the same good cause; if they were providing intelligence that the British government had not seen fit to communicate, they were only making good the government's failure to act as a loyal ally should. This was, of course, a specious argument: the British and Soviet governments might be at one in seeking to defeat Hitler, but they were not in agreement about how to achieve this aim. The major source of disagreement concerned when and where to open a second front, which would take the strain off the Red Army. As early as September 1941, when British forces were retreating in North Africa and the USA was not yet in the war, Stalin had already begun to demand that Churchill should open a second front in Western Europe and the obedient CPGB furtively daubed blank spaces with the slogan 'Second Front Now'. When Maisky got wind of the projected Anglo-American landings in French North Africa, code-named 'Torch', he insisted to all who would listen that such an operation would not meet Stalin's demands. Three weeks before the landings, which took place on 7th November 1942, Oliver Harvey wrote in his diary:

'Maisky ... has told Cummings of the *News Chronicle* ... all the details of Torch. This is extremely serious, hazarding as it might the lives of thousands.'[25]

Maisky may well have derived at least part of his information from Maclean, whose Department had assumed responsibility for legal and administrative matters arising from the stationing in British territory of Allied armed forces, of which the most numerous in 1942–3 were French and Polish. Maclean's contacts with these forces, if tenuous, would have provided some insights of interest to the NKVD. For example, he would have been aware of the lamentable impression made on the Poles by the discovery by the Wehrmacht in the forests of Katyn of the bodies of Polish officers and fighting men, buried there whilst the area was still in Russian hands. This led in April 1943 to the break in relations between the Soviet government and the Polish government in exile in London. At this time Blunt in MI5 was responsible for the security of the Missions of Allied governments in London, including the governments in exile and their couriers, who could sometimes be parted from their diplomatic bags. Philby was in close liaison with MI5, as head of the Iberian section of the counter-espionage branch of MI6, which monitored peace feelers emanating from the anti-Soviet German resistance movement. At the centre of the web sat Gromov, drawing together the various threads for the edification of Stalin.

The war was creeping up on the Maclean family. In 1943 Alan left Cambridge to join the Army. In October of the same year the eldest brother, Ian, was killed. He had abandoned the legal profession with a sigh of relief and joined the RAF in July 1940, rising to the rank of Flying Officer. He became navigator of an aircraft on loan to the Special Operations Executive (SOE), which was operating out of Tempsford in support of the Danish resistance movement. He was shot down over Esbjerg in Denmark and there buried; he was posthumously awarded the Distinguished Flying Cross and his name was added to the octagonal plinth under the cross on his father's grave in the churchyard at Penn. Forty years on, Donald, too, would find a place there.

5

Washington: The Cold War

Towards the end of April 1944 the Macleans set sail in convoy for New York, where they arrived on 6th May. It was not a comfortable journey; male and female passengers were segregated and their opportunities for relaxation were frequently interrupted by boat-drill. Melinda was three months pregnant and found it tiresome to keep pulling on a life-jacket. She was delighted, however, to be escaping from wartime London and returning to her own country, where she hoped to bear her second child in safety. Had their departure been delayed another six weeks, the V-1 'flying bombs' would have been landing around them. Donald was equally glad to leave London and improve his prospects in the Service. In New York he briefly met William Hayter (Sir William), whose post he was taking at the Embassy. As Hayter was already a First Secretary, Maclean was confident that his promotion would follow shortly, as indeed proved to be the case. Arriving in springtime in the New World, with infinite opportunity before him, he experienced an unfamiliar elation. He was glad, too, to find petrol unrationed and, instead of scouring the corner-shops of London for a packet of ten, he could now buy cigarettes by the carton.

Melinda settled in with her mother, Mrs Dunbar, and her step-father, who had an apartment in Park Avenue and a farmhouse at South Egremont, Massachusetts. Maclean had been unable to take on Hayter's rented house in Washington and was faced with a long search. The capital city had proved unable to accommodate the great influx of soldiers and civilians and their families that the war had brought. For the British, whose dollars were severely rationed, the housing problem was particularly acute; it was not until the Foreign Office raised Maclean's rent allowance to $175 per month that he was able to sign the lease of 2710 35th Place and move there in mid-January 1945. Melinda had been delivered by Caesarean section of her son, Fergus, on 22nd September 1944. In one important respect the long delay in becoming reunited with his family had suited Maclean very well. As we shall see, he needed an impeccable pretext for travelling regularly to New York to see Melinda there or join her for a weekend at South Egremont.

Washington in 1944 was still little more than a large country town, embellished with a few fine buildings and monuments. One of the finest buildings was the Embassy designed by Lutyens in Massachusetts Avenue; unfortunately accretions of staff had rendered it inadequate and it had spawned alongside a hideous, modern annexe. The Chancery, however, where Maclean worked, was housed in the Lutyens building. He found old friends there and soon made new ones. He got on well with the Ambassador, Lord Halifax, and frequently joined his foursome on the tennis court behind the residence before the day's work began. Old friends from Paris days included Michael Wright, who was head of Chancery, and Roddie Barclay, one of the First Secretaries; but the most important was Ronnie Campbell, who was the senior Minister and had become Sir Ronald. It was mainly to him and his high opinion of Maclean that the latter owed his assignment to work connected with development of the atom bomb, which was soon to be the NKVD's top priority. This work, known to the British as 'Tube Alloys' and to the Americans as the 'Manhattan Project', was a closely guarded secret even within Chancery. In 1946 when George Carey-Foster, head of the Foreign Office Security Department, visited Washington, Campbell's successor in the atomic work, Sir Roger Makins (Lord Sherfield), asked him to set up a special security zone for 'Tube Alloys' files, to which only Makins, Maclean and their respective secretaries should have access. The arrangements were made in close consultation with Maclean, who had a good sense of humour and would have appreciated the irony of it all.[1] It has been supposed that his connection with this top-secret work began in February 1947, when he was appointed joint secretary of the Combined Policy Committee on the departure of Makins; but the fact is that this appointment was the culmination of over two years' study of this vital area of policy.

The Combined Policy Committee (CPC) had been set up in the wake of the meeting in Quebec in August 1943 of Churchill and Roosevelt, who agreed that for the duration of the war there should be an Anglo-American-Canadian partnership, from which all other countries, and specially the USSR, should be excluded. Nominal representatives of Britain on the CPC, which had a joint Anglo-American secretariat, were Lord Halifax and Field Marshal Sir H. Maitland-Wilson; but they seldom attended and Halifax was represented by Campbell until March 1945, when Makins replaced him on appointment as Economic Minister. The economic aspect had become of great importance, because the CPC supervised the work of a subordinate body, the Combined Development Trust (CDT), which pre-empted and allocated scarce minerals, including uranium. General Leslie Groves, who was in charge of the 'Manhattan Project', had become aware early in 1943 that the USSR was trying to acquire uranium ores in the USA. These ores were known to exist in the USSR, but wartime conditions made it difficult to mine and transport them. The CDT was able to claim by September 1944 that it directly or indirectly controlled over ninety per cent of known deposits of high-grade uranium outside the USSR.[2] Maclean was well placed to notify the Russians of this virtual monopoly. Not until 24th July 1945 was Stalin informed in general terms by Truman that the USA possessed 'a new weapon of unusual destructive power', which was to be used against the Japanese.[3] On 14th August the Japanese surrendered.

Washington, where some four months earlier Victory-in-Europe Day had been greeted in relatively sober fashion, went mad with joy over the final end of the Second World War. Everyone kept open house and Maclean, for once, was able to follow his inclination and wander festively from door to door, joining in the almost universal intoxication of that night. Reaction in the Kremlin was very different. The abrupt ending of the war had only just allowed time for the USSR to join in against Japan and so claim a share of the spoils, including the occupation of North Korea. The Soviet press played down the importance of the Hiroshima bomb and did not mention at all the second bomb that had fallen on Nagasaki. It now became apparent to Stalin that an entirely new factor had entered into international relations. The work of the Special Committee on the Uranium Problem was assigned the highest priority and instructed to produce a Soviet bomb as soon as possible. On 22nd August 1945 the NKVD sent a signal requesting Colonel Nikolai Zabotin, the GRU representative in Ottawa, to supply with maximum speed 'documentary materials' on the bomb;[4] similar instructions, we must assume, were sent to Anatoli Yakovlev, the GRU representative in New York, who was in touch with Maclean. Stalin reflected bitterly that it was now plain why the Anglo-Americans had delayed the second front in Europe; whilst the Red Army was bleeding, these false allies had prolonged the war until they had perfected the master-weapon that would enable them to dominate the postwar scene. It was not a comforting note on which to greet the new dawn of peace and plenty.

An indication of the entire confidence placed in Maclean is to be found in his participation in the planning of Prime Minister Attlee's visit to Washington in mid-November 1945. Attlee had met Truman a few months earlier at the Potsdam Conference, but this was his first formal visit to the President. The timing was largely dictated by the pressing need to define international policy concerning the atom bomb and, if possible, to influence American policy in the right direction. In the British view, this meant, first and foremost, reaffirming the wartime understanding that Anglo-American co-operation in the linked fields of research and development should continue as before. Closely allied to this, however, was the need to formulate international policy in such a way that the USSR should not feel threatened by an Anglo-American monopoly, since signs were accumulating that the sense of common purpose that had briefly marked the war years was vanishing fast.

The intention that atomic energy should hold first place on the Truman-Attlee agenda was underlined by the simultaneous visit to Washington of Mackenzie King, the Canadian Prime Minister. When Sir John Balfour, who had replaced Campbell as the political Minister, went to the State Department to concert plans for the joint visit, it was Maclean whom he took with him.[5] They were at pains to ensure that the press corps should not be alerted to the chief topic to be discussed; but it would all have been known to the NKVD. The three statesmen, when they met, agreed that some role must be found for the UN, which would satisfy the Russians. The logical course was to entrust international control of the atom bomb to the Security Council, which was charged with peace enforcement. On the other hand, the USSR, like Britain and the USA, had the right of veto in the Council; it would therefore be possible for the USSR to veto progress there whilst secretly developing a Soviet bomb.

The tripartite conference was able to come to no more far-reaching decision than that they should launch in the UN an Atomic Energy Commission, consisting of the Security Council with the addition of Canada, where all these delicate issues would be debated. Attlee went home without any clear assurances about the future of Anglo-American collaboration. The group of Ministers, whom he consulted about atomic energy, was already agreed in principle that, whatever the US attitude, Britain must have her own research establishment and that development of a bomb must have top priority. If, however, American co-operation were not forthcoming, a great deal of 'blood, tears and sweat' would have to be expended. In due course Harwell was set up and in mid-summer 1946 Klaus Fuchs returned from the USA and was appointed Head of Theoretical Physics Division. He had first made contact with the GRU in England in 1942, but had been taken over in the USA by the NKVD, whose sub-agent, Harry Gold, had been given full information about the bombs that had been dropped on Hiroshima and Nagasaki. The success of the Russians in obtaining so much secret information by devious means greatly reduced any lingering wish the USSR may have had for international co-operation in the atomic field.

I arrived at the Embassy in April 1945 as one of the numerous Second Secretaries. It was soon borne in on me that Donald Maclean was regarded as a coming man; he had acquired an air of authority, tempered by just sufficient consideration for others to pass as a good fellow. I detected no signs of anti-Americanism; but outside the Embassy he was less discreet. In the spring of 1945, an old school-friend turned up in Washington; he was George Judd, now a colonel and on official business. Maclean had greeted him cordially and took him on a sight-seeing tour of the city. The San Francisco Conference, which gave birth to the United Nations, was in full swing and in Western newspapers there was criticism of Soviet insistence on the right of veto in the Security Council and on UN membership for the Ukraine and Byelorussian Republics, as if these had been genuinely independent states. Much to Judd's surprise, Maclean defended the Soviet position and added a number of anti-American comments. Judd was also surprised that Melinda did not demur. The conversation only came back into his mind six years later, when he read of Maclean's disapperance.[6]

If in 1945 Maclean had been what he appeared to be, it would have been plausible to prophesy for him not only a successful career but also a contented home life, as he and Melinda, with Fergus and a nurse, installed themselves in the new house. One of their first visitors was Lady Maclean, who had had an operation and needed a change from the rigours of London life. In Washington she met Mrs Dunbar for the first time; there was not much cordiality about the encounter between Mrs Dunbar in her silk dress and high heels and Lady Maclean in tweed coat and skirt and sensible walking-shoes. Melinda's sisters, Catherine and Harriet, were regular visitors, especially the latter, whose charms so inflamed a bachelor Second Secretary that, when repulsed, he threatened suicide and had to be sent back to London. Donald handled the business without sentiment, but with good sense. The episode did nothing to dispel Mrs Dunbar's residual doubts about the British Diplomatic Service.

In addition to Maclean's work on 'Tube Alloys', he had been entrusted with a wide range of other duties. Soon after his arrival he had been put to work with Barclay on an Anglo-US committee, which was urgently elaborating terms for a peace treaty with Italy. Barclay has recorded that he was impressed by Maclean's 'skill at drafting and his ability to unravel complex issues'.[7] This was indeed the secret of his rapid entry into vital areas of work at the Embassy, which in collaboration with the State Department was trying to give shape to the post-war world. No task was too hard for him; no hours were too long. He gained the reputation of one who would always take over a tangled skein from a colleague who was sick, or going on leave, or simply less zealous. In this way he was able to manoeuvre himself into the hidden places that were of most interest to the NKVD. By the time Wright left Washington in March 1946, Maclean was marked down as the man to take over as acting head of Chancery until the arrival of the new Counsellor, Denis Allen (the late Sir Denis). These points have to be emphasised, because certain writers, basing themselves on ignorance, lightly salted with imagination, have depicted him at this stage of his career as a shambling pederast, who was seldom sober.

If distrust of the atom bomb was at the core of the emerging Cold War, there were other aspects of it that were exercising the minds of those State Department officials who had once shared Roosevelt's belief that he could do business with 'Uncle Joe'. As the situation changed, the same officials were beginning to wonder if the Labour government of Clement Attlee would prove sufficiently robust in standing alongside Truman in his resistance to Soviet encroachment. As the British Embassy was brought into constant consultation, no member of it was in more demand than Maclean to handle the contentious issues that arose all along the periphery of communism. On one day it would be the civil war in Greece; on the next, trouble with Yugoslavia over Trieste or occupied Austria. Soon after Maclean's arrival at the Embassy he had begun to apply his mind to matters requiring liaison with the British Joint Staff Mission (JSM). Some of these related to British and Commonwealth bases, which had been used during the war by both British and US forces, such as those in the Caribbean and Pacific. These regions were still remote from direct

Soviet influence, but his interest in them paid an early dividend as he became familiar with the personnel and methods of the JSM in ways that he could exploit in due course. The NKVD was avid for information concerning bases within range of Soviet territory, especially bases equipped for the B-29 bomber, which was capable of delivering an atom bomb. It became an essential feature of Soviet political warfare to depict all US bases as outposts of imperialism and such propaganda was a staple of 'front' organisations like the World Peace Council.

In the autumn of 1946 the USSR placed on the agenda of the UN General Assembly a resolution requiring member states to declare the number and location of forces maintained on the territory of non-enemy states (i.e. excluding those, like Germany and Austria, with which no peace treaties had yet been concluded). The resolution was clearly aimed at the USA and, to a lesser extent, at Britain; and consultation followed between Maclean, representing the Embassy, and the Director of the State Department's Office of Special Political Affairs, which dealt with the UN.[8] The Director was Alger Hiss, who had attended the Yalta Conference and the inaugural session in London of the UN General Assembly (UNGA). Maclean had already corresponded with him in 1945 about the abortive UN Military Staff Committee. He welcomed tasks that provided official pretexts to visit the UN, which was then located at Lake Success on Long Island. As we shall see shortly, liaison with the GRU and NKVD required him to visit New York and domestic reasons for these visits were not always sufficiently plausible.

In September 1946 Hiss and Maclean exchanged statistics of overseas troops and discussed how to tackle the Soviet resolution; one suggestion, emanating from the Foreign Office, was to broaden it to include ex-enemy states, such as Hungary and Romania, where the USSR kept troops. It must certainly have been useful for the Soviet delegation to have known in advance of the UN debate that the USA had military personnel, in excess of a hundred, in as many as thirty-eight overseas locations; the exact number in South Korea, for example, was 52,590. In the course of these Anglo-American negotiations, Hiss paid a visit to Maclean at the latter's house.[9] This would not necessarily have been unusual at a weekend, if a communication needed to be made urgently, for which the telephone was insufficiently secure. The visit, however, took place on Wednesday, 30th October, and is therefore something of a curiosity. Whatever the reason for it — and here it must be stressed that Hiss was not convicted of espionage and has always insisted on his innocence – there can be no doubt that he had a good relationship with Maclean. In after years, as the ordeal by Grand Jury ran its course, ending in the conviction of Hiss for perjury, Maclean heatedly championed him on occasions when it would have been in his own best interest to have kept silent. Some twenty years after these events, I had an opportunity at a social gathering to ask Hiss how well he had known Maclean. He replied tersely: 'I know why you ask that question,' but declined to say more.

Intensification of the Cold War was accompanied by inroads into the Soviet networks in North America, which Maclean would have found deeply disturbing. The direct involvement of the Communist Party of the USA in espionage and the reluctance of Roosevelt and the State Department in wartime to give the FBI a free hand in countering this activity had induced a certain laxity and failure to observe NKVD precautions relating to the size of networks and their segregation from one another. When in July 1944 Gromov, who in the USA was known to sub-agents as 'Al', not 'Henry', followed Maclean to Washington, he began to enforce the usual NKVD practices, known as *conspiratsia*; but he could not undo damage already done through widespread and incautious contacts between agents and informants.[10] In August 1945 disaster struck with the defection of Elizabeth Bentley, who had provided liaison between the NKVD in New York and a large number of informants strategically placed within the US government machine. Because Gromov had had the wisdom to keep Maclean apart from these other agents, he was untouched by these revelations; but Gromov's own position, as First Secretary in the Soviet Embassy, became so precarious that he had to leave the USA. It was fortunate for Maclean that, as suspicion grew concerning the communist contacts of Hiss, there appeared to be adequate official reason for liaison between them. In March 1946 Secretary of State Byrnes warned Hiss that he was likely to be attacked by right-wing Congressmen and in the following year he withdrew from the firing-line by becoming President of the Carnegie Endowment for International Peace. It was in that year that he became fatally embroiled with a former communist, Whittaker Chambers, who was in touch, like Elizabeth Bentley, with the FBI.

The destruction of Soviet networks in Canada had begun in September 1945 with the defection of Igor Gouzenko, cypher clerk to Zabotin, the head of the GRU in the Soviet Embassy in Ottawa. Mackenzie King was uncertain how to handle the disclosures that followed and these were discussed at his meeting with Truman and

Attlee in Washington in November. No public announcement was made until mid-February 1946, but it is probable that Maclean became aware earlier, because of his connection with the Washington meeting. In addition to Zabotin, who left Canada in a hurry, one of the casualties was Maclean's Cambridge friend, Alan Nunn May, who had also left Canada and taken up a post at King's College, London. The NKVD in London, knowing Nunn May was at risk, did not attempt to make contact and he behaved with equal restraint; but this did not save him. The decision to arrest him was taken at a meeting between representatives of the Foreign Office, MI5 and MI6; the representative of MI6 was Kim Philby.[11] Under investigation Nunn May, who was sentenced to ten years' imprisonment, explained:

> 'The whole affair was extremely painful to me and I only embarked on it because I felt this was a contribution I could make to the safety of mankind. I certainly did not do it for gain.'[12]

Maclean in a similar situation might well have used the same words. Many years later in Moscow, speaking to an English visitor, he summed up espionage in these words: 'It's like being a lavatory attendant; it stinks, but someone has to do it.'[13] He never took that subtle pleasure in deception for its own sake, which marked the careers of Philby and Blunt.

Since the evidence, on the strength of which Maclean was eventually unmasked, is connected with the way in which at this time he was controlled, something more detailed needs to be added. As he never had a 'dark room' in his house and was notably unhandy in using a camera, he must have made frequent use in Washington of *duboks*, as the NKVD termed 'dead drops', from which documents could be collected. It would have been far too risky for him to have had frequent meetings with 'Al' in Washington, which at that date was still little more than an overgrown town, where evasion of FBI 'watchers' would have posed grave problems. These problems were much reduced in the teeming and cavernous city of New York, where the NKVD had its headquarters. Their recognition of Maclean as an agent with exceptionally good access made them anxious to debrief him about files that could not safely be copied and high-level meetings, which he had attended. The fact that he had valid reasons, both official and personal, for coming to New York, especially in the first two years (1944–6), further promoted this arrangement. There was also a factor arising from his growing involvement in the nuclear work.

As he was in no sense a technical expert, it was necessary for a Soviet expert to explain to him in detail exactly what information was most needed. The GRU had such an expert in New York in the person of Anatoli Yakovlev, who had been appointed a Vice-Consul at the Soviet Consulate-General in March 1944.[14] Those who maintain that, because Maclean was non-technical, he cannot have done much damage, have overlooked his capacity to act as a conveyor-belt for those who did have the requisite qualifications.

Over the years Melinda's sisters joined the Macleans for holidays in Long Island or in the Cape Cod area, and such journeys provided Maclean with further opportunities to keep in touch with the Russians in New York. In July 1946 Melinda returned to the New York hospital where Fergus had been born and there had another successful Caesarean operation, giving birth to young Donald. It was one of Maclean's expeditions to Melinda's bedside, when she was in child-birth, that in due course supplied a vital clue, leading to his exposure. When in June 1941 Britain and the USSR became allies against Hitler, we were not reading Soviet cyphers and during the war no attempt was made to do so. As collaboration between Anglo-American crypt-analysts developed, however, some Soviet traffic was inter-cepted for future investigation. At the beginning of 1949, fragments of a cypher telegram, emanating from the NKVD in New York, were elucidated, indicating that some five years earlier an agent code-named 'Homer' had had access to messages exchanged between Roosevelt and 'former naval person', as Churchill used to describe himself.[15] Efforts to discover the identity of this agent continued, and in April 1951 a further cyphered fragment came to hand, establishing that on one occasion 'Homer' had been in New York because of the birth of his child. Whether this apparently irrelevant detail was included because visits had become less frequent, or in order that a present might be made to this valuable agent, who received no regular remuneration, we do not know. What we do know is that it was this clue that convinced British investigators that Maclean was their man.

An episode in the summer of 1946 has left me, with hindsight, in no doubt that Maclean was aware that one of the chinks in his armour was the need to make regular journeys to New York. His appointment as acting head of Chancery made it harder to leave Washington and, in the days before shuttle services by air, the normal means of travelling to New York was by train, taking nearly four hours. I was myself very well aware of the inconvenience, because that summer I was trying as often as I could to attend lectures given in New York by the exiled

Russian mystic and philosopher, P. D. Ouspensky. As this meant leaving my office early on Wednesday afternoons, I decided to consult the acting head of Chancery about the propriety of absenting myself and invited Maclean to lunch at the Wardman Park Hotel, where uninterrupted talk would be easier than in the crowded Embassy canteen. As we walked through Rock Creek Park, Maclean was strangely silent and, by the time I opened the conversation by saying, 'It's about going to New York I want to talk to you,' the tension was palpable. I came to think in later years that Maclean was at first ascribing to me the role of interrogator, which I never had in mind and for which I lacked the qualification. His suspicion may have been aroused by the fact that for the last two years of the war I had been one of the personal assistants of 'C', the head of SIS. Whatever the truth of the matter, tension was immediately dissipated when I made it clear that my enquiry related to my own journeys. He showed not the smallest interest in Ouspensky, but asked only: 'Is it very important to you to go?' When I insisted that it was, he told me to go but to make up time on Saturday afternoons.

This was a minor decision, but typical of his understanding attitude, which made him well liked in his post of authority. Tribute to him in this capacity has also been paid by Walter Bell, who arrived in Washington in May 1946, as private secretary of the new Ambassador, Lord Inverchapel. Bell was married to the daughter of US Airforce General Carl Spaatz and had many American friends, but he was not a member of the diplomatic service and had to deal with an Ambassador of uncertain temperament and idiosyncratic habits. Bell found the acting head of Chancery a tower of strength in helping him to master Embassy procedure and handle the Ambassador. Only once did hackles rise; the subject of Christianity cropped up in the course of casual conversation; Maclean with sudden asperity exclaimed, 'Jesus was a shit – cause of all our troubles!'[16] Walter Bell, whose father had been Canon of Rochester, was both surprised and disconcerted.

Maclean had no difficulty in establishing with the new Ambassador the same happy relationship he had had with his predecessor; Lord Inverchapel soon pronounced him to be 'a sweetie'. Writers who did not know Inverchapel and lack a sense of history have accused him of being a fellow-traveller, if nothing worse. The fact of the matter is that for four wartime years in Moscow he cultivated good relations with Stalin, as it was his duty, as Ambassador, to do. By the time he left Moscow in January 1946 he was already sixty-three and past his best.

He ought to have retired, but Ernest Bevin liked him, regarding him as less of a 'stuffed-shirt' than some Ambassadors of his acquaintance. Inverchapel arrived in Washington, however, without having grasped the important point that wartime attitudes had changed and everything Russian was coming to be regarded with suspicion. At the time of his departure from Moscow Stalin had asked what farewell present he wanted. Inverchapel replied that he would like to have released to him a young Russian, named Evgeni Yost, whose sister worked in the Embassy and who had himself worked there before Hitler's invasion. Yost was in trouble with the Soviet authorities, but Stalin overrode objections and Yost was allowed to leave Russia with Inverchapel, who decided to employ him as his valet. All might have been well if the Ambassador had left Yost behind in Scotland (where he now lives), but he insisted on taking his valet with him to Washington and boasting, 'I have a Russian slave given to me by Stalin.' This was a conversation-stopper, but did not strike American press men as being as funny as the Ambassador thought.

The implications of Inverchapel's indiscretion were not lost on Maclean; it risked drawing attention to the security of the Embassy as a whole. There was also the disagreeable possibility that the NKVD wished to keep a closer watch on Maclean himself. In parenthesis, it seems unlikely that this was the case; Yost belonged to the suspect race of Volga Germans and in any case the NKVD had had no time to brief him before his abrupt departure from Moscow. One day Maclean appeared in the Ambassador's servants' quarters and asked Yost how he liked the life, compared with that in Russia. Yost made some comparisons highly unfavourable to the USSR. Maclean's face dropped and he quickly left the room. His next step was to approach Balfour and suggest that they jointly confront the Ambassador and urge him to send his valet to Britain.[17] This they did, but six months passed before Inverchapel, returning home on leave, finally took Yost with him. Whatever Maclean's motives may have been, the incident did nothing to harm his reputation as a sound man with a proper appreciation of the hard realities of the Cold War and the delicate state of American public opinion.

At the end of November 1946 Denis Allen arrived in Washington and took over as head of Chancery. He also took over the pass into the Pentagon building, which Maclean, in his acting capacity, had been using. The latter, having acquired an overview of the work of the Embassy as a whole, was now able to concentrate on those areas of particular interest to him – and to the NKVD. Chief of these was the development of the atom bomb. When in February 1947 Maclean was appointed British co-secretary of the CPC, there were no doubts among the few who knew what work the position entailed that he was the man for the job. It was important to make the right choice, because Makins' place was taken not by a specialist but by Sir Gordon Munro, the head of the Treasury Delegation in Washington. In this latter capacity Munro already had heavy responsibilities connected with the sterling-dollar rate of exchange, as well as representing Britain on the International Monetary Fund; it was clear that he would want to delegate to Maclean as much of the CPC work as he properly could. If he had hitherto had opportunities to pick up useful information, his new post allowed him better access to the 'documentary materials' on which the NKVD had laid stress. He was able to expand his contacts among American officials, such as Carroll Wilson, the General Manager of the US Atomic Energy Commission (AEC), and make discreet enquiries in sensitive areas without arousing suspicion. FBI files, relating to the investigation mounted after Maclean's flight in 1951, show that none of the American officials, who were interviewed, had had any suspicion of him, or had heard him make any anti-American remarks; his outstanding ability to differentiate between hearers in the safe and unsafe categories had stood him in good stead.

These informal contacts with American officials had acquired special importance since passage in 1946 of the MacMahon Act, which inhibited the AEC from disclosing information about atomic weapons. Those who knew that it had been enacted in disregard of wartime agreements had some sympathy with the British point of view; others, as the Cold War began to bite, thought it unwise to alienate the most important ally of the USA in any coming struggle with the USSR. In November 1946 the US State-War-Navy Coordinating Committee issued a new directive on exchange of military information with Britain, which went some way towards preserving the intimate links that had existed earlier. It fell to Maclean to communicate this good news to the British Joint Staff Mission and the Commonwealth Scientific Office and both organisations expressed their appreciation.[18] There were other legitimate paths into the forbidden territory of weapon technology. One of these was a conference in Washington in November 1947 to determine which wartime secrets could now be declassified. Discussion of what need no longer be regarded as top secret lends itself readily to discussion of what must remain secret and why; an American official, interviewed by the FBI after Maclean's flight, admitted that at the conference 'a discussion did take place regarding atomic weapons.'[19] The British delegates included Fuchs, as well as Maclean. It is unlikely the one recognised the other as working undercover for the same employer. After Fuchs' arrest in February 1950 he disclosed to MI5 and the FBI all his clandestine contacts, including Harry Gold. In his confessional state of mind he would almost certainly have named Maclean, if he had known about him.

One of the topics discussed at the declassification conference was detection of nuclear explosions at a distance; American minds were beginning to concentrate on the question of how soon the USSR might be expected to catch up. The US military were thinking in terms of up to ten years; but scientists were much less optimistic. Meanwhile Anglo-US co-operation was improving. The worsening international situation raised American anxieties about adequacy of stocks of uranium and thorium and in this context relations with Canada, and British relations with South Africa and India, assumed growing importance. As the work of the CDT went on apace, it became possible to trade Anglo-Canadian access to raw materials against American know-how. In January 1948 a tripartite *modus vivendi* was initialled, but had to be kept under wraps, in case Congress might consider that it infringed the MacMahon Act.[20] It was not until 1956 that the State Department, in response to a query from Senator Eastland, chairman of the Senate Internal Security subcommittee, reluctantly admitted that, in pursuance of the *modus vivendi*, Maclean had had

> 'access to information relating to the estimates made at that time (January 1948) of ore supply available to the three governments, requirements of uranium for the atomic energy programmes of the three governments for the period 1948–1952, and the definition of the scientific areas in which the three governments deemed technical co-operation could be accomplished with mutual benefit.'[21]

Access of this quality could not have failed to delight the hearts of the NKVD; for example, insight into American stockpiling would have provided indications of production schedules. For the Russians, the crucial questions were: how many bombs had the USA got? How would these be used in time of war? American demobilisation after the war had at first gone ahead at great speed until suspended in April 1946. The USSR had never demobilised and, as the Cold War intensified, the US Joint Chiefs of Staff became increasingly perturbed by the discrepancy between the conventional forces of the two superpowers. Realising that the disparity could only be made good by taking the atom bomb into their strategic calculations, they belatedly embarked on an investigation that further alarmed them. It transpired that bombs were not stored ready for use, but needed to be assembled; the trained civilians, who had formerly undertaken this task, had returned to their peacetime occupations and military replacements would not be fully trained until December 1947. There was also a marked deficiency of processed uranium and plutonium. General Carl Spaatz later gave it as his estimate that, whilst he was Chief of Air Staff (February 1946–April 1948), only a dozen atom bombs were available; at the beginning of the period the number was certainly less. In those early days no more than twenty-seven modified B-29 bombers capable of delivering the bombs were available; the only bases from which they could have operated against the USSR were those in Britain and in the Cairo–Suez area.[22] In short, the US monopoly of power was much less impressive than world opinion at that time supposed.

It goes without saying that any intimation of this relative weakness, however tentative and imprecise, that reached Stalin would have been of the utmost value to him. How much did reach him we shall never know, except in the very unlikely event that Kremlin archives are one day opened for research. What we can affirm is that Beria, who was close to Stalin, controlled not only the NKVD's network of agents, but also the production of atomic energy for military purposes. We can also affirm that, in the period up to the first Soviet nuclear explosion in August 1949, Stalin was acting with marked self-confidence; he was in no way deterred by any fear of the US bomb from consolidating his hold on Eastern Europe and, at the time of the Berlin blockade, bringing the world to the very brink of war. Stalin was never a rash operator in the international field and it is tempting to believe that he had at least one very well placed source of intelligence in Washington. No candidate comes near to Maclean in his qualification for this vital role. In November 1947 he was provided with a pass, allowing him to enter the AEC building and move about it unescorted; this was a coveted privilege, denied to many high American officers. He is recorded as having made use of it on twenty occasions over a ten-month period up to June 1948.[23] The pass allowed him to visit the AEC in the evening, when few of the regular staff would have been on duty; one begins to understand the reiterated complaints of

Melinda that Donald's late hours disorganised the household. It is, of course, unlikely that even on clandestine visits out of hours he could have unearthed documents explicitly confirming the relative naked-ness of US defences; but the fact that he had become a familiar and well-liked figure would have enabled him in conversation to elicit information that would have given substance to what might otherwise have remained in the realm of supposition. Nothing could have been more natural than that American colleagues should have confided to him their hopes and misgivings; the alarm and indignation generated in Washington by his disappearance less than three years later strongly suggest that revealing conversations took place. In the late summer of 1948 the AEC gave Maclean a farewell lunch at the prestigious Hay Adams Hotel. Nothing could have been more comradely: once more the deception had worked.

In discussing this, the most significant, phase of Maclean's spying career, we have tried to remain within the realm of plausible recon-struction, avoiding exaggerated claims for his impact on events. There is one area of speculation, however, which deserves at least a brief mention, because of its historical importance. There has been a tendency to assume that the bombing of Hiroshima and Nagasaki led those who were contemporaneous with it to the immediate and irrevocable conclusion that the whole character of warfare had changed and that, in future, the most terrible of all weapons must be targeted not against warships and troop concentrations but against densely populated industrial areas. This was not the automatic assumption made, even in military circles, at that time; there was, rather, an inclination to regard what had happened as a 'one-off' act of destruction necessitated by the obduracy of Japan in fighting a lost cause to the bitter end. It was not at once conceded that there had been a total diversion of military effort against the civilian sector. Late in 1945, General Groves was considering whether to try out the bomb against an obsolete battleship; such a test was carried out at Bikini atoll in the summer of 1946. What concentrated the minds of the US JCS on the use of the bomb almost exclusively as an instrument of terror was the intensity of the Cold War, coupled with their recog-nition that fissionable material was scarce and their stockpile of bombs inadequate. Up to that date (it was about six months after Maclean had taken up his CPC duties) no clear strategic doctrine about employment of the bomb had been laid down. The US JCS then formulated what one commentator has described as 'the chilling concept of "killing a nation"'.[24] This concept was, of course, taken over without question by the USSR two years later, when the first Soviet bomb was exploded. As adopted by both superpowers, it led inexorably to the horrifying culmination expressed in the acronym MAD – Mutual Assured Destruction. Whether intelligence supplied by Maclean up to his departure from New York on 1st September 1948 contributed in any way to this lamentable development we cannot know; by the same token, we cannot exclude the possibility.

The year 1948 saw a further increase in tension in Europe with the eye of the storm moving to Czechoslovakia and culminating in February with the communist take-over in Prague and the defenestration of Jan Masaryk, who was regarded, perhaps too confidently, as the last pillar of Western influence. Bevin judged that the time had come to propose to the State Department that the US government, having already decided to invest in Western Europe's recovery through the Marshall Plan, should agree to undertake the defence of its investment, if this should prove necessary. It was essential, however, to proceed with caution, since Republicans dominated Congress and Congress had never sanctioned a military alliance in time of peace. On 22nd March, with no fanfare and no accompanying staff, Sir Gladwyn Jebb (Lord Gladwyn) came out from London and Lester Pearson from Ottawa. The State Department, fearing that their joint arrival on their doorstep with delegations drawn from their Embassies might provoke press enquiries, decided to hold the initial meetings at the Pentagon, which in those days was less haunted by the press corps. Further to discourage premature leakage, it was stipulated at the opening meeting that no notes should be taken and that we should not disperse for lunch, which was eaten at the long table where discussion took place.

These precautions did indeed defeat the American press, but not the NKVD, since Maclean was a member of our delegation. I was the junior member and suffered for it. It was a Foreign Office rule that the record at *ad hoc* meetings, for which no regular secretariat was provided, should be taken down by the junior participant; it was, however, highly unusual for such meetings to last nearly six hours with note-taking banned. As we drove away from the Pentagon, I cherished the hope that Maclean might volunteer to draft the telegram to London, summarising our discussion. He did not do so; no doubt he was preoccupied in making his own summary for a recipient to whom it would be a good deal less welcome than it was in Whitehall. In the end it was Jebb who reduced my musings to a concise form, suitable for digestion by the Secretary of State for Foreign Affairs.

Some thirty years later, Lord Gladwyn cast doubt on the damage Maclean may have done on that momentous day, which heralded the signature one year later of the North Atlantic Treaty, the foundation on which our security has rested ever since:

'Looking back, I can only assume that the likelihood ... of the Americans' coming into a powerful Western Alliance may well have exercised restraint on any Russian 'hawks'. In other words, but for Donald, there might have been a different issue to the subsequent grave crisis over Berlin.'[25]

Lord Gladwyn's views naturally merit respect; one may doubt, however, whether he would have expressed them at any time during the year that elapsed before – in April 1949 – NATO came into being. He could scarcely have wanted the Kremlin to know how anxiously we debated the constitutional restrictions requiring the US government to consult the Senate before engaging in hostilities (undeclared wars, which have since become commonplace, were still only a gleam in a general's eye). As a result of American misgivings, the obligations incurred by the NATO allies towards one another are less binding and specific than those accepted by the Western European powers in the Brussels Treaty of 1948.

There is also some evidence that the Russians may have tried to make trouble over the territorial scope of the North Atlantic Treaty, which provoked much discussion at our secret sessions. On 4th April 1948 a Warsaw newspaper featured an article alleging that there were Anglo-American plans to form a North Atlantic *bloc* and apply pressure to Scandinavian countries. Swedish newspapers took up the theme a few days later. There was never any prospect that Sweden would abandon neutrality; but participation in NATO of Denmark and Norway hung for a long time in the balance. At one of the secret sessions it was suggested by Canada that the western zones of occupation of Germany and Austria should also be covered by the proposed treaty.[26] This suggestion was not adopted and only someone who was present, or had access to the record, would have known that it had been made. At that date negotiations with the USSR for a peace treaty with Austria were well advanced; for reasons that have never become clear the Russians went into reverse; seven years elapsed before they were finally convinced that we envisaged a neutral, independent Austria on the model already under discussion in 1948.

Maclean could have reported another important area of debate that was not reflected in the text of the North Atlantic Treaty, namely what forms of aggression should bring the treaty into operation. The US delegation, with Czechoslovakia in mind, wished to define 'indirect aggression'; others objected that to spell out how far a potential aggressor could safely go, without precipitating war, would enable him to adjust his strategy accordingly.[27] This may have been exactly what the Russians were doing. Our discussion in Washington took place at a time when only the preliminary hint of what was to become in June the full-scale blockade of West Berlin had so far taken place; the Red Army, on various specious pretexts, was beginning to close access routes by road, rail and canal. By midsummer it was clear that the Soviet intention was to hold hostage the Western garrisons and the population of West Berlin, in order to bring about reversal of allied policy, designed to unify the three Western zones of Germany and create the state that became the Federal German Republic.

Maclean would not only have known about this policy; he would also have known that – unlikely as this may seem in retrospect – there was no Western contingency planning to deal with a crisis such as that which the blockade had brought about. The Berlin air-lift was a brilliant improvisation in the best Anglo-Saxon tradition. Before the end of Maclean's Washington career in late August, he would also have known that General Lucius Clay, who was directing the air-lift, had been instructed that his transport aircraft should not open fire, unless fired upon, and should not have fighter escorts. As the Russians were continuing to take part in the quadripartite control of air traffic over Berlin, it is clear that both sides had embarked on crisis management designed to render open hostilities less likely. It is highly probable that Maclean's reports that the US government, despite its monopoly of the atom bomb, was determined to exercise restraint may have contributed to preventing a cataclysm.

There is no British damage assessment relating to Maclean in the public domain; but in addition to one produced in July 1951 by the US Atomic Energy Commission, there is a curious document, prepared in October 1955 by a Colonel in US Military Intelligence for the US JCS, which relates also to Burgess. The timing of this assessment is presumably related to publication two months earlier of the Australian government's report on the defection of the KGB agent Vladimir Petrov, who had thrown new light on the two missing British diplomats. The US JCS assessment enters into no details, but summarily concludes:

'In the fields of US/UK/Canada planning on atomic energy, US/
UK postwar planning and policy in Europe all information up to
the date of defection undoubtedly reached Soviet hands probably
via the Soviet Embassy in London.'[28]

This is a surprisingly broad, general statement; it is inconceivable that
even two such active agents, in addition to performing their legitimate
functions, could have conveyed such an immense volume of illicit
information to the Kremlin. On the only point on which the report is
specific it is clearly wrong: as we have seen, Maclean's main control,
Gromov, who had followed him to Washington, had been attached to
the Soviet Embassy in London only from 1939 to 1944.

The US JCS assessment also concludes that 'all UK and possibly
some US diplomatic codes and cyphers in existence prior to 25 May
1951 are in possession of the Soviets and of no further use.' This vague
and alarmist statement fails to take into account that in the period
1944–8 nearly all secret Anglo-American cypher traffic was en-
cyphered on One Time Pads (OTP), randomised sheets of figures
which, if correctly used, could not have given away subsequent
messages. Only a well-placed spy in the Government Code and
Cypher School (GCCS) could have had foreknowledge of OTPs to be
employed in the future. The days of stealing cypher-books were over,
except in relation to countries still relying on inferior systems. This
does not preclude the possibility of decrypting isolated messages, or
fragments of telegrams, but the wholesale revelations envisaged in the
US JCS assessment belong to the realm of fantasy. Apparently with
the intention of making it more plausible, the assessment leaps to a
further conclusion that Burgess and Maclean 'throughout their time in
public office ... were apparently protected by others in even higher
places, some of whom are alleged to be still occupying key positions
... particularly in the Foreign Office.' The context suggests that this
allegation, for which no evidence is given, may have derived from the
FBI. It illustrates how deep a wound had been inflicted on the vital
Anglo-American relationship: the bitter resentment that followed
upon the defection of Maclean is the measure of the confidence
formerly accorded to him.

For Donald and Melinda the Washington years, filled, as they had
been, with both promise and foreboding, were coming to an end.
In December 1947, when the owner of their house wished to sell,
they had moved to 3326 P Street; it was in a fashionable part of
Georgetown, but did not stand in its own grounds, as the previous

house had done. There in August 1948 Maclean gave a farewell cocktail party for about fifty of his American friends and colleagues on the CPC and CDT. Then they packed up and went together for the last time to New York for the voyage home. They stayed at the Plaza Hotel and in the lobby Maclean ran into his friend of Paris days, Valentine Lawford, who was serving with the British delegation to the UN. Lawford wrote later:

> 'Donald looked a bit strange . . . sort of puffed-up and beaten-down simultaneously . . . But both he and Melinda were very nice to me, and we laughed at some of the good old jokes.'[29]

They told him they were bound for Egypt, where Maclean was to take up the post of head of Chancery at Cairo on promotion to Counsellor; at thirty-five he was the youngest Counsellor in the Diplomatic Service. The prospects for 'Sir Donald' had never shone brighter.

There was, however, a darker side. Melinda used occasionally to murmur to sympathetic Embassy wives, my own included, that Donald often seemed moody and preoccupied. Now that the war was over, she could not understand why he still had to work so late and sometimes at weekends. He loved his two small boys, but never had time to play with them. There were, too, the drinking bouts that occurred from time to time. Some hold that Melinda already knew, if not in detail, that Donald was betraying her country, as well as his own. I do not share this view. If she had been in any sense a fellow conspirator, she would not have risked speaking of him in such a manner; she would have swallowed her unease. It could be argued that her apparent candour was a double-bluff; but she was not by nature an actress; she lacked her husband's capacity for dissembling her feelings. She lacked, too, the stimulus to deceit that devotion to an ideology supplies. She was indeed in a much more banal situation, or so it seemed; she was a wife whose husband has a problem that she cannot fathom and about which he cannot, or will not, speak.

For Maclean, despite his promotion, the skies were darker than they had been when he had arrived in the USA over four years earlier. Then the anti-Hitler alliance had been poised for the final thrust and the fascist beast was about to be buried in the ruins of Berlin. Four years later new alliances were forming, but these stood opposed to one another. What must have seemed even worse to Maclean, who studied events through a thick haze of Marxism, was that the beast of fascism was not dead, but was being reborn on the American continent. In the elections of 1948 Truman had been re-elected, but had lost control of Congress. The era of Senator Joseph McCarthy had scarcely begun, but already there were ambitious young politicians, like Richard Nixon, who had seen that the anti-communist bandwagon would carry them to prominence. It was not only Maclean's friend Hiss who was in jeopardy; several members of the British Embassy, including Maclean, knew Gustavo Duran, a former Loyalist General in the Spanish Civil War, who had become an American citizen and married the sister of Michael Straight, who had returned to the USA after being recruited at Cambridge into the ideological struggle by Blunt. Duran was working as a Latin American expert for the UN, but this did not save him from the attacks of the Committee on Un-American Activities and its running dogs, the syndicated columnists, Walter Winchell, Fulton Lewis and Bob Considine. We know now that this wave of opinion, which was to rise higher during the war in Korea and was indeed much aggravated by the flight of Maclean himself, did not in the long run damage the solid structure of American democracy. This confidence in the fundamental sanity of the American people was not shared by Maclean; it seemed to him that the fascist monster had lifted its ugly head and that in its hand was the atom bomb.

6

Cairo – Eastern Reproaches

The 'Jewish desk' at the British Embassy in Washington was one of the most onerous and least relished of all. It had never fallen to Maclean's lot for any length of time; but as acting head of Chancery he had had plenty of opportunity to familiarise himself with the problems that it posed, both in terms of Middle East politics and in terms of Anglo-American relations. In any case, the Palestine problem intruded itself into diplomatic life in a way that, in those days, was highly unusual. The numerous and vociferous Jewish community of New York, wishing to make itself heard in the tranquil – and predominantly Gentile – environment of Massachusetts Avenue, Washington, DC, rented a mob on several occasions; the Embassy staff, as they arrived for work, were affronted by anti-British slogans and placards denouncing the inhumanity of restrictions on Jewish immigration. One of these demonstrations, coinciding with the demolition by the Irgun gang of the King David Hotel in Jerusalem with heavy loss of British life, struck many of the Embassy staff as singularly ill-timed.

The Foreign Office, from Ernest Bevin downward, was widely regarded as incurably pro-Arab. Maclean did not share these sympathies; if anything, he was a Zionist; but he was necessarily caught up in the common endeavour of the Embassy to stitch up the fissures that kept appearing in what the Foreign Office like to regard as the seamless garment of Anglo-American policy in the Middle East. For in the decade before the disastrous Suez aberration it was a constant aim of British foreign policy to secure American backing for British efforts to maintain the *status quo* in the Near and Middle East and keep oil flowing. It was this aim that was so gravely threatened by the vote in the United Nations in November 1947 to partition Palestine, and the establishment of the Jewish state of Israel, which followed some six months later. The British could usually count on a friendly hearing in the State Department; in the White House it was a different story. There were votes in Zionism and, as the threat grew to the re-election of President Truman in 1948, he became increasingly prone to listen to psalms sung in New York. Thus in June 1948, after the barest minimum of notification to his Secretary of State, Truman appointed, as his Special Representative in Tel Aviv, James G. McDonald, a well-known Zionist sympathiser, at a time when the Foreign Office was dragging its feet, reluctant to grant Israel even *de facto* recognition.

One of the few points on which Foreign Office, State Department and White House saw eye to eye was in believing that only increased violence would result from arming Jews and Arabs. Denial of arms to both sides, however, could only have operated even-handedly if armaments on both sides were already balanced, or if the United Nations and its mediator, Count Bernadotte, had been able to keep the peace. Egypt, Iraq and Jordan, however, had treaty relations with Britain, on which they depended for the equipment of their armies. As soon as the state of Israel was proclaimed in May 1948, the Arab states attacked; Israel was saved by her own exertions, by Arab disunity and by the timely supply of arms from Eastern Europe, mainly Czechoslovakia. This last factor aggravated Foreign Office suspicions that the new state was likely to become a centre for diffusion of Soviet influence in the Near East. That the USSR did at first cherish such hopes is indicated by the very prompt appointment of a Soviet Representative in Tel Aviv; Pavel I. Yershov slipped in just ahead of McDonald, his American diplomatic colleague.

Within a week of Maclean's arrival in London in September 1948, Folke Bernadotte was assassinated in Jerusalem by the Stern terrorists; it was clear that Maclean's assignment as Counsellor in Cairo would be no sinecure. Egypt boasted a Department to itself in the Foreign Office and Maclean was chiefly briefed by its head, George Clutton (the late Sir George). The Eastern Department, which dealt with Palestine, also took a hand, and its head, Bernard Burrows (Sir Bernard), gave a dinner-party to enable the Macleans to meet people who knew the area. Among the guests were the journalists Geoffrey Hoare and his wife, Clare Hollingworth. The former, as might perhaps be expected, was more impressed by Melinda, whom he found 'utterly charming', though in such company 'rather out of her depth'. She was 'thrilled at the thought of going to Cairo'. Donald, however, 'showed no marked enthusiasm'.[1] His promotion had certainly pleased him; but he left Washington with a certain regret. There he had been at the heart of Anglo-American decision-making and could feel that his reports were eagerly read in the Kremlin and might be exerting influence on Soviet policy, which in the Near East was not yet clearly formulated.

Peace or war – that was the issue, as the forces that were beginning to crystallise into NATO and the Warsaw Pact lined up on opposite sides of the Iron Curtain. In Germany the process of constituting two antagonistic states was under way and West Berlin was being blockaded by the Red Army. But the direst threat, in Maclean's eyes, was that the USA still had the monopoly of the atom bomb. In the last week of September his former colleague in Washington, Philip Jordan, who was now Press Officer at No. 10 Downing Street, invited Donald and Melinda to dinner and to meet Malcolm Muggeridge and his wife. As at the Burrows' party, it was Melinda who earned the acclaim; Donald's achievement was to keep silent, as the talk moved into the crucial area. Muggeridge recorded:

'Discussed everlasting question of Russia and the possibility of war. Philip is quite certain that there was no question of appeasement. He expected that the Americans would act ... Then it really does begin to seem as though the inconceivable must happen, and that an atomic war with Russia is almost a certainty.'[2]

Maclean would have known of Muggeridge's wartime service in MI6 and may well have thought he was trailing his coat: in any case he made no comment.

There were other reasons why Maclean should have approached his new assignment with caution. He had left behind in New York the Soviet 'control' with whom he was familiar and would have to foster a new relationship in a strange environment. Then there was the ambivalence of Soviet Palestine policy to consider. The USSR had voted for partition and approved supply of arms to the Jews. Maclean, as a moderate Zionist, would have thought this right; but the growing influence of New York on Tel Aviv could not be overlooked. A majority of post-war Jewish immigrants had come from Eastern Europe and the MAPAM party was Russophile; but until elections were held there was no way to be sure which horse to back. Dollars might speak louder than ideology. So long as so many Arab countries were ruled by autocratic monarchs in league with Britain, it might be difficult for the Kremlin to swap horses; but such rulers could not last forever. One day, surely, the impoverished, semi-literate masses would assert themselves.

The Macleans arrived in Cairo in October 1948 and Donald's misgivings soon began to sprout. If the Foreign Office had wished to put his loyalty to the test, they could scarcely have chosen for him a more exacting post, in which he would have to call continuously upon the capacity for deception that sustained his 'cover'. Almost by heredity, he was anti-imperialist; yet Egypt was a country in which defence of imperial interests appeared at its least attractive. In the Sudan the superstructure of an Anglo-Egyptian condominium disguised an enlightened colonial administration by British civil servants, who could apply revenues to the relief of poverty and disease. The ostensible independence of King Farouk, however, inhibited British intervention to bridge the chasm between the penniless *fellahin* and the rich sugar and cotton magnates, who haunted the Turf Club and Shepherd's. Britain's strategic interest in the Suez Canal and the Delta brought with it the need to bolster this deplorable regime in peace, as had been the case during the war.

On the surface, life was pleasant. Maclean could stand, with a glass in his hand, watching the sunset from the terrace of the elegant Semiramis Bar; but he could not for long ignore the fact that, less than a mile up-stream, the teeming slums began. Cairo was the most densely populated city of Africa. Plague accompanied poverty; one year before the Macleans arrived, cholera had broken out and, in a single day in October 1947, 175 deaths had been registered. It was not necessary to be a communist to see that what the country needed was not more luxury hotels, not more arms to fight Israel, but an intensive programme of technical assistance to raise living standards. Super-imposed on this tottering economy was the frenetic social life at the heart of which was the diplomatic corps. Maclean observed it with a jaundiced eye – and refilled his glass.

Egypt provided also his first experience of a country where the British presence was resented. Under Egyptian pressure the British army, which had taken root during the war, had retreated to the Canal Zone. In the eyes of most Egyptians this was not far enough; Cairo was still full of British uniforms and buildings appropriated for British use. Hostility to Farouk expressed itself in hostility to Britain; even in the Canal Zone, British soldiers were not safe going out singly in the evening. In 1947 the Moslem Brotherhood, an Islamic Fundamentalist organisation with a terrorist wing, had declared a *Jihad*, or holy war, against the British. The organisation had links with the Free Officers' movement, which finally overthrew Farouk in 1952. The small Egyptian Communist Party, being secular, attracted little support. In a report to the Foreign Office in August 1949, Maclean referred to it dismissively as 'a bogey'.[3]

The political and economic problems of Egypt made small impact on Melinda, who was soon enjoying life in a way she had seldom done in Washington. There they had had to hunt for a rented house and compete for servants in a seller's market; the dollars had never flowed freely. Donald's new seniority meant that a fine house in Gezira, originally built for British servants of the Egyptian Government, was at his disposal. It was furnished by the Ministry of Works, who also kept up the garden, where mimosa and jacaranda bloomed. His higher allowances enabled them to employ an English nurse for the two boys and four well-trained servants. Relieved of most of the cares of being a mother and a housewife, Melinda began for the first time to enjoy entertaining in her home. The Ambassador was a bachelor and she soon found herself in demand as a hostess. In March 1949, when Prince Philip came to Cairo and stayed with the Ambassador, she was asked to arrange a young people's evening for him. They sat down fourteen to dinner and afterwards, when other guests came, played games around the house. The party was a success: Melinda had won her spurs. As her self-confidence grew, she began to attract admirers.

If Maclean had been a more loving husband or a more convention-ally ambitious diplomat, these developments might have delighted him. Instead, he found himself resenting the loss of privacy, as his house filled up with guests and servants. Stories that he was a master-photographer and had his own dark room are pure invention. He was notoriously unhandy and could not even take family snapshots without getting his thumb in the frame; reading such stories later in Moscow, he used to become convulsed with laughter. Nevertheless, he needed some peace and quiet for his nefarious work. He un-doubtedly took documents home and made notes, though his chief strength, as a spy, must have been his retentive memory, which enabled him to rehearse a sequence of facts and figures almost verbatim long after the event. He could not share these concerns with Melinda, who for the first time in their marriage was evolving her own way of life. He had always adopted a rather patronising attitude towards her and her growing power to assert herself was unwelcome. Even before they were married she had been critical of his bouts of drinking; the habit was growing on him and, as it did so, he found it harder to tolerate her criticism. Drink, as she well knew, brought out a strain of violence in him. It also touched off his latent homosexual tendency, as she confided to my wife after his flight.

One of the expeditions that they made together was to Khartoum, where they stayed with the Chief Secretary, James Robertson (the late Sir James). Maclean was not in tune with the paternalist assumptions that, in his view, prevailed in the Sudan; at dinner one evening he directed to his host a series of searching questions which, in the thinking of at least one of his fellow guests, exceeded the limits of good manners. Relations were not in any case comfortable between the Embassy in Cairo and the Sudan civil service, which was inclined to suspect the Foreign Office of being less interested in Sudanese independence than in making concessions to Egyptian ambitions to control the entire course of the Nile. It was not a very happy visit, though Lady Robertson found Melinda 'a very pleasant, easy guest'.[4] The same could not be said for Donald.

A more agreeable evening has been recorded by Sir William Hayter, whose post in Washington Maclean had taken five years earlier. Hayter had recently become an Assistant Under-Secretary in the Foreign Office with responsibility for the Department that maintained liaison with the Armed Forces. He was on a tour that took in military installations at Ismailya in the Canal Zone. In Cairo he transacted most of his business with Maclean and found nothing untoward in his behaviour. He dined *en famille* with the Macleans 'in their nice house ... a cosy, conventional F.O. evening'.[5] Such evenings were becoming rarer, as the Macleans were increasingly drawn into the hectic night-life of Cairo where dinner-parties began around 11 p.m. and continued into the small hours. On one of these occasions Maclean was seated next to the wife of the Netherlands representative and horrified her by observing, 'If Alger Hiss felt as he did about communism, he was quite right to betray his country.'[6]

Most diplomatic martyrs to high living took a prolonged siesta in the afternoon; but at the British Embassy the pressure of work was unremitting and even Maclean's robust constitution showed the strain. The Hoares, returning from Beirut to Cairo in the spring of 1949, observed changes in both Macleans. 'I found Melinda on top of the world,' he recalled later. Donald, however, 'was developing a deep dislike for Egypt,' though his work at the Embassy still seemed to be going well.[7] He was fortunate in having about him staff who liked him and proved exceptionally loyal. The Ambassador was Sir Ronald I. Campbell, who had formed a highly favourable impression of Maclean at previous posts (he is to be distinguished from the Campbell who had been Ambassador in Paris) and was determined that nothing should spoil their very friendly relations. Second in the hierarchy was the Minister, Edwin Chapman-Andrews (the late Sir Edwin), an expert on the Near East, but who seemed willing to give Maclean his head. His right-hand man was the First Secretary, Lees Mayall (Sir Lees), who liked Maclean well enough to forgive physical injury, as events would shortly show. Donald and Melinda also got on well with Michael Maude, who was Campbell's private secretary. None of them had the least suspicion that Maclean was a member not only of their team but also of another team, pulling in a very different direction.

In the early summer of 1949, as the heat increased, there occurred an episode that was to cast a long shadow. Harriet had come to stay with her sister, and another visitor to Cairo was David Scott-Fox (the late Sir David), who was on local leave from his post as Counsellor of Embassy at Jedda. Melinda had the idea of making up a party, hiring a *felucca* and sailing up the Nile to Helouan, where there were friends who would give them late dinner and put them up for the night. Arrangements were made for cars to be brought to Helouan next morning (Sunday) to take them all home. The party of about ten was completed by Lees Mayall and his wife and two local businessmen, one English and one American. From the start everything went wrong; either the craft was undermanned, or the wind changed or the Egyptian skipper had underestimated the time the journey would take. In any case, he was soundly berated by Donald, and Melinda, too, did not escape his criticism, as they crept up-river in the gloom of a moonless night. They had brought no food, but plenty of alcohol and Maclean began to go out of control.

The climax was reached when around midnight they finally arrived at their destination. An Egyptian nightwatchman, carrying an ancient fire-arm, made as if to dispute the landing of a party that sounded noisy and quarrelsome. Maclean laid hands on the weapon and Mayall then intervened to prevent serious injury. Maclean, who weighed about fourteen stone, rolled down the bank with Mayall, whose leg was broken. It was thought best not to move him till first light and Scott-Fox sat with him by the river for the rest of the night. He was taken to hospital in Cairo next day. Maclean, however, spent most of the day sun-bathing near Helouan with Scott-Fox. He was penitent, the latter subsequently recalled, and talked about the strains and stresses of diplomatic life; but no whisper of the strains and stresses of disloyalty escaped him. On Monday he duly presented himself in Alexandria, where the bulk of the Embassy had taken up summer quarters, and explained to Campbell that Mayall had met with a mishap and was remaining in Cairo. It seems that Campbell realised that he was not being told the full story, because some weeks later, seeing Mayall again, he asked, 'What really happened?'[8] But he did not persist with his enquiry, in the face of Mayall's loyal reticence, and made no report to the Foreign Office.

Beneath the incidents, the private lives and emotional tensions, which form, as it were, a descant, there continued relentlessly the melody represented by a discordant phase of international relations. An Israeli-Egyptian armistice had been signed in February 1949, but it had done nothing to settle disputed frontiers, nor bring about Arab recognition of the Israeli state. Both Britain and the USA were becoming increasingly worried that the instability of the whole area would lead to Soviet intervention. At the beginning of the year, the US Embassy in London had had a depressing conversation about Egypt with 'the responsible official' (probably Clutton) in the Foreign Office. The latter said that the Palestine war had aggravated all Egypt's problems and, sooner or later, revolution there was inevitable.[9] There was, however, no alternative to dealing with Farouk and his government, even though the main nationalist party, the WAFD, remained in opposition. Field Marshal Slim had visited Cairo, warned the King that the USSR had designs on Suez and the Delta, and suggested Anglo-Egyptian staff talks. The US Embassy in Cairo reported to the State Department that Maclean had kept them fully informed; presumably the Kremlin also felt gratitude.

It will be recalled that the US Chiefs of Staff regarded the Cairo-Suez area as one from which in an emergency a nuclear threat to the USSR could be mounted. This led to a proposal that there should be Anglo-American staff talks at Fayid, the HQ of the British Middle East Land Forces (MELF). This was an embarrassment to the British, who were already sufficiently hesitant about embarking on Anglo-Egyptian staff talks; these, as Maclean informed the US Embassy in Cairo, 'could be dynamite to the present government'. The American Admiral in the Eastern Mediterranean, Admiral Connolly, was undeterred; to avoid curiosity and suspicion on the part of the Egyptians he suggested that twelve US officers be flown direct to Fayid without observing the formality of obtaining Egyptian visas. No sooner was he dissuaded from this undiplomatic evasion than he countered by proposing that the British Embassy be asked to use its close relations with Farouk to tie up arrangements. This placed the American Ambassador, Jefferson Caffrey, in a dilemma; he did not want the British to be seen as 'acting as agents of the Americans'; on the other hand, he recognised that his country was unpopular in Egypt, because of 'distrust in US intentions in Palestine'.[10]

The outcome of these negotiations need not concern us, but two points require to be emphasised: first, the US Embassy appreciated Maclean's helpful attitude in keeping them fully informed. Secondly, Maclean avoided any temptation to leak information to the vernacular press, which could have created a great deal of mischief by revealing what the Anglo-American Generals and Admirals were up to. Maclean always gave top priority to preserving the 'cover' that enabled him to keep abreast of developments without arousing suspicion. This, as he saw it, was what the NKVD required him to do; it was up to them to decide what use to make of the intelligence provided. In the Kremlin there would have been growing concern about this extension to Egypt of American influence, which was already taking root in Israel. In December 1949 the UN General Assembly, meeting in Paris, voted to internationalise the city of Jerusalem, military occupation of which was uneasily shared between Israel and Jordan. Significantly, the majority included the USSR and all Arab states except Jordan; the minority included Britain and the USA, as well as Israel. The future pattern of great-power involvement in the area was beginning to take on its definitive shape. As it did so, Maclean was once more the right man in the right place.

He was not destined, however, to be there much longer; pressure of work, hectic social life and deteriorating relations with Melinda were destroying his morale, and bouts of heavy drinking were becoming more frequent. Away from the city for a few days' local leave at Luxor or Assouan he seemed to be his old self, playing family bridge and tennis and showing his affection for his small sons; but back in Cairo it was another story. More and more frequently he would set out with Melinda on the nightly round of cocktail parties, followed by a dinner engagement, which Melinda alone would keep. On occasion he would fail to return home at all and once on the next morning he was found slumped on a bench in the Esbekieh Gardens. The diplomatic staff remained loyal to him and Campbell either heard nothing or decided to ignore these misdemeanours. Even so, word reached the Foreign Office through the Embassy Security Officer, Major Sansom, that all was not as it should be and early in 1950 George Middleton (Sir George), head of Personnel Department, wrote to Campbell to enquire. Campbell was a diplomat of the old school, who had not been enthusiastic about the amalgamation of the Diplomatic and Consular

Services in 1945. He replied sharply to Middleton (who had been a member of the Consular Service) that he disliked hearing tittle-tattle about an able officer like Maclean: such an enquiry would never have been made in the old days.[11]

There is likely to have been a more sinister reason why around this time Donald's *sang-froid*, which had served him so well, had begun to give way. As we saw, it was early in 1949 that Anglo-American cryptanalysts discovered that there had been a high-grade Soviet agent, code-named 'Homer', who had been purveying secret intelligence from Washington. It had taken time to investigate this alarming discovery, but the hunt was now on. Maclean would not have known about it at first; but in August 1949 Philby was selected by SIS to represent them in Washington with cover as First Secretary at the Embassy for liaison duties with the CIA and FBI. Before leaving London he was briefed about the quest for 'Homer' and soon realised that Maclean was at risk.[12] As interrogation of Maclean might well endanger both Burgess and Philby, the latter would have conveyed some warning to Maclean, so that he might redouble his precautions. This warning would have confronted Maclean with the stark alternative that he eventually had to face: gaol in England or exile in Stalin's Russia. It was an alternative calculated to send even a teetotaller to the bottle. Further bad news followed: at the beginning of February 1950 Klaus Fuchs was arrested, made a full confession and at the end of the month was condemned to fourteen years' imprisonment. No doubt Maclean had a reasonable degree of confidence in the humane methods used by MI5 to extract confessions; but Fuchs' failure to put up any resistance was not reassuring.

It was at this juncture, with storm clouds gathering and lightning beginning to play, that a new and combustible element was added. As we have seen, Philip Toynbee was a good friend to Donald, though they had been together only once since the end of the war. On that occasion Donald, on leave from Washington, had stayed on the Isle of Wight with Philip and his first wife, Anne. It had been a pleasant encounter, except for the evening on which Philip played a recording of T. S. Eliot reading his religious poems: *The Four Quartets*. Donald had surprised his friend by the violence of his reaction, dismissing Eliot as 'decadent' and 'effete'.[13] The truth, however unpalatable to Donald, was that Philip had abandoned his youthful communist phase, though his mind had not yet taken on the Christian coloration that would eventually suffuse it.

In the meantime, however, the outlook was sombre. Philip's wife had left him, taking the children, and his finances were also in disarray; his literary talent, though full of promise, was not proving remunerative. At this crisis in his affairs, his father, Arnold, discreetly intervened by suggesting to David Astor that *The Observer* might be able to find work for Philip. Astor rose to the occasion by offering to Philip a roving commission in the Near East, starting in Cairo. It was a generous offer, but as Philip boarded his aircraft it filled him with apprehension. He did not know the countries on his itinerary, nor their languages, and he lacked experience as a foreign correspondent. If ever a man needed a well-placed friend, it was Philip, as on 9th April 1950 he recorded in his diary: 'Ancient hell of Shepherd's Hotel. Wretched humiliation of not speaking the language.' He telephoned to Maclean.[14]

For Maclean, too, it was a call full of promise, as the mercury in his barometer dropped towards danger point. He desperately needed some outlet; he could not talk freely with his colleagues and had never rated highly the intellectual pleasure of conversation with Melinda or Harriet, who was staying with them. Philip Toynbee was an ideal companion both for talk and for drink. Both men were ambitious, but had grown up in the shadow of distinguished fathers. Both, as they began to examine the outside world, had been struck by its inequalities and miseries. Both had in common a certain duality in their natures, even though its roots in each case were dissimilar; but for both of them alcohol seemed to supply the brief illusion of unified personality. The conjunction between them had a fatal charm.

The weekend of Toynbee's arrival in Cairo was that of the Coptic Easter and Maclean was relieved of some of the immediate official and social duties of his position. 'Suddenly Donald arrived, called me "Philippo", his old private nickname. Tall, graceful, delightful old friend! With his pretty little son. Then I was at a roof party, among bougainvillaea, military attachés, thin colonial women.' Maclean was able to do more than welcome Toynbee as an old friend; he warned him against a female colleague in the local press corps, who resented his assignment and had depicted him to all and sundry as anti-Egyptian and a communist. American diplomats in the area, as later transpired, gave credence to the second charge. Before the day was out, Philip had met, and liked, both Melinda and Harriet; he was soon being treated as one of the family. Donald at first impressed him as resigned to, rather than rebelling against, a life that was obviously bringing him neither pleasure nor reward. 'Like Donald, every one of us to be wise and tolerable must be defeated yet not defeated, dead but not lying down.'

Among the brash, throat-slitting fraternity of the international press corps, Toynbee continued to feel insecure. Here again Maclean was able to help. Toynbee, commenting in his diary on a party given by the British Information Officer, wrote: 'Donald was there at first to offer some protection . . .' Dining with the Macleans afterwards, he complained of his hotel, whereupon they offered him their spare room as soon as it was vacated, despite the fact that it had already been offered to old friends from Washington days, Walter and Katherine Bell. It was the Bells who had to go into the hotel when they arrived in May. Not until Philip Toynbee had been ten days in Cairo does his diary contain any explicit mention that Maclean was doing more than keeping up with the steady drinking that was a feature of the daily life of the foreign community: 'Whirling into a wilder and wilder world. Dinner with Donald on Sunday, then both to the Izzards [Daily Mail]. Very drunk. Relax! as Melinda sweetly and often said to me.' On 21st April Toynbee moved in with the Macleans: 'Delightful to have moved to Donald's where I have my own little white flat at the top of the house . . . It even seems cooler (yesterday 105°!).'

The relative calm was not to last. On the night after Toynbee had come to stay Maclean showed the side of his personality that puzzled and, at times, alarmed his friend: 'Extraordinary conversation with Donald. I find him more and more fascinating and delightful. His extreme gentleness and politeness – the occasional berserk and murderous outbursts when, so to speak, the pot of suppressed anger has been filled.' The anger, for which alcohol provided a vent, derived not only from the restraints imposed by his double life and by the diplomatic social life that cloaked it; there was also instilled into it a hostility to the women around him. In the less active phase of their social life in Washington Donald and Melinda had harmonised reasonably well; but in Cairo, whilst he had become increasingly allergic to the constant round, Melinda, abetted by Harriet, who had arrived in March, had entered into it with enthusiasm and, as she became more animated, attracted admirers. The most persistent of these was a princeling of the royal house. Melinda was coming to symbolise for Donald a way of life that he detested; she, together with the Embassy, were the cords that bound him to it. After one of these drunken evenings Philip recorded: 'Donald told me he wished, still, for the death of his wife. He was in a queer and terrifying condition . . .'

On 26th April Toynbee wrote: 'Donald and I tumbled into a two-day trough together . . . I was back and in bed by midnight, but

Donald rushed out again to disaster after disaster, ending by hitting Eddie [Gathorne Hardy] and throwing glass after glass against the wall.' Philip undertook the task of getting his friend to work next day: 'Donald was still rather drunk, but I forced him out of bed, sobered him with talk and took him all the way to his room at the Embassy. Somehow, once there, he managed to heave on his armour and become a good semblance of a Counsellor. I admired it.' That night Philip got to bed at 2 a.m., only to be aroused by his host: 'So, over weak whiskies, we sat there till 5.30 a.m. Birds loud in the jacaranda trees . . .' It was on this night that for the first time their talk began to bump on the rock which Maclean, however drunk he became, usually steered clear of: communism. Toynbee in his diary described this part of their long conversation as 'fanciful and light'; but in an article written with hindsight in 1967 it took on for him a more sinister meaning: 'We were to form, we decided, a new Communist Party, whose only members would be oursleves. "We must have one other member," he suddenly insisted; and when I asked who, he spat out the word "Stalin!" with preposterous venom.'[15] Toynbee, like all the others, failed to read aright the signs and portents. At a party at the beginning of May he was surprised to overhear Maclean, in conversation with an Egyptian, who worked at the University and had once been a communist, urging the latter 'not to betray his past by writing an anti-communist article'.[16]

Through the haze of alcohol the events of the world outside kept reappearing, like a ship looming up in fog. On one morning of repentance after orgy, news came through that Jordan had annexed most of Arab Palestine, so offending the Arab League, which was currently meeting in Cairo. *The Observer* demanded a story from Philip Toynbee: 'Talked to Donald, read the evening French paper – and wrote my story.' On 4th May there took place what Toynbee termed 'an evening of rabelaisian exhibitionism' at the expense of the Marling sisters, marked by 'wilder and wilder attempts to shock them. Failure. They retired in good order long before we did. Donald began to become aggressive . . .' Eventually Maclean went out with one of the guests, a known homosexual, and did not reappear that night. The next day was Saturday: 'All that day I was affected by Donald's gigantic grief. When he came back for lunch, Melinda was upstairs in her bedroom. I told him the headmaster was waiting in his study.'

The lost weekend was merging into the last week. On Monday morning 'Donald came down with those terrible, tell-tale bleary eyes, and told me that he had gone wild again last night, publicly insulted

Harriet, hit Melinda . . . "I really am getting near to the point where I shall have to be shut up." I tried to say, "How absurd!", but of course it's terrifyingly true . . . I am now convinced that he must at once, and at whatever cost, be analysed – even if it means asking for two years' medical leave from the foreign service. It can't go on . . .' Melinda was coming to much the same conclusion. The only effect of her disapproval was to ensure that the final orgy of drink and destruction took place in the apartments of others. It began in that of John Wardle-Smith, who had replaced Lees Mayall: 'All yesterday we drank and drank, mostly sitting on a balcony in the sun, very happy for several hours and very certain that what we were doing was the best thing we could possibly be doing. The snarling hog's head on the gin bottle, whom we named Gordon and whom we emulated by drinking, in all six bottles . . . Then, girl-hounding, we went to another flat and, finding nobody, smashed it to pieces.' It is not clear how they got into the second flat, but it must have been known to Maclean that it was normally occupied by two American girls working for the US Embassy. Drawers were emptied and underclothes ripped apart; the climax was described by Philip some years later: 'Donald raises a large mirror above his head and crashes it into the bath, when to my amazement, and delight, alas, the bath breaks in two while the mirror remains intact.'[17]

Wardle-Smith tried to intervene. 'Donald's colleague, a nice responsible man, came back from the Embassy to warn us that a furious complaint had already been made by the owner of the ravaged flat . . .'[18] Maclean was unimpressed; in the end it was the Marling sisters who brought the two men home. It was not to be home much longer for either of them. Melinda insisted that Philip should leave: 'I am banished as the serpent in Eden, and am back in the Metropolitan Hotel,' he recorded on Wednesday, 9th May. On the same day Melinda, white-faced, but resolute, went to see the Ambassador.[19] She got her way; that evening Toynbee wrote in his diary: 'Donald is to be sent back at once to England for treatment.' This prompt decision must have taken some of the heat out of the protest subsequently lodged by Caffrey with Campbell. It appears that the former, though regarded in the British Embassy as Anglophobe, made no formal report to the State Department. When after Maclean's disappearance the FBI enquired into the episode, they had to rely on such information as they could glean from Americans who had been serving in Cairo. One of the inmates of the 'ravaged flat' in her interview stated: 'It was agreed not to make an official protest.' She added that on the following day she had 'received a written apology from Maclean and he offered to pay for the damage and also informed her that he intended to see a doctor'. In no other respect did any of the FBI's informants know anything to his detriment; one remarked that he was 'quite certain Maclean ... had absolutely no contacts with Russians'.[20]

Maclean accepted his fate with resignation. Toynbee commented that 'he seemed relieved to have given up the terribly unequal struggle.' Early on Friday, 11th May the Minister, Chapman-Andrews, escorted his Counsellor to the airport, Farouk Field. By one of those coincidences that colour the careers of successful journalists, Geoffrey Hoare was booked to fly out by the same aircraft. 'A rather strained and unhappy Melinda was there to see him off, with Harriet ... I asked Donald why he was flying to London and he replied merely that he was going home on private business for a few days ...' Hoare found him a silent travelling companion, but 'noticed nothing wrong with him in any way ... He had none of the external signs of a person suffering from a severe nervous breakdown.'[21] One week later an Arabic language newspaper carried an account of the unsavoury incident, which ended (according to Philip) 'by insinuating that he [Donald] had been sent home and dismissed from the service'. Philip, whose contacts with the British and American Embassies were no longer what they had been, made a comment indicating that he was unaware that Caffrey had protested. 'If the newspaper is seen by the American Ambassador he will *have* to make the complaint to our Embassy which the paper claims that he's made already. And the British Ambassador, who refused to enquire closely, who covered up for Donald, who is in every way nice, arranged that he should be going home only on medical grounds, will *have* to take official notice and inform the FO that Donald is no longer fit to belong to the Service.'[22]

No aspect of this strange story is stranger than the behaviour of Campbell. His conspicuous failure either to conduct a full investigation or to make a detailed report to the FO cannot be extenuated as a straightforward desire not to injure the career of a subordinate, whom he regarded as a friend. Campbell was an experienced Ambassador, who well knew that the Personnel Department in London relied on the reports of Heads of Mission in making appointments. Campbell's sin of omission had a disastrous consequence; if he had provided a full account of the final episode, with an adequate portrayal of earlier incidents, all pointing in the same direction, it is scarcely conceivable that the FO would have selected headship of its American Department as the post to be entrusted to Maclean after his supposed cure. It was this appointment that so largely fuelled the resentment felt in Washington after his disappearance.

The importance of this issue justifies some investigation into Campbell's reason for acting as he did. Those who served with him in the later stages of his distinguished career knew that at these posts he was accompanied by an efficient and faithful servant, against whom he would not have a word spoken. It was widely believed, rightly or wrongly, that this man had homosexual proclivities. Campbell was a much respected and long-serving member of the Diplomatic Service and it is not suggested that there was any impropriety in his relations with his manservant. In so far as the latter's behaviour gave rise to criticism, however, it may well be that his master came to adopt a defensive attitude, which predisposed him to ignore all stories about the private lives of his staff, whether diplomatic or domestic. In any ordinary community such an attitude would command respect; but a diplomatic mission in foreign parts is in no sense an ordinary community and it requires more rigorous standards. The reluctance of some Ambassadors of Campbell's generation to apply such standards was illustrated in an earlier chapter by the cautionary tale of Lord Inverchapel and his Russian valet.

Campbell's role is not the only one that merits further examination. It is necessary to emphasise that of Melinda, if only because of the widespread belief that she was privy to her husband's espionage, perhaps even an active member of his spy ring. This latter, and graver, supposition does not stand up to the new evidence brought to bear by Toynbee and Maude upon the modalities of Maclean's removal from Cairo; the initiative was not taken by the British or the American Ambassador, but by Melinda herself. Moreover she took it, when the final crisis was reached, without any hesitation or delay. If she had been in any degree under the orders of the NKVD, or apprehensive about their reaction, she would never have ventured, without first consulting them, to remove one of their most important agents from the post where he was proving increasingly useful, and expose him to a searching examination in London into his conduct. Melinda did not act as someone who might herself fall under suspicion, but as any other woman would have done, whose first priority was to preserve the decency of the home in which she was raising her children.

Finally, the role of Maclean himself excites some queries. After his return to London, he wrote to Toynbee, who was suffering remorse both about the incident itself and gossip about it, in which he had been involved, 'a very affectionate letter,' containing 'an absolute assurance that he didn't hold me responsible for his misfortune'. Regarding Toynbee's subsequent indiscretion with an Egyptian journalist, Maclean made the strange comment: 'It would be no use concealing it. After all, we broke up that room in order that it shouldn't be concealed.'[23] If one takes this at face value, it seems to explain both the extravagance of his actions and the fact that these took place in an apartment occupied by Americans. Why, when the urge to violence overcame him, did he not break up the flat of his own Embassy colleague, where the drinking bout had begun? It can be argued that it was an anti-American gesture; but Philip Toynbee's diary gives no support to this view. Such a gesture in the heat of drink would surely have been accompanied by some familiar anti-American slogan. It is more plausible to assume that Maclean did not ravage a British flat for the very reason that this could so easily have been covered up. If, on the other hand, he had become desperate to get away from Cairo, he would, consciously or perhaps subconsciously, have gone over the top, knowing what the consequence must be. Entering the realm of speculation, we can test a further possibility: it may have been a Russian, rather than a British, veto on his leaving Cairo that he was desperately trying to overcome. If he had approached Campbell and asked for sick-leave, it is unlikely that it would have been refused. His Soviet control, valuing his reports, might well have proved less sympathetic, as the USSR veered more and more towards the pro-Arab policy that has ever since prevailed.

7

His Last Post

The supposition that Maclean had been determined to quit Cairo at any price and may even have contemplated ending his dual career gains some strength from the ineptness of his behaviour on arrival in London. Instead of reporting at once to the Foreign Office and throwing himself on the mercy of his friend, George Middleton (later Sir George), who was head of Personnel Department, he left it to the latter to get into touch and even then declined to present himself at Carlton House Terrace, where the administrative departments were then located. When they finally agreed to meet on neutral ground for lunch, things went better than Maclean could reasonably have expected. He wrote on the same day to Melinda:

> 'I lunched with George Middleton today and told him the score. He was very understanding and has fixed for me to see a Dr. Wilson tomorrow morning, who is said to be a leading psychiatrist and who the F.O. employ as a consultant when their employees' psyches miss a beat. I still have my lid off and I am prepared therefore to ask help; if he says I need more exercise I shall go round the corner to Erna (from Harley to Wimpole – not far).'[1]

He spent a blameless evening watching V. de Sica's famous film *Bicycle Thieves*.

Two days later he wrote again, after his examination by Dr Wilson in Harley Street, who advised going into a clinic 'for no specific period for tests of all kinds'. Maclean rejected this advice: 'At the moment of writing I do not feel I can face going into a clinic; fear plays a leading part in my resistance, but I also much doubt that there is any point in it.' The letter does not explain the nature of his fear, but it is easy to suppose that he was afraid that under the sedation he might say more

7   Philip Toynbee

Dining in Cairo: Donald,
Melinda and Harriet; Michael
Maude (right of picture)

9   Kim Philby

10   Tom Driberg and Guy Burgess in Moscow

than was prudent about the strains to which he had been exposed in Cairo. In the first week of June he had various tests in Maida Vale Hospital including an encephalograph, which proved negative. Meanwhile, with the approval of the Foreign Office and at their expense, he had begun a course of treatment with Dr Erna Rosenbaum, a female psychiatrist of his own choice, whom he always referred to as 'Rosie' or 'Dr Rose'.

Dr Rosenbaum, practising in Wimpole Street and preserving the secrets of her patients, has left few traces. She is reported to have been a follower of Jung; if this was so, nothing could have been better fitted to Maclean's case, nor more threatening to his survival as a spy. Jung has written:

> 'Clinical diagnoses are important, since they give the doctor a certain orientation; but they do not help the patient. The crucial thing is the story. For it alone shows the human background and the human suffering, and only at that point can the doctor's therapy begin to operate.'[2]

Jung found, as other psychiatrists have been doing ever since, that neurotic symptoms could be alleviated, or even cured, if the patient could be led to tell his or her story and, in the process, bring to light the hidden fears, resentments, or other negative emotions deeply lodged in the subconscious. Maclean had for years been trying to cover up both his homosexual tendency and his betrayal of his family, friends and colleagues. There might have been a time during the war when one or two of them might have understood, even if they could not approve, his pro-Soviet activities, much as Goronwy Rees tacitly condoned the activities of his friend Guy Burgess; but as the Cold War became more intense, this hope of confession, to be followed, perhaps, by absolution, had sharply receded. Maclean was never inclined to concede that he might have been wrong; but he was not so cut off from family and friends as to be indifferent to the wrong he was doing to them by deceiving them. He had not separated himself from them in the way adopted by Philby, who rejoiced in every discomfiture he could inflict on the British and American security forces; nor did Maclean share Philby's dog-like devotion to the NKVD.

Maclean's distaste for what he was doing led him to try to suppress his awareness of its true significance. One way of doing this was by excess doses of alcohol. Here, too, Jung could have enlightened him:

'Every form of addiction is bad, no matter whether the narcotic be alcohol or morphine or idealism.'[3]

By 1950 idealism was functioning no better than alcohol. Even if Maclean and his fellow-communists outside the USSR were still unable to see Stalin's Russia for what it was, they could no longer see it as the great experiment, the dawn of a new day, as it had seemed twenty years earlier, when young men threw away their lives in Spain, or plunged into the deep, cold waters of espionage. What Maclean was doing for Russia in 1950 was being done from necessity, operating, as he saw it, at two levels. At international level he believed that peace between the two superpowers could only be preserved by maintaining an even balance between them; this meant helping the Soviet cause. At the personal level it was necessary to continue to do this because the NKVD had the means to compel him to do so. This was the dark side of his life, which had to be obscured not only from the outside world, but even, to the extent that this was possible, from himself. If he had gone to Dr Wilson's clinic, elements of the suppressed life might well have come to the surface; Dr Wilson would no doubt have put loyalty to his country before loyalty to his patient.

Were these priorities reversed in the eyes of 'Dr Rose'? We do not know; but it seems probable. She was an immigrant from Eastern Europe and suspicions about her arose in the minds of Middleton and Carey-Foster; her particulars were sent to MI5 but the familiar answer came back: 'Nothing Recorded Against'.[4] There remains, however, another unanswered question: how did Maclean know about her in the first place? He had served abroad continuously for seven years without requiring the services of a psychiatrist; it is strange that, on arrival in London, he at once knew of one and where to find her, as an alternative to the practitioner who had been officially recommended. Maclean's troubled head was the repository of much highly secret information; on this ground alone it is remarkable that the Foreign Office, who were paying, did not insist on their man. It should be made clear, of course, that 'Dr Rose' reported on her patient at regular intervals; she ascribed his condition to overwork, marital troubles and repressed homosexuality. Nothing more sinister emerged.

With hindsight one might perhaps suppose that a guarded mention of homosexual tendencies would have alerted the Personnel Department to the risk of employing such an officer on highly secret and responsible work. It would be unhistorical to think in this way: it was indeed the defection of Maclean and Burgess, followed by the prosecution in 1962 of John Vassall, the homosexual Admiralty clerk, that finally drove home the lesson that a deviation in one direction may indicate deviation in another. This deduction continued to hold good even after the risk of blackmail had been much reduced, following the change in the law on adult homosexuality; but it was not a deduction generally accepted forty years ago. The most notorious homosexual traitor of modern times was probably Sir Roger Casement, to whom Burgess in one of his lighter moments once compared himself; but the practices recorded in Casement's diaries were not regarded by his contemporaries as explaining his treason so much as reinforcing the demand for his execution by destroying any sympathy for him.

Maclean's abrupt departure from Cairo left Melinda with many problems. As usual, when at a loss, she appealed to her mother, who duly arrived in Cairo on 1st June. The Macleans had rented a house for July in Alexandria, where most of the Embassy moved in the summer, and the first question to be decided was whether to cancel the letting. No firm guidance was forthcoming from the Ambassador, and Maclean's letters were confused and contradictory. The only definite offer – an attractive one in the circumstances – was from Melinda's Egyptian admirer, who proposed a long holiday in Spain. This had the advantage of removing the family from Cairo, where they were an object of gossip, without their having to go to London, where the future of Donald and Melinda was in the melting pot. Mrs Dunbar paid outstanding bills and they all sailed from Alexandria on 18th June. Melinda had been in Cairo less than two years and would never again experience diplomatic life; but this relatively short period had changed her. She was no longer the rather retiring, lackadaisical wife and mother that she had been, ready to let life flow over her and around her. She was now more confident and self-possessed: better equipped for a life of adventure. It was just as well.

With Donald drinking himself silly in London and Melinda in Spain, living with a man of means, it might be thought that their marriage was at an end. If it had been a childless marriage, it would probably have petered out; but there was another factor, in addition to the two boys, that contributed to bring them together again – the Foreign Office. Preservation of marriages, under the strains to which diplomatic life exposes them, has always been an aim of the Foreign Office, which has a strictly pragmatic attitude towards matrimony. The happiness of couples is a secondary consideration; but keeping them out of the divorce courts and so avoiding publicity is primary.

Even separation is regarded as very undesirable, since it deprives the Service of the unpaid hostesses and housekeepers who accompany their husbands to their exacting posts. These important, if utilitarian, factors have sometimes led the Personnel Department to take up the unlikely role of mediator and conciliator. For this role George Middleton, who was on friendly terms with both Macleans, was well fitted. The reports reaching him from 'Dr Rose' suggested that, if Donald and Melinda could be brought together and a job could be found for him in London, where friends could keep an eye on him, a useful career would be salvaged and the Service would benefit.

The chief obstacle was Maclean himself, as his disordered life in London continued, despite the efforts of those who had known him and liked him in better times. These latter included the Bonham-Carter sisters, with whom he had once attended 'deb dances'. Cressida, whose husband, Jasper Ridley, a close friend of Philip Toynbee, had been killed in the war, invited Donald for a quiet weekend in the country. Her sister, Laura, who had married the Liberal MP Jo Grimond, accepted an invitation from Maclean to lunch with him; the Grimonds tried to probe into his state of mind but met with an impenetrable barrier:

'There was nothing wrong with his memory, nor with his grasp of the international situation. He made light of his own troubles too, even suggesting that he might soon be going back to rejoin the Embassy staff in Cairo.'[5]

As always, Maclean could pull himself together when he most needed to do so; but on evenings when it seemed safe to let go everything fell apart. One of those who observed his disintegration was Cyril Connolly, in whose house Maclean's friend, Robert Kee, had a flat. Connolly wrote:

'He had lost his serenity, his hands would tremble, his face was usually a livid yellow and he looked as if he spent the night sitting up in a tunnel. One evening a man leaving a nightclub got into an empty taxi and found him asleep on the rug. When awakened he became very angry and said he had hired it for the evening as his bedroom.'[6]

Another old friend who tried the remedy of a weekend in the country was Robin Campbell, married to Lady Mary St Clair

Erskine (Lady Mary Dunn), whom Maclean had known briefly in Munich before the war. The Campbells were living at Stokke, near Pewsey. She met him one sunny afternoon at Hungerford Station and, as he seemed in a bad way, took him first to the house of a friend who had a quiet garden. They piled up cushions under a weeping beech, where she hoped he would be able to relax. Instead of that, he was seized by an attack of *delirium tremens* and would not lie still. He kept getting to his feet and fighting the overhanging branches, shouting, 'They're after me!' 'Who are?' she asked. 'The Russians.'[7] She dismissed this remark as a symptom of his clinical condition and only remembered it one year later. Once she got him home, he became more manageable and during the next few days did no more than drink level with the Campbells, who were not prosperous at that time and kept no extensive cellar. Maclean had several long talks on this and a subsequent visit, in the course of which he came close to disclosing the root cause of his trouble. As Campbell later recalled,

'He talked on several occasions about communism in the same way that a potential Catholic aware that he lacked the gift of faith might discuss religion.'[8]

In August, when Donald was staying with another friend near Oxford, he wrote in a letter,

'There are two men in a car waiting outside. They've been there for four hours. Are they after me?'[9]

If his doubts about communism had been juxtaposed to his fear of pursuit, an insight might have resulted into the predicament of a spy, who had grown weary of the underground struggle and uncertain whether the ideology still rang true enough to make up for loss of integrity and peace of mind, let alone the prospect of separation from his family through imprisonment or self-imposed exile. But his friends refused to think the unthinkable; it was easier to ascribe random remarks to drunken self-dramatisation, aggravated by manifest dislike for diplomatic life and all its trappings. In general, he continued to reserve his wilder utterances for old friends, such as Campbell and Mark Culme-Seymour, on whose goodwill he could rely. There was an evening when he challenged the latter to denounce him for having said that he was working for 'Uncle Joe' (Stalin). Culme-Seymour was sufficiently perturbed next day to consult Cyril Connolly, but both finally agreed that Maclean in his drunken state had probably been submitting his friend to some kind of test.[10]

A potentially more serious episode occurred at the Gargoyle, involving Goronwy Rees, who had not seen Maclean for fifteen years and did not at first recognise him. Maclean, however, had no difficulty in recognising Rees; crossing the crowded dance floor, he hissed: 'You used to be one of us, but you ratted.'[11] This was very near the bone; indeed the late Anthony Blunt insisted that Rees had been a fellow member of the ring up to the time of the Nazi-Soviet Pact of 1939, which caused him to drop out, after promising not to give his friends away. He was in intermittent touch with MI6; but it would have been very awkward for him to have reported the incident witout revealing more of his own past than was comfortable. Although Maclean was unlikely to have known of Rees' Intelligence link, the extravagant nature of this indiscretion, coming on top of other such lapses, does raise the question whether at times he half-hoped to end the suspense and the ordeal by finally bringing down upon himself the whole edifice of deceit and betrayal. If so, he hoped in vain; after his flight a number of people claimed to have felt concern, even consternation; but only one report reached the Foreign Office, emanating from a departmental secretary-typist, and that failed to arrive on Carey-Foster's desk.

At the beginning of September Maclean wrote a depressed letter to his wife, expressing doubt whether he would ever make a satisfactory husband or father and suggesting that she would do better without him. On receipt of this letter Melinda, with some encouragement from the Foreign Office, decided to come to London, leaving the boys in Paris with Mrs Dunbar. She was at first circumspect and did not stay at the same hotel as Donald or with his mother, though she did call on Lady Maclean. Middleton brought husband and wife together and confronted them with the need to decide whether to try to reconstruct his career and so enable him to support his family.[12] The family weighed with both Macleans. Donald had shown himself an affectionate elder brother to Alan, who was nine years his junior, and there is no doubt about his feelings for his own two boys. As for Melinda, if the marriage broke up, she would have little alternative but to take the children with her to the USA and become dependent upon her mother. This was clearly not a favoured option; two years later, when she left England for good, it was in Switzerland that she temporarily settled; she evidently had no wish to go back to her homeland. Ten years of married life, troubled as these had been, had not only given them two children, but had linked them with the ties that grow between a couple who have faced hard trials together and surmounted them, however precariously. There had been happy days, as well as nights of fear, during air-raids on London, and more recently nights of shame in Cairo.

In the end they decided to try again; Melinda stayed two weeks before returning to Paris to fetch the boys. Their pact was sealed by sleeping together for the first time for at least four months and Melinda became pregnant. After Maclean's flight she decided to imply that this had been their intention, setting a seal upon their reconciliation. One may be more disposed to believe that this was a rationalisation after the event. It certainly had the effect of erecting a barrier between Melinda and her Egyptian princeling; but it added a further complication to the delicate balance on which Donald teetered. From Paris Melinda wrote a letter to Harriet to explain her decision:

'Donald had grave doubts at first about our ability to be happy together but we decided to try it again. To me it was the only decision to take on account of the children, and I think Donald has already benefited tremendously. He realises many things which he never allowed himself to think before. We have both, alas, developed in opposite directions. I have become more extroverted and enjoy gayer and simpler people, but Donald will have none of that at all. However, if we are frank and above all don't repress our feelings perhaps we will work something out. He is going back to the Foreign Office on November 1st – poor lamb!!'[13]

There has been speculation that Burgess was instrumental in persuading Maclean to resume his dual career; but there is no evidence of this, nor of any regular contact between the two up to the date of Burgess' departure at the beginning of August to take up his new post at the British Embassy, Washington.

There was, however, a major international event that cannot have failed to influence Maclean's thinking. On 25th June 1950 the forces of communist North Korea invaded South Korea, carrying all before them. At that time the Soviet delegation to the UN was boycotting all meetings as a protest against refusal to seat the People's Republic of China (CPR) in place of Chiang-kai-shek, who was confined to Taiwan. In default of a Soviet veto, the UN Security Council took the decision, with only India and Egypt abstaining, to constitute a UN force to restore the situation. This force, to which Britain was the main contributor after the USA, was placed under the command of General MacArthur, who by the end of September had liberated South Korea up to the 38th parallel, which divides the two parts of the peninsula. The situation remained one of great tension and uncertainty. Would MacArthur push on into North Korea in an attempt to unify the country, which had been partitioned after the war into two zones of occupation? If he did so, would this lead to an intervention of the People's Republic of China, as Indian diplomatic representatives in Asia were already warning? It was clear that, as these and other crucial questions were being determined, London would be an excellent listening-post for the NKVD, both on account of the Anglo-American special relationship and of Britain's ties with India and other Commonwealth countries.

Whatever the true state of Maclean's health when he left Egypt, and whatever his relations at that time with the NKVD, it must be assumed that there had been an interval, during which he had been virtually out of touch with the NKVD, to whom the leniency with which his misdemeanours in Cairo had been treated by the Foreign Office would have appeared incomprehensible. The NKVD must surely have assumed that the Foreign Office would have received a full report on his conduct and that he would have been subjected, if fit enough, to rigorous cross-examination. In any case it would have taken time for the NKVD, pursuing its usual prudent procedures, to set up new control arrangements in London, necessitated by Maclean's unforeseen and unheralded arrival there. Maclean himself would have welcomed some respite from the pressure and would have been in no hurry to resume contact. By September, however, the NKVD would certainly have been anxious to reactivate their agent; the news that he was to be made head of the American Department must have come to them as a scarcely conceivable stroke of good fortune. His new 'control' was Yuri Modin, code-named 'Peter', who also kept in touch with Blunt, though the latter had been allowed in 1945 to leave MI5 and become a 'sleeper'.

There is no evidence that Maclean himself was able to exert influence to bring about his new appointment, though he may have known that the headship was vacant, because of the illness of the previous head, Stanley Fordham (the late Sir Stanley), and that no other Department was available to him. He was eligible for the post, because of his service in Washington and the favourable reports of at least two of the Ambassadors under whom he had worked there. He was well-known to Sir Roger Makins, who as Deputy Under-Secretary was the senior member of the Promotions Board, which made the appointment, after its chairman, Sir William Strang (later Lord Strang), the Permanent Under-Secretary. Strang himself held a good opinion of Maclean. When in the early spring of 1951 Carey-Foster broke to him the news that Maclean had become the prime suspect, Strang went quite white: 'I just can't believe it,' he exclaimed.[14] In the summer of 1950, when the Promotions Board made its fateful decision, it had before it nothing against him, apart from some doubts about his general health and his inclination to drink too much. Nonetheless the identity of 'Homer' had not yet been determined and Maclean, if only on the strength of having been in Washington at the critical time, could hardly be absolved from suspicion. In this connection it must be noted that Carey-Foster, who was responsible for liaison with MI5 about the case, was not a member of the Board; nor was his superintending Under-Secretary, Patrick Reilly (Sir Patrick), although he later became a member. The plain fact was that at that time the Foreign Office did not give a sufficiently high priority to security; it was the defection of Maclean and Burgess that taught this belated lesson. On the credit side, it must be added that the Board took fully into account – indeed too fully – the humanitarian considerations. Maclean would soon have exhausted the six months' leave allowable, after which he would have to go on to half-pay. On half-pay, and without private means, he could not hope to support his family; his rejection for the appointment would virtually have signalled both the end of his career and of his marriage.

In the final analysis the Promotions Board, in making this appointment, which later contributed so much to the exacerbation of American opinion, was the victim of bad timing. In the first place the vital evidence of 'Homer's' visit to New York, which pin-pointed Maclean as the man, was not received from the cryptanalysts until April 1951. Secondly, the process of elimination up to that point had necessarily been slow and laborious; accusations of treasonable behaviour could not be lightly tossed around among members of one of the most trusted sectors of government. In the House of Commons in November 1955 Harold Macmillan referred to 'a search in a field of about 6,000 people'. In arriving at so large a figure, he was probably including possible American suspects, as well as the British. The latter would have included not only the staff of the British Embassy in Washington, but also that of the Joint Staff Mission. In Philby's book, which had, of course, a polemical and propaganda purpose, he derided the insistence of the FBI on screening all kinds of menial employees. In doing so, he ignored the way in which the immense proliferation of documentation and, in particular, the expansion of copying facilities, has expanded the range of espionage. A spy need no longer be a person whose importance gives him access to secrets; he can be a humble typist, or a lowly functionary charged with disposal of confidential waste. MI5, as always, were short-handed; but by the end of 1950 they had reduced the number of suspects to thirty-five. This list had been further reduced to nine by the time that the final piece of the jigsaw fell into place.

In considering how much scope for damage Maclean's new appointment allowed, we can start from the bland statement made in November 1955 by the Foreign Secretary. In the Commons debate Macmillan described Maclean's new post as follows:

> 'This Department ... deals principally with Latin-American affairs. Major questions relating to the United States are dealt with regionally – for instance, N.A.T.O. affairs would come under the Western Organisation Department ... the United States questions which are dealt with by the American Department are largely routine, welfare of forces, visitors, and the like. The appointment implied no promotion for Maclean and provided an opportunity to watch his conduct and health.'[15]

Like many of the best parliamentary statements, this one contains no falsehood, but reveals no more than absolutely necessary. It presupposes that it is the duty of an enemy agent to intervene directly in the conduct of public business. This is not so; on the contrary, his first duty is to preserve his 'cover', whilst securing access to as much secret information as possible. By virtue of being a head of Department, Maclean achieved access to most of the important telegrams passing between the Foreign Office and posts abroad, as well as a selection of Cabinet papers, designed to keep senior officials abreast of the thinking and decision-making of Ministers. As we shall see, the supply was later attenuated; but not before much potential damage had been done, especially in the context of the Korean War. Because of the volatile nature of American public opinion in relation to the war, the American Department was frequently consulted and shown information by Departments, such as Far Eastern Department, which had the executive responsibility.

An unusual feature of the American Department was that it had two Assistants and served two Under-Secretaries. The Assistant

Under-Secretary supervising the Latin-American section, which was in my charge, was the late Sir Andrew Noble; but Sir Roger Makins, although holding the senior rank of Deputy Under-Secretary, supervised the US section, which was under John Curle (later Sir John). Makins, who was being groomed to become the next Ambassador in Washington, had undertaken to keep a special eye on Maclean. Curle's comment on him is as follows: 'I never noticed him the worse for drink. I thought him a good head of Department; he was never fussed or flustered.'[16] It is a comment that I can endorse; Maclean was not much interested in Latin-America and left me to get on with it; no Assistant could ask more. Geoffrey Jackson (the late Sir Geoffrey), who was in the Latin-American section, was another who found him remote, but reasonably relaxed. One afternoon, Jackson, going into the office of his head of Department, found him

'with his heels on his desk, and reading a paper-bound French novel. For once he was less impersonal than usual. Had I read it? Did I like it? It was Camus' *La Peste* ('The Plague'), and I told him that I liked neither it nor *L'Etranger* ('The Outsider') . . .'[17]

There was a gulf between Maclean's communism and the existentialism of Camus; but the latter's vivid description of bubonic plague in Oran and the deficiencies of French colonial administration would have touched a chord in his anti-imperialist heart. There had been an outbreak of plague in Cairo in the year before he took up his post there; he may well have been thinking that he was better off in London, whatever the anxieties under which he laboured. We were all mildly surprised that he never asked any of us out for a meal, or even a drink, and courteously evaded any attempts to establish closer relationships. We accepted, however, that he was still recuperating from a nervous crisis, of which we knew no details, and that, living as he did in the country, he usually went straight to Charing Cross to catch his train home. Of nights spent in London in haunts rarely frequented by his colleagues, we knew nothing.

The decision of Donald and Melinda to look for a house in the commuter belt was a natural one for them to have taken. In those days members of the Service working in London received none of the allowances available to those serving abroad. Maclean had no money of his own and, if he was to live on his salary, it was obviously necessary to avoid the higher cost of buying or renting a house in London. No doubt Melinda also hoped that Donald, faced with the journey home, would catch his train, instead of staying in London to drink in congenial company. She wrote to Harriet:

'Donald is still pretty confused and vague about himself and his desires but I think when he gets settled he will find a new security and peace. I hope so. He hasn't had any drinking bouts since I have been back but I can see that the root of the trouble is still not cleared away. He is still going to R. however and is definitely better. She is still baffled a bit about the homosexual side which comes out when he is drunk and I think slight hostility in general to women.'[18]

They decided to look for a house on the Kent-Surrey border and, whilst doing so, went to live in a residential hotel near Sevenoaks. Eventually they found what they wanted in the village of Tatsfield, raised a mortgage, partly through Mrs Dunbar, and moved in a few days before Christmas. 'Beaconshaw' was a large, late Victorian house with garden and gravel drive, but it had a dilapidated appearance and Melinda found that, by American standards, it was woefully lacking in labour-saving appliances. They had a country girl to help with the boys, but Melinda sorely missed the numerous and well-trained staff who had looked after them in Cairo. Many years later in Moscow Maclean described the garden as 'lovely': distance may have lent enchantment.

At first all went reasonably well; the children caught colds, but Maclean was still catching the early train. In January 1951 they paid a brief visit to Paris to attend Harriet's marriage to James Campbell Sheers, an American official, who was working there. He and Harriet promised a return visit to the Macleans in the spring. As Donald's sister Nancy was about to marry an American, Anglo-Saxon ties seemed to be holding firm. Once back in London, however, the old trouble soon began again. More and more often, after a long alcoholic evening at a club, such as the Gargoyle or the Mandrake, he would miss the last train home. One of those who befriended him on such occasions was Robert Kee, who was working as a journalist in London. He found Maclean good company in the early stages of the evening, but recalls no anti-American talk and little comment on the Korean War, apart from some murmurs about the cost in human suffering.[19]

With a friend of longer standing, however, Maclean, as usual, lowered his guard. Toynbee reappeared in London early in 1951 with a new wife, Sally, an American, to whom Maclean at once took a liking. She had been private secretary to the US Ambassador in Tel Aviv, where Toynbee had met her on his journalistic tour of the Near East. They had got married in Tehran in November and Toynbee, once his tour was over, brought her to London, where she had few English friends. At parties Maclean several times took charge of her, introduced her to his friends and showed great kindness.[20] Unfortunately it was not long before she also saw the other side of his character. In the third week of January a jury in New York convicted Alger Hiss for perjury and he was sentenced to five years in prison. Toynbee wrote an article in *The Observer*, in which he conceded that there might be some validity in the evidence given by the ex-communist, Whittaker Chambers, on the strength of whose testimony Hiss had been convicted. Next time Toynbee encountered Maclean in the Gargoyle, he was already very drunk and showed him his most menacing face. Maclean advanced on his friend, muttering, 'I am the English Hiss.' As Toynbee wrote later, 'Donald threw me backwards into the band, pint-glass in hand.'[21] He was becoming increasingly unpopular with night-club proprietors.

In the office at this stage he was still preserving a certain reticence. His views on the Korean War were forcibly expressed, but hardly stood out against the general background of apprehension about where American policy might be leading. The US Embassy in London noted nothing amiss in his dealings with them. Early in 1951 the Unity Theatre, a theatre club under left-wing management, staged a revue, *Here Goes*, which contained sketches highly derogatory to the US Army in Korea. The theatre, being a club, was not subject to licensing or any form of censorship, but the audience was required to take out membership. When the police interviewed some of those connected with the revue, the latter counter-charged that two Americans, suspected of belonging to the US Embassy, had tried to gain admission without signing on as members. When the case was taken up by the National Council of Civil Liberties and publicised in the *Daily Worker*, Jim Penfield, Counsellor of the Embassy, called on Maclean to deny that anyone on the embassy staff had acted as *agent provocateur*, as alleged.[22] Maclean's sympathies must have been with the theatre, but his behaviour occasioned no adverse comment then or later from Penfield.

At the beginning of July 1950 Dick Brooman-White, Conservative MP for Rutherglen, who had formerly worked both for MI5 and MI6, complained to Malcolm Muggeridge that 'the young men in the F.O.

are all anti-American and against the Korean intervention.'[23] If this was a true verdict, as it probably was, the reason is not far to seek. Like a great majority of the British people, little more than five years after the end of the Second World War and still subject to some privation, they did not want war with China, which would have been (to quote General Omar Bradley) 'the wrong war, at the wrong place, at the wrong time, and with the wrong enemy'. It was feared, however, that the sage views of the General were not widely shared in the USA at a time when Senator McCarthy was lifting up his voice and attracting most of the publicity. The opinion almost universally prevailing in the Foreign Office was that the more pressing dangers to peace were in Central Europe and the Middle East: by comparison Korea was a diversion. If officials had had any doubts on this score, Ministers in Attlee's government would have been quick to set them right. When John Strachey, who was in charge of the War Office, wrote to Emanuel Shinwell, Minister of Defence, complaining about the aggressive posture of the US Seventh Fleet in waters round Taiwan and MacArthur's wish to use Chiang's troops in Korea, he sent a copy to Herbert Morrison, who had just become Foreign Secretary. The latter had no hesitation in replying that he 'shared many of the fears expressed by John'.[24] The atmosphere was not one in which anti-American sentiments expressed by Maclean would readily have been regarded as treasonable.

It is only fair to add that this view does not seem to be shared by Sir Nicholas Henderson, if we are to judge by a television interview in which he said:

'Maclean took a rather odd line in the Foreign Office on the Korean War, an anti-American line, and I remember being astonished by that at the time. Then I had some argument with him in which he showed, to me, totally irrational views from the Western standpoint. So when he ultimately left I wasn't actually surprised. I knew exactly what had happened.'[25]

Not many of us had Sir Nicholas' prescience and even he does not appear to have propagated his opinion very widely at the time when it would have been of most value. Personally, I recall only one remark, made at teatime soon after Maclean had taken over the Department. It was at the time when MacArthur was in full retreat in the face of massive Chinese forces, described as 'volunteers'. He observed that the General had been stupid to move up to the Yalu River, forming the frontier between China and North Korea; I could find no argument to counter him. As the weeks went by, however, there is no doubt that his behaviour and remarks outside the office became less and less discreet. His increased drinking kept pace with his growing anxiety about the war: each fed the other.

There was, in fact, a crisis in Anglo-American relations within the larger international crisis. As MacArthur retreated around the turn of the year, the US Joint Chiefs seriously considered withdrawal from Korea altogether; but the inflamed state of opinion in Congress and the country meant that such a move would have had to be accompanied by direct retaliation against the People's Republic of China. The least aggressive measure would be some form of economic sanctions, which would have had drastic implications for Hong-Kong. The most violent step would be to play the nuclear card. There was acute fear in Britain and throughout the Commonwealth that MacArthur, rather than accept defeat, would persuade Truman at least to threaten use of the atom bomb. Truman had no such intention, but this was scarcely better understood in London than it was in Moscow. Moreover he was trapped early in December into making an indiscreet reply to a press enquiry whether the bomb might be used: 'Consideration of the use of any weapon', he said, 'is always implicit in the very possession of that weapon.'[26] This set all the alarm bells ringing in Whitehall and was the main reason for Attlee's hurriedly arranged visit to Washington later in the same month. Maclean's initials appear on the briefs prepared for this visit and a Cabinet paper reporting on it was among secret documents that I retrieved from his steel filing cabinet after his flight.

At this period Maclean was able, for once, to salvage a little integrity by openly criticising the US Government in ways that would not threaten his 'cover' by striking others as too far out of line. He could feel also that British influence was being exerted in ways that made extension of the war less likely. In mid-March in a comment on Anglo-American relations he wrote:

'There is a good deal of disquiet here about American leadership, particularly fear that their fire-eating in the Far East and generally will land us unnecessarily in war.'[27]

One week later, when the Ambassador in Washington, Sir Oliver Franks (later Lord Franks), was on a visit to London, the Permanent Under-Secretary held a meeting at which there was an anguished discussion of the declining 'special relationship'. Maclean was not present, but would have seen the record. The two countries were like men tied together in a three-legged race; they had to go forward together, but neither could move freely. The USA needed allies to preserve the appearance that the UN was fighting the war; but as American casualties mounted, pressure increased on the US government, which was bearing the brunt, to take firm decisions unencumbered by European misgivings. The forward pressure of the US administration was countered in Whitehall by the backward movement of opinion in the Labour Party, which resented the close American link and tended to overlook Britain's financial dependence on the dollar.

Intelligence reports about these rifts within the alliance would have been sweet music in Stalin's ear. He was also keenly interested in shifting alignments in the UN, which increasingly reflected Asian mistrust of American aims. Because of the important role of India in the Commonwealth and in Asia as a whole, London was a vital listening post, as Attlee and Bevin struggled to keep emergent nations in line. In October 1950, when the Political Committee of the UN General Assembly (UNGA) debated the war, India, Yugoslavia and three Arab states voted with the USSR. When in February 1951 the UNGA, on US insistence and with the reluctant assent of Britain, branded the CPR as the aggressor, no Asian state, except the American client states, Thailand, the Philippines and Taiwan, supported the motion. It was this vote that led Stalin to denounce the UN as 'the tool of aggressive war ... an organisation for the Americans'. He was learning, however, that it was possible to chip away at the American majority, as the general yearning for an end to hostilities became more emphatic.

Although in the spring of 1951 the military situation in Korea improved, a new crisis in Anglo-American relations followed Truman's dismissal of MacArthur, who was the hero of 'Pacific First' and other Rightist elements in American politics. The restraint that had been imposed on his conduct of the war, aggravating (as was alleged) the loss of American lives, was largely attributed to British influence exerted on the US State Department and, in particular, on the anglophile Secretary of State, Dean Acheson. The US Ambassador in London, calling on Morrison, Bevin's successor, referred to 'a very strong wave of anti-British feeling'.[28] There was discussion in the Foreign Office whether Truman's firm stance and his determination to avert world war would enable him to ride the storm provoked by

MacArthur's reappearance in Washington, where he addressed both Houses of Congress. Maclean minuted as follows:

'Americans have for some time had steady diet of "punishing the aggressor", "fighting communism", etc. and the President's present accent on "avoiding a third world war" will have an unfamiliar ring . . . it is difficult to see much stability in the position of the President and his Administration unless they can lead strongly in favour of some comprehensible policy in China and Korea.'[29]

After the flight of Maclean and Burgess, MacArthur alleged that they had sabotaged his operations by their disclosures to the Russians. This goes too far; it is unlikely that intelligence supplied by Maclean was of immediate military value. It is true that regular appreciations of the military situation were provided in Tokyo by MacArthur's staff and telegraphed by the British Embassy there to London; but these telegrams had an operational prefix and went straight to the Ministry of Defence without receiving a distribution within the Foreign Office. What Maclean's reports would have made clear to the Kremlin was that everywhere the desire for a truce to hostilities was growing and that the CPR and North Korea could drive a hard bargain once the fighting had become stabilised on the 38th parallel.

Truce talks finally began in July 1951, but by that date Maclean's usefulness to the NKVD was at an end, though his services to the Soviet state in other capacities were to continue for over thirty years. Almost to the end he had been able from a position of great advantage to promote Soviet strategy in ways that were of incalculable benefit to the advance of world communism. The Soviet tactic of holding back from direct participation in war and supporting the communist cause through a surrogate communist army had proved notably successful in Korea; it was to be applied in the future with equal success in other parts of the world. In Korea the truce talks dragged on for two years; the USSR was in no hurry to end the tension in the Far East and allow the USA to concentrate its attention on Europe. In particular, the Kremlin had no wish to see a normalisation of American relations with the CPR; even so, Stalin's successors in their most optimistic moments could have scarcely guessed that this process of conciliation would take another twenty years.

8

Final Night Exit

Lord Sherfield, who takes a less serious view than most of us of the damage done by Donald Maclean as a spy, shares the generally held opinion that his defection 'undoubtedly did cause very major problems'.[1] These problems mainly concern Anglo-American relations, to which so much of Lord Sherfield's long and distinguished career has been devoted. We must therefore examine in detail what precipitated his defection, what measures were taken to prevent it and why these met with failure. In doing so, we shall be hampered by the official reticence that continues to veil the subject, a veil that is only partially lifted from time to time, when some new disclosure makes this inescapable. This point needs to be stressed, because British reticence in the immediate aftermath of the defection was one of the factors that most exasperated American opinion. In subsequent years Americans interested in the subject have come no nearer to understanding why British officials remain so tight-lipped; indeed the enactment of freedom of information in the USA, which has made much documentary material available, has rendered even less comprehensible the official British attitude.

This lack of candour is all the more regrettable because there was nothing discreditable in the planning for Maclean's interrogation, however lamentable the outcome may have been. Silence, then as now, has left the door open for allegations that there has been a cover-up and that the Foreign Office were secretly relieved to see the backs of Maclean and Burgess. More recently a different allegation has been made by a senior officer of the FBI, namely that his organisation was kept in the dark about the progress of the British investigation that led to Maclean's identification as 'Homer'; Robert Lamphere has complained that months passed, during which he was told nothing. This statement is remarkable because on an earlier page Lamphere himself has told us that the crucial cryptanalytic evidence pinpointing Maclean only came to hand in 'late 1950 or early 1951'.[2] The fact is that from the start the British had regarded the investigation as a joint one: the offence had been committed on American soil and had come to light through co-operation in cryptanalysis. Those most directly connected on the British side, who still survive, all agree on the cardinal point that until mid-April there was close liaison with J. Edgar Hoover. It does not, of course, follow that Hoover thought it necessary to keep Lamphere informed. Moreover, when disaster occurred and the quarry had got away, Hoover may well have decided to dissociate himself from the whole unfortunate business by maintaining that he had been kept in ignorance. However that may be, Lamphere's Chapter XIII clearly shows that even today resentment caused by the defection still smoulders. Researchers in Washington, who fail to find traces of MI5's communications to the FBI (these were in MI6 cyphers and passed through Philby) should not be misled into believing that there were none. The US Freedom of Information Act does not absolve the US government from its obligations to friendly foreign governments, including HM government.

We cannot elucidate these events without reverting to the careers of Philby and Burgess. The covert careers of Donald Maclean and Kim Philby since both left Cambridge had moved, like parallel lines, in the same direction, but without touching. It would have been elementary prudence on the part of the NKVD to have kept it that way; it was the decision to involve Burgess in Maclean's escape that virtually ended Philby's nefarious career, which eventually petered out in Beirut in 1963. In Washington in 1951 he was at the pinnacle of effectiveness; located at the focal point of co-operation between the British and American intelligence communities, he was able to inflict maximum damage on both. He might have risen even higher if he had not then made a series of uncharacteristic and ruinous errors of judgment. When in September 1949 he was briefed about 'Homer', he had at once realised that Maclean must be the man and that, if he was unmasked, all earlier members of the 'Cambridge Comintern' would be at risk. On the other hand, he 'had only seen Maclean twice, and briefly, in fourteen years ... both times on a conspiratorial basis'.[3] If he was careful and Maclean was discreet, he might hope to avoid involvement. He had powerful friends in both MI5 and MI6, who thought highly of his wartime services and would resent the imputation that he had all the time been working for the NKVD.

The contrast between Philby and Maclean, as spies, is a striking one. Maclean was essentially a loner: he fed his 'control' but never formed part of a spy ring. Allegations have been made by Andrew Boyle that Maclean was associated with a British-born physicist, code-named 'Basil'.[4] This could not have been Dr Wilfred Mann, since he left the USA in September 1945 and only returned in December 1948; he subsequently became an American citizen. No shred of hard evidence for this association has been produced: Andrew Boyle's 'Basil' seems to inhabit the world of fiction. The fact is that Maclean, as he showed after he got to Moscow, did not much like fellow spies and certainly did not like spying. He regarded it as a dirty trade, which had to be practised by those few capable of it, because of the paramount need to enable the USSR to catch up with the USA in the superpower stakes. He derived no pleasure from what he did, apart from the satisfaction that any craftsman gets from a job well done.

Philby, by way of contrast, was a born spy, who revelled in deception and had no compunction about sending agents to their death, some of them men whom he knew. In this way he was like some of Himmler's SS-men, who worried about their wives' migraines and the loss of domestic pets, but could distance themselves from the human tragedies on the other side of the barbed wire. Unlike Maclean, who was not proud of being a spy, Philby was delighted to belong to what he called 'an élite force'.[5] His account of his service in it is redolent of schoolboy gratification at having fooled innocent companions and mocked obtuse authorities. In Moscow, Maclean began, as soon as he could, to work in the Institute of World Economics and International Relations. Philby, on the other hand, stayed with the KGB (as the NKVD had come to be called) and rose to high rank in it: that was all he could do and all he wanted to do.

Maclean once said of Guy Burgess, 'Guy's my evil genius.'[6] Philby would never have made such a remark, but there was a sense in which it proved to be true. After the fall of France in 1940, Burgess had been responsible for Philby's recruitment into Section D of MI6, which soon after became part of SOE. This launched Philby on his career in the intelligence community; afterwards he was able to make his own way; but he never cut loose from Burgess, whose company he enjoyed. This was a mistake, which became apparent as Burgess' own career began to go downhill. Early in 1948 Burgess was given a trial with the new Information Research Department (IRD), which pro- vided briefs about communism and Soviet policy. To make known the wares of the new Department, Burgess was allowed to make a tour of diplomatic posts around the Mediterranean; it was marked by his customary alcoholic indiscretions and on his return to London his connection with IRD was terminated. In the course of his tour, he stayed in Istanbul with Philby, who was serving there with cover as First Secretary. Aileen Philby hoped this disorderly guest would never again be inflicted upon her; but her hopes were dashed when in the late summer of 1950 Burgess was transferred to Washington as a Second Secretary.

Burgess was aware that his arrival would arouse mixed feelings in the Philby household; he wrote to Philby, 'I have a shock for you. I have just been posted to Washington.' He asked if he could stay with the Philbys at 4100 Nebraska Avenue. Philby faced a dilemma. He wrote later:

> 'In normal circumstances it would have been quite wrong for two secret operatives to occupy the same premises. But the circumstances were not normal. From the earliest days our careers had intertwined ...'[7]

No doubt Philby hoped he could keep Burgess under control; he should have known better. An illustration of the disadvantages of having Burgess under the same roof is provided by the notorious dinner-party given by the Philbys on the night of 19th January 1951. The chief American guests were Lamphere of the FBI and two rising CIA officers with their wives: Bill Harvey and James Angleton. The British guests included Wilfred Mann and Sir Robert Mackenzie, who was the Embassy's regional security officer. Significantly, Burgess had not been invited; but this did not stop him from joining the party, full of mischief, after dinner. He had already met most of the guests except the Harveys and soon made a comment on Libby Harvey's face, which she misguidedly took as a compliment. This led on to the suggestion that he should sketch her. When she looked at the sketch, she saw that it was a clever, but malicious, caricature; the Harveys left with minimal formality.[8] Philby called next day to apologise, but the damage had been done. Harvey's resentment took the form of judging Philby by the company he kept and he began to look into the background of the two Englishmen.

If having Burgess to stay was Philby's first error, his second was even graver; he initiated Burgess into the secret of the hunt for 'Homer'. He claims to have obtained the approval of his Soviet 'control'; it may be so, but this hardly absolves Philby, who knew all about Burgess and how unreliable he was. Moreover his reason for initiating Burgess is so bizarre that it requires further analysis. He states that 'Guy's special knowledge of the problem might be helpful.'[9] Since Guy did not know there was a problem, it is not clear what special knowledge of it he could have had. When he had left London in the previous year, Maclean had not yet been appointed head of the American Department, nor had he gone to live at Tatsfield with Melinda. It is wholly implausible that, with the entire resources of the NKVD in London, and the services of Anthony Blunt, if needed, there was no way of cutting Maclean free other than by despatching Burgess from Washington to undertake the task.

If, in the light of these facts, one looks for a more sensible explanation of Philby's decision, it is not difficult to find one; he was desperate to get Burgess away from Washington at almost any price. The contagion of Burgess had begun to affect Philby's standing both with his Embassy colleagues and with his counterparts in the FBI and CIA. Burgess' growing sense of failure had been aggravated by his short stay and a corresponding deterioration in his behaviour had set in. He had been sent out from London as a Far Eastern expert, after working in that Department in the Foreign Office; but Hubert Graves, the Counsellor in charge of the Far Eastern work of the Embassy, had refused to employ him and he was increasingly used for odd jobs, such as replying to hate-letters blaming Britain for Truman's decision to sack MacArthur. As his conduct got worse, it was clear to Philby, and probably also to Burgess, that the patience of the Ambassador, Sir Oliver Franks, or of the US State Department, would sooner or later be exhausted; but before that moment arrived irreparable damage might be done to Philby's very promising aspirations. His problem was how to prise Burgess out without giving offence and so precipitating a crisis in which Philby himself might also fall victim. 'Brigadier Brilliant' (to use Connolly's apt soubriquet) must go out with a bang, not with a whimper; instead of crawling home with his tail between his legs, he could go as the leading figure in a gallant and secret exploit – nothing less than the rescue of an old comrade.

The scenario appealed to Burgess, who no doubt embroidered it. One of his additions must have been his wild drive in February through Virginia; his Lincoln convertible was three times stopped for speeding; he had picked up a young American suspected of being a homosexual. As Burgess had diplomatic immunity, the Virginia state police could do no more than lodge a complaint; in due course it reached the Governor, who passed it on to the State Department. When it finally reached Sir Oliver Franks, he acted and Burgess was ordered home. Philby could sleep more soundly at night and Aileen, too, was relieved to be rid of such an unwelcome guest. There were, of course, risks involved; the most serious of these was that the unpredictable Burgess would himself go into exile. Philby had a last moment of *Angst*; his parting admonition to Guy was, 'Don't you go too!'

Around this time Philby made a further mistake, designed to restore his reputation as a skilled and reliable operator: 'I could help to divert suspicion by making a positive contribution to the solution of the British Embassy case.'[10] His contribution was to draw attention in London to Krivitsky's earlier report about the idealist of good family, who worked without payment. This did not much expedite the investigation in London, where by that time more recent evidence was pointing to Maclean; but perusal of Krivitsky's report was later to prove damaging to Philby's own case. Krivitsky had mentioned another unnamed agent, who had worked in Spain as a journalist during the Civil War. When MI5 came to cross-examine Philby, this led to some awkward questions, such as how he had financed his freelance work in Spain before the London *Times* took him on. His stammer became more pronounced, as he talked his way out of that one.

Why did Burgess defect? At what point did he make up his mind? Differing answers have been given to these questions by different people, including Burgess himself. No convincing answer can be given without an understanding of his eccentric personality, which, like Peer Gynt's onion, contained many layers, each half-hiding the next. Burgess has been included in a BBC Radio series under the general heading 'Rebels', in company with Paul Robeson, Albert Luthuli, Countess Markievicz and others. This is a basic misapprehension about his character and career. A rebel is usually one who, sometimes because he is an idealist, sometimes because he is a misfit, aims radically to change both his own circumstances and the society in which he finds himself. This definition does not fit Burgess at all. He had no trace of idealism; when recruited by the NKVD and instructed to erase his past as a student communist, he transformed himself without the least misgiving into a convincing Germanophile, who seemed quite at home at one of Hitler's Nuremberg rallies and at the Berlin Olympic Games of 1936. Nor was he in any true sense a misfit. He had been a homosexual, of course, ever since his years at Eton; but he had no feeling of being an outcast, because he lacked all sense of shame. He had no particular wish to change the law on homosexuality;

so long as he succeeded in defying it, the risk involved gave an added *frisson* to his exploits. He fitted excellently into the interlocking circles on the fringes of politics, art, letters and intellectual debate, in which as a younger man he had shone. It was because he had fitted so well into this raffish sub-culture that he was so unhappy in Moscow and, unlike Maclean, so nostalgic about the past. Anthony Blunt, who moved in similar circles at a higher level of attainment, understood perfectly that the tolerant and cosmopolitan city of London was where he belonged and when, at the end of May 1951, the NKVD advised him, too, to escape, he refused to do so and brazened it out.

Why, then, did Burgess go? The first point to grasp is that his overinflated ego needed constantly to be nourished if not by admiration, then at least by close attention; to decline into mediocrity was a little death. In Washington his failure to impress had brought home to him that he was nearing the end of his chosen road; at the age of forty he was a juvenile lead running out of roles. His antics, designed to draw attention to himself, had finally brought even the Foreign Office to the point of dispensing with his services; this was double death, since it would also end his usefulness to the NKVD. There was talk, it is true, that he might find a niche in journalism; but after so many years close to the levers of power the humdrum life of a middle-aged Fleet Street hack could not be expected to appeal to him. He was therefore in a state of mind in which a dramatic adventure, followed by a new start in another country, where his past services would be appreciated, looked like supplying a fitting climax. Philby's apparent confidence in him gave him the chance to return to London, knowing that he was to play a hero's role at last; instead of making an humiliating exit, he would come as a *deus ex machina* and Maclean would be saved.

The second point to recall is that Burgess was himself at risk. If the despised sleuths were catching up with Maclean, they might be on his trail also. He was prepared to have a laugh at the expense of the heavy-handed men of the CIA and FBI, but in his more sober moments he must have realised that to make enemies of them had not been very prudent. There had been another worrying incident shortly before he left Washington. Outside the Embassy he had encountered Michael Straight, who knew all about his past, but had been under the impression that he was no longer in government service. They had an acrimonious conversation about the Korean War, in which American casualties were still rising, and Straight threatened to give his friend away.[11] This may have been an idle threat; but Burgess could not have been sure. Twelve years later Straight did at last tell on one of his old Cambridge friends – Anthony Blunt.

Despite Burgess' secret mission, he seemed in no hurry to leave the fleshpots of Washington and New York; but from a personal stand-point his sailing in the *Queen Mary* was well-timed. On board he struck up a friendship with Bernard Miller, a young medical student, of whom he hoped to see more. By the time he reached Southampton on 7th May much of his old self-confidence had returned. He had no misgivings about calling on the head of the American Department and they lunched together at the RAC, where they might well have been observed by someone wondering why so junior an official at the Washington Embassy had so much to say to a Counsellor. At some point Maclean's anxiety began to infect Burgess. Maclean certainly told his friend that he was being shadowed and some chance incident may well have convinced Burgess that he, too, was under surveillance. He decided to break off direct contact with the NKVD in London and Blunt and his control, 'Peter', were inserted as links in the chain.[12] Here Blunt's testimony is reinforced by that of the Soviet defector, Vladimir Petrov.

It is not easy to evaluate Petrov's evidence, as it relates to Maclean and Burgess, since it is not at first hand but derived from his NKVD colleague, Filip Kislytsin, who had been a cypher clerk in the Soviet Embassy in London from 1945 to 1948 and was serving at NKVD headquarters in Moscow in 1951. It was there that he claimed to have seen a joint appeal for help from Maclean and Burgess. At a meeting called by Anatoli Gorsky, the deputy head of the First Directorate, who as Gromov had at one time been Maclean's control, it was agreed to respond to the appeal and provide asylum.[13] Events validate this information; on the other hand at least one part of Kislytsin's evidence was manifestly false, when he testified:

'The most astonishing fact about the whole extraordinary affair is that the two men, though they became close friends after their Cambridge days, did not know of each other's spying activities. It was not until they were almost ready for their flight to Moscow that they learned they were both linked in highly secret MVD work.'[14]

This erroneous statement may have been made to make the story more sensational, or as testimony to the skill of the NKVD in keeping their agents isolated from one another. One interesting deduction from it is that, during Gromov's time in London, he cannot have been running

Maclean and Burgess as a team; otherwise Kislytsin could hardly have made such a statement. We shall have to take a further look at Kislytsin, as a witness, in due course. Whatever Burgess may have thought, he was not under surveillance and there was no dossier about him, on the strength of which charges could be brought. If he had kept his head and denied everything, nothing could have been proved. His best defence would have been that later used by Philby:

> 'It was almost inconceivable that anyone like Guy, who courted the limelight instead of avoiding it and was generally notorious for indiscretion, could have been a secret agent, let alone a Soviet agent from whom strictest security standards would be required.'[15]

Maclean would have viewed Burgess' reappearance in London with mixed feelings. Around this time Maclean lunched with Philip Toynbee in a public house near Leicester Square. When Toynbee happened to mention Burgess, 'Donald told me that he had been a friend of Guy's at Cambridge but had seen little of him since. It seemed he no longer liked him.'[16]

Maclean needed someone who shared his political opinions and to whom he could talk freely; even more urgently he needed this new channel through which to communicate with 'Peter'. On the other hand, he had never since Cambridge liked or trusted Burgess, who in any case was the last person anyone would have selected to make plans for a dangerous journey and carry them out efficiently. Maclean would also have sensed that Burgess, though posing as his saviour, was himself in a very uncertain state of mind. He was still toying with the idea of working for the *Daily Telegraph*, after first taking a continental holiday, perhaps in the company of his new friend, Miller. How seriously he entertained these possibilities and to what extent he talked of them in order to put others off the scent we do not know; till the last moment Maclean may well have been one of those put off in this way. What we do know is that Burgess' decision was taken some days before his final departure, since he had to obtain approval from 'Peter' and this necessitated reference to Moscow. Here again, the evidence of Kislytsin and Blunt corroborate one another. In April 1982 I asked Blunt how he could be so sure that the NKVD had authorised Burgess' departure, in view of the danger in which Philby was placed. In reply Blunt pointed to the fact that he, too, had been told by 'Peter' to make his getaway.[17] Evidently the NKVD underestimated his capacity to stand up to interrogation and overestimated the degree of pressure that would be applied; in the USSR such pressure would, of course, have had a much better prospect of leading to a confession. The need to await a reply from Moscow also explains what otherwise seems to be surprisingly dilatory behaviour on Burgess' part; this, as we shall see, was beginning to worry Philby in Washington, since the NKVD had not informed him of the new development.

The fact that in the end Burgess cut it so fine has given rise to another myth. It is known that the final decision to interrogate Maclean was taken by the Foreign Secretary, Herbert Morrison, on the morning of Friday, 25th May and that it was on the same evening that the fugitives got away. It has been assumed that Morrison held a meeting and that someone present at that meeting tipped off Burgess, who put on a burst of speed. The charm of this scenario for those who make a living out of spy stories is that it provides more 'moles' – preferably dead ones – who can be hunted down first in newspaper articles, then in hardback and paperback and finally in TV pseudo-documentaries. The familiar scenario relating to the events of 25th May 1951 has generated so much income and excitement that it may be now out of reach and no longer subject to correction by someone who knows what actually happened. Nevertheless the attempt must be made, if only because the main beneficiaries by the slanted version have been Philby and the KGB, who have watched with a mixture of delight and incredulity, as the British and American intelligence communities have split apart, attacked one another and fanned the flames kindled with so much enthusiasm by the media in both countries.

The first and simplest point to make is that there was no meeting on Friday, 25th May and that the decision taken on that day by Morrison, on the basis of a written submission, drafted by Carey-Foster and Patrick Reilly and endorsed by William Strang, did not lay it down that Maclean was to be taken in for questioning precisely on Monday, 28th May. When Morrison took over from Bevin in mid-March, he had been told that a serious investigation was in progress and that the suspects had been reduced to a short list. By mid-April the final piece of cryptanalytical evidence had come in and it was clear that Maclean was 'Homer' and would have to be watched; the highest category of intelligence was at the same time withheld from him. Up to this point the FBI had been conscientiously informed of the progress of the enquiry by means of messages from MI5, transmitted in MI6 cyphers and thus accessible to Philby in Washington. At the April meeting it was decided to delay further communication with the FBI until the time came to set a date for interrogating Maclean. The reason for this decision was that, because of his key position in Anglo-American relations, it was feared that the FBI would feel obliged to inform the State Department that the net was closing on him. This extension of number of those in the know would greatly increase the risk of premature leaks.[18]

Among the small number of Foreign Office officials who were privy to the enquiry there was at least one who would have liked to move on more rapidly to the crucial stage of interrogation. At the mid-April meeting, however, the decision had been taken to entrust the case to MI5 and its Director, Sir Percy Sillitoe, was insistent that his men must have time to observe Maclean, his habits and his contacts. Whitehall might be convinced of his guilt; to drive it home in a court of law was a very different matter, especially if the cryptanalytical evidence could not be used. It was not very likely that Maclean would be caught red-handed with 'Peter', but it was hoped that he might be found keeping dubious company or acting indiscreetly in ways that would make it easier to extract a confession when the time came. This tactic had worked well with Nunn May and Fuchs, both of whom had confessed. Maclean's low spirits seemed to suggest that he would give way under cross-examination; this was certainly what the NKVD feared. If he cracked, it would be the end of the 'Cambridge Comintern'.

Another meeting of officials was held in the second week of May, at which it was decided to increase the number of 'watchers' in London, but not to extend surveillance to Maclean's house in Tatsfield. To have done so would have meant assigning twenty trained men to the case and the resources of MI5 were insufficient. In any case the attempt to watch an isolated house in a small village would probably have alerted not only Maclean but most of the village to what was going on. Unfortunately Maclean's expertise in the field of espionage was underestimated; as we shall shortly see, he had already become aware that he was being shadowed in London. At the same meeting it was agreed that MI5 should send through Philby's channel a telegram to their representative in Washington, who was required to clarify a technical point about the original 'Homer' telegram by interviewing a cypher officer who in 1944 had been on duty in the Embassy and was once more serving there. It was stated that an answer was required by 23rd May for a meeting to be held on the following day.

This telegram, arriving on Philby's desk after over three weeks' silence, greatly alarmed him and led him to the conclusion that the next meeting might well be the last before Maclean was taken in for questioning. He sent an urgent airmail letter to Burgess, which was ostensibly about the car left by him in the Embassy car park; but Philby added a postscript, which was not lost on his friend: 'It's getting *very* hot here.'[19] When Burgess left London for good, he typically left this letter in his bedroom. There it was picked up and pocketed by Blunt, whose help had been imprudently invoked by MI5 in order to obtain entrance to Burgess' flat, in the absence of his flat-mate, Jack Hewit, and without incurring the risk of publicity by applying for a search warrant. If Burgess had benefited ever since his return to London from leakages from someone present at Strang's series of meetings, he would have known that Philby's alarm was premature and that no date had yet been set to bring Maclean in; he would also have known that he was not himself a suspect and was not being shadowed. This point needs to be stressed, because a wholly speculative attempt has been made to ascribe MI5's failure to prevent the flight of Maclean and Burgess to the supposed treachery of the late Roger Hollis. Not only is there no scintilla of evidence for this, but also no record that Hollis attended any of Strang's meetings.

The last of these meetings, which took place on Thursday, 24th May, approved the recommendation to Morrison, which cleared the way for Maclean to be interrogated on or after Monday, 28th May; but the exact timetable remained flexible. Sillitoe's first priority was to inform Hoover of what was intended; for this purpose he favoured a personal visit to Washington early in June. This would mean some further delay, but would bring one advantage with it. Melinda was due to go into hospital in the second week of June for her third Caesarian birth; this would provide an opportunity to conduct a clandestine search of 'Beaconshaw' in her absence, whilst Maclean was at work. It is easy to see in retrospect that this programme was altogether too leisurely; MI5 underestimated the back-up provided by Burgess and Blunt and believed they would be alerted to any signs that Maclean was planning his getaway. If their watchers detected such signs, the way would be clear for him to be taken in for questioning.

To the myth-makers, believing, as they are disposed to do, that there must be a direct connection between the imaginary meeting on the morning of 25th May and the departure of Maclean and Burgess that same evening, it has seemed unlikely that this could be a coincidence. Two theories have therefore been devised: the first postulated a leak in London to Burgess; the second, a series of exceptionally rapid communications to and from Philby in Washington.

Given the time differential, it might just have been possible for Philby to exchange messages with the NKVD in London before the evening of 25th May; but the latter would have had to alert Blunt, who in turn would have had to locate Burgess. When I put this sequence to Blunt as being a possibility, he derided it, pointing out that on the previous day Burgess had already purchased the two boat-tickets that were to take him and Maclean to France. It has been suggested that, until the last moment, Burgess intended the second ticket for his American friend, Miller; but his decision to go with Maclean to Moscow had, as we have seen, been taken some days earlier.

Burgess, too, was an old hand at deception and had good reason to leave a few false trails. Talk of a trip with Miller was a 'cover' story to throw Hewit and others off the scent. When on 30th June 1951 the FBI interviewed Miller, he 'denied any plans to go to France with Burgess'. He very reasonably pointed out that he had come to London from France as recently as 21st May and was already preparing to return to the USA.[20] Guy's telephone call to Stephen Spender to ask for Auden's address in Ischia falls into the same pattern of deception. When it came to saying goodbye to an old friend, who knew all about his subterranean career, his tone was completely different. Before Burgess finally left the Reform Club on 25th May, he tried to telephone to Goronwy Rees. Rees was spending the weekend at All Souls and the call was taken by his wife, who knew nothing of her husband's former association with Burgess and his spy ring. Burgess was therefore obliged to speak less frankly than he might have wished, but he did make it clear that he was about 'to do something which would surprise and shock many people', and that Goronwy would not see him again for some time. Goronwy, he concluded, would understand. Rees did indeed understand and, when he returned home on the evening of Sunday, 27th May and learned of this conversation, he telephoned to Blunt, who came to see him on the following day and tried to persuade him not to tell MI5:

'He was the Cambridge liberal conscience at its very best, reasonable, sensible and firm in the faith that personal relations are the highest of all human values.'[21]

Rees felt matters had gone too far; even the E. M. Forster syndrome failed to move him. When he got to see MI5, he learnt that not only Burgess, but also Maclean, was missing.

The accumulation of instances, in which everyone delayed just too long, has fuelled the supposition that these were not coincidental and that officialdom was reluctant to act in time. The actions of officialdom, however, represent only one side of the equation; on the other side, Burgess had plenty of time to act and plenty of warning that he should do so. That he left everything so late and got away with it is completely in character. There is no need to resort to conspiracy theory in order to explain the sequence of events; nor at this remove in time is it useful to go on hunting for scapegoats. Maclean and Burgess slipped through a net that was, admittedly, full of holes; those who would like to live in a country where the nets catch all the 'moles' should go and live in the USSR or South Africa. Sometimes the price of liberty is eternal inefficiency.

Although Maclean was out of touch with all his fellow conspirators except Burgess, he was certainly well aware before seeing Burgess that his days were numbered; the end was in sight of the two careers that had twined themselves round his life to the point of suffocation. Latterly his access to top-secret reports had been restricted; he was still receiving the normal distribution of telegrams and printed despatches sent daily to all heads of Departments and above; but boxes requiring special keys were withheld. Maclean had not been a spy for fifteen years without developing very fine antennae; he would have read the signs. If any confirmation were needed, this was provided when he became aware that, at least in London, he was being shadowed. His low spirits did not inhibit him on one occasion from playing a game with his pursuer. One of the few Under-Secretaries who was in the know recalls crossing St James's Park after lunch on a warm spring afternoon and being surprised to see Maclean following a diagonal course at great speed. This focused his attention on the spectacle of another man, with much shorter legs, moving at a similar speed, but at a fixed distance.[22] It may have been in order to upset his 'watchers' that Maclean sometimes varied his routine by travelling to Victoria, instead of to Charing Cross. On two or three occasions when he did so, he encountered a fellow commuter in the person of Fred Everson (Sir Frederick), who had been his colleague in better days in Washington. The latter recalls:

'I was struck by Donald's shabby dress and moroseness. He wore an untidy, worn, brownish tweed coat and a crumpled trilby hat, when we were wearing Anthony Eden homburgs. He walked, untalkative, with his hands thrust deep into the coat pockets and his shoulders hunched.'[23]

Whilst Burgess dithered and delayed, Maclean tried to carry on at the office, as if no disaster impended. It must have consoled him to observe that none of those with whom he had regular dealings were treating him in an unusual manner; indeed none of us in the American Department was aware that anything was amiss. The sound reputation that he had built up in earlier years stood him in good stead. One Under-Secretary, when told that a former colleague of Washington days was about to be called in and accused of espionage, leaped to the conclusion that the suspect must be Paul Gore-Booth (the late Lord Gore-Booth). This distinguished public servant was regarded as something of an eccentric, partly because he was a strict Christian Scientist and partly because he was the nephew of Constance Markievicz, who had been sentenced to death, but reprieved, after the Easter Rising in Dublin. This association seemed to make him a more likely black sheep than the son of a former Cabinet Minister. By a curious coincidence, Gore-Booth, whilst he was serving with Maclean in the Washington Embassy, had also visited New York, where his wife gave birth to twins.

In the last, miserable week an old friend from Cairo days, Michael Maude, came back to London. At first he had difficulty in getting Maclean to return his calls, but on 22nd May they met for lunch in the Sloane Square area. Maude found his friend looking ill and unhappy, and asked if anything were wrong. Maclean replied that the Foreign Office were insisting on his having another examination at the hands of the Treasury doctor.[24] Maude did not pursue the point, but wondered if Maclean were facing the end of his career; it was a correct diagnosis, though not in the way he thought. Three days later came Donald's thirty-eighth birthday. Either that morning or, more likely, on the previous evening, word reached him that the day of departure had come at last. He said nothing to Melinda, who was preparing a special birthday supper for his return that evening. The only other celebration was to be lunch with Robin and Mary Campbell and he decided to stick to their plan; any change might have excited questions.

For Donald Maclean that Friday was to be the longest day; he began it unusually early and was in his office by 9.15. Next door was the office of the Assistant Labour Adviser, Frederick Mason (Sir Frederick), who walked into his room with a telegram just received from Ciudad Trujillo: a prominent trade unionist in the dictator-ridden Dominican Republic had disappeared and was believed to have been kidnapped.[25] Maclean spared it a languid glance; it was his own

11   Guy Burgess

12   Donald and Melinda at
       Burgess' funeral

13   Maclean memorial at Penn

disappearance that was on his mind. Soon after noon Mary Campbell, driving her jeep, collected him in the cobbled courtyard of the Foreign Office. She noticed at once that he was in good spirits; the recognised sign of this was that the brim of his hat was turned up all round. He was wearing a jaunty and very unproletarian bow-tie. Some years later, when Mary Campbell was able to write to him in Moscow, she asked him whether, when they met that day, he had already known that it was the day of his final departure. Yes, came back the answer: he had known.[26]

It is easy to understand how his spirits had risen, as soon as he knew the die was cast: after the long period of suspense the very thought that the time for action had come must have been a stimulant. His Russian friends were living up to the confidence he had long ago placed in them; on the far side of what the capitalists foolishly called the Iron Curtain he would be recompensed for his secret years of service to the cause. There he could at last lead an honest life and put behind him the precarious deceits and the furtive meetings. Above all, he would not now have to face his inquisitors and the pressure to give away the names of those who had shared his clandestine struggle. No half-promises of leniency, if he co-operated, followed by renewed pressure to tell all. He could not have stood up to all that: he was too tired.

So he gave Mary his tired, but grateful, smile and she took him first to Wheelers, off St James's Square, for oysters and a half-bottle of champagne. They talked about Melinda's baby and he promised that, when she went into hospital, he would come and stay with the Campbells at Stokke. In was a 'dutch' party and, by the time Maclean had paid his share, he was out of cash; he went across Pall Mall to the Travellers' Club and cashed a cheque for £5, which in those days was the permitted maximum. They then went to Bertorelli's in Soho to meet Robin Campbell and eat the rest of their lunch. On the way they ran into Connolly and some of his friends. Donald, he thought, was

'looking rather creased and yellow, casual but diffident .... He seemed calm and genial, and went off gaily to continue the luncheon with his friends.'[27]

By this time it was late and a certain amount of drink had been consumed. For some reason Maclean, instead of going straight back to the office, telephoned to Geoffrey Jackson, who was in charge of the Latin American section, during my absence on leave. It was, according to Jackson, a rather incoherent conversation on a bad line:

'Would I hold the fort? There followed a rather garbled explanation of meeting his sister-in-law, due at Tilbury from abroad.'[28]

Evidently Maclean was covering his tracks and accounting for his absence on the following morning, since at that date Saturday in Whitehall was a regular half-day. He did not speak again to Jackson, but he returned to the office in time to receive the visit of the Argentine Minister-Counsellor and record, with his usual accuracy, Señor Leguizamon's communication about Anglo-Argentine trade negotiations. He also signed a clear, concise letter to Sir Nevile Butler, the Ambassador at Rio de Janeiro. He had missed his usual train – the 5.19 from Charing Cross; it was about six o'clock when he put his head round the door of John Curle's room: 'I shan't be in tomorrow morning.'[29] That's my final word, he must have thought, but it was not so. In the courtyard he unexpectedly ran into Makins (Lord Sherfield), who was also leaving, and they exchanged a few casual remarks. Sherfield's main concern was to give Maclean no ground for suspicion; he was under the impression that watch was being kept at Tatsfield, as well as in London. Maclean decided to repeat the 'cover' story that he had already used with Jackson and said that on Saturday morning he would be meeting Harriet, whom Sherfield had known slightly in Washington. Sherfield has since said, 'There was nothing fishy about him. In any case, I knew he was being tailed.' Nonetheless he decided to go back into the Foreign Office and alert Carey-Foster; but both he and his secretary, who was also in the know, had gone home. Next morning, when MI5 met the usual train and failed to see Maclean, telephones began to ring and this episode came to light.

An ill-informed academic writer, embroidering a reference I have made elsewhere to this episode, accuses me of having implied that

'Lord Sherfield was, in the final analysis, responsible for Burgess and Maclean's defection, since if he had told Carey-Foster of Maclean's request, MI5 would have been alerted and steps taken to prevent Maclean from leaving England.'[30]

This is a false deduction and one that I have never made. Even if Lord Sherfield had known that Maclean was not under surveillance at Tatsfield, there was no warrant for detaining the fugitive; to have imposed restraints at ports and airports would have required the authority of the Home Secretary. This was, in fact, obtained in the late afternoon of Monday, 28th May; but by then, of course, the birds had flown.

The fate-lines of Maclean and Burgess, which since Cambridge days had been performing a dance – now nearer, now farther – were once more converging. Burgess had hired an Austin A40 and begun to pack; he slipped in the collected works of Jane Austen; as he said later to Tom Driberg, 'I never travel without it.'[31] At Charing Cross, Maclean, duly observed by his 'watchers', had caught his later train; the temptation to wave them goodbye must have been very strong. Melinda had cooked a ham for his birthday supper and it was awaiting him on the dining-room table; but they had scarcely begun before Burgess drove through the open gates and insisted that, if they were to catch the boat, they must go at once. He was introduced to Melinda, who had a hazy recollection of having seen him somewhere before, as 'Roger Styles'. She was incensed by his sudden appearance and Donald's failure to tell her what had been planned; her supper grew cold. Maclean raced up the stairs to say goodnight to the boys, then he was gone. They shared the driving. Even in these days of dual carriageways it is a slow cross-country journey from Tatsfield to Southampton; Burgess had left barely enough time to reach the quayside before the *Falaise* sailed at midnight. 'We'll be back on Monday,' he shouted, as they ran out of the car-park.

Donald Maclean's thirty-eighth birthday was over. The elation of the morning would have given way to a state of exhaustion and confused reactions to the drama of this last day in England. As the ferry moved out into the Channel through the darkness, he was not just between two coastlines but between two worlds. The capitalist world, which he had so often condemned, would soon be behind him; the untried world of communism, for which he was bound, had not yet taken shape in the dark ahead. How much remained of his youthful enthusiasm for life under Stalin? He would not have been human if, when no turning back was possible, some doubt, and indeed self-doubt, had not assailed him. He would have disowned Auden's verse, if it had come into his mind; but it applies all the same:

'And, alone with his heart at last, does the traveller find
In the vaguer touch of the wind and the fickle flash of the sea
Proofs that somewhere there exists, really, the Good Place,
As certain as those the children find in stones and holes?
No, he discovers nothing; he does not want to arrive.
The journey is false; the false journey really an illness ....'[32]

As the harbour of St Malo loomed up in the grey light of morning, he would have put such misgivings out of his mind. England could do one last thing for them; they went to the restaurant and ate an English breakfast of bacon and eggs. They sat over it so long that they missed the boat-train to Paris. A taxi-driver named Albert Gilbert drove them to Rennes, where they caught up with the train. He was until February 1956 the last inhabitant of the Western world to identify them.

When in the summer of 1956 Tom Driberg visited Burgess in Moscow, the latter devised for the visiting journalist – and through him for *Daily Mail* readers – a fictional account of his journey as a fugitive five years earlier. No doubt he had been encouraged to do so by the NKVD; but he was also serving his own aim to convince opinion in England that he had never been a spy and that his flight had been a haphazard one undertaken to help an old friend, who was in trouble. Burgess' imaginary odyssey took in Berne and Prague; it seems, too, to have taken in Driberg. We now know, however, that the NKVD had made careful arrangements to provide the defectors with false papers and exfiltrate them through the Soviet zone of occupation in Austria.[33] A rather similar route was used two years later to enable Melinda to rejoin her husband.

9

The Miseries of Melinda

The orchestration of events after Maclean and Burgess absconded is Wagnerian in character: it begins around 10 a.m. on the morning of Monday, 29th May 1951, with the gentle piping of the woodwind, as Melinda makes two telephone calls to the Foreign Office. The Maclean-Burgess *motif* makes its entrance in muffled form, as the small circle of officials in the know try to keep the dreadful news from radiating more widely. With the hunt continuing, however, more and more people come to know for whom they are looking and why, until finally on 7th June the news bursts forth in the *Daily Express* with a crescendo of horns, trumpets, tubas and trombones. High above the din can be heard the shrill piccolo of Lord Beaverbrook, taunting the Foreign Office with malicious glee. On both sides of the Atlantic there are instant repercussions; at the rear of the operatic stage the towers of Whitehall can be seen to totter.

Of Melinda's two calls, which were the prelude to these convulsions, the first was to the American Department. 'By my recollection', wrote Geoffrey Jackson many years later, 'she simply asked if her husband was around, or expected, without comment, or leaving a message.'[1] Her second and subsequent call was to Carey-Foster, whom she had met in Washington a few years earlier and knew to be head of Security; in this conversation she was more specific about Maclean's departure with 'Roger Styles'. Why, if at this point she had no suspicions about the reason for her husband's disappearance, did she telephone to the Security Department? It might have been expected that she would wish to speak to the Personnel Department. No doubt she would have done, if the Macleans' old friend, Middleton, had still been in charge there; but he had been transferred to another post and replaced by Robin Hooper (Sir Robin), whom she did not know. In any case Hooper was on sick-leave at that time. On the whole, her decision to speak so early in the day to Carey-Foster militates against the thesis that she was part of the conspiracy. If she had been, she would have wanted the fugitives to have maximum time to get beyond the Iron Curtain; by calling Carey-Foster, she ensured, either deliberately or inadvertently, that the hunt would begin with the least possible delay. She was within two weeks of going into hospital for the birth of her child; the simple explanation of her action seems the most likely: she wanted to know where her husband was and was doing her best to find out.

Carey-Foster had no doubt where Maclean was going; the crucial question was how far he had got. As soon as he had verified that the 'watchers' had not picked up Maclean at Charing Cross, he called a hurried meeting of the officials concerned. Scotland Yard set on foot an enquiry at ports and airports and before long confirmed that the car hired by Burgess had been found at Southampton. The news about Burgess turned the day into a nightmare for Guy Liddell, Sillitoe's deputy, who over the past decade had consorted more freely with Burgess than prudence would have dictated. On the previous evening he had received a telephone call from his friend in MI6, David Footman, who had recounted to him the forebodings of Goronwy Rees.[2] With Burgess had vanished all hope that Liddell would in due course succeed Sillitoe: he ended his career looking after security at Harwell. Before the end of the day Carey-Foster had telephoned to Paris, where his regional Security Officer, Robert Mackenzie, was attending a meeting; the latter invoked the help of the French Sûreté, but by that time the trail was cold.

In a country in which investigation into treason is conducted with ruthlessness the next step would have been to grill Melinda and search 'Beaconshaw' for clues. The proposal was indeed made, but was vetoed by Strang.[3] Presumably he was influenced by Melinda's delicate condition and lack of any firm evidence that Donald had gone for good. On 30th May, MI5 at last had a chance to question Melinda, who was in London for a medical check and met the MI5 representative at Lady Maclean's flat, Iverne Court, Kensington. It was a disappointing meeting for all concerned; nobody went away any wiser. Both ladies were advised to say nothing to anyone. The same advice in even more stringent terms was given to those of us in the Foreign Office, from whom the fact of Maclean's unexplained disappearance could no longer be concealed.

On the very day of the flight Makins had submitted to Strang his appreciation of the state of Anglo-American relations derived from his recent transatlantic visit. His view was encouraging; seen from the American east coast, relations 'did not seem to be as bad as they looked from London'.[4] The events of that weekend were to bring about a sharp deterioration. The defection plunged Whitehall into a state of shock, in which nobody, Ministers included, grasped the need to recognise what had happened and limit the damage. Instead, all hopes were pinned on recapturing the defectors and repressing all information. It was an understandable reaction, but it resembled that of a driver who, after a fatal accident, walks away from the scene, trying to convince himself that it was all a nightmare that will eventually go away. The Diplomatic Service with its links to the throne had always gone on the assumption that its loyalty was irrefragable; that its status and tradition set it apart from, and above, the rest of the Civil Service. In pursuance of this belief, it had long been administered much as a kindly Victorian paterfamilias would run a large family. As in any family, there would be the occasional black sheep, who could be sent to vegetate in Tegucigalpa, much as the Victorian wastrel might be despatched to the colonies; but alcoholism and adultery were assumed to be the worst vices of which a member of the family was capable. Once the diplomatic family had accepted its child, as Maclean had been accepted, ties of mutual obligation, leading upward to the Crown, were supposed to hold it together without the necessity for much formal regulation.

In the debate in the House of Commons in November 1955, Richard Crossman observed:

'There was a curious perverted liberalism which tolerated as eccentricity inside the Foreign Office conduct which would have been condemned if anybody else had done the same thing outside the Foreign Office.'[5]

At one blow this whole framework of mutual confidence and trust had been shattered; it had been built up over more than a century and it could not be reconstructed. Reconstruction was impossible partly because it no longer corresponded to the spirit of the times and partly because it was shown to have been predicated upon a false assumption: in the twentieth century class and status did not provide the required assurance of loyalty to the Crown and to the Service. Two intelligent men from the right class had been practising disloyalty for some sixteen years. In the Commons debate already mentioned Macmillan correctly summed it up:

'Our Foreign Office regards this case as a personal wound, as when something of the kind strikes at a family, or a ship, or a regiment.'[6]

The immediate effect of this desperate wound was to produce near-paralysis in the Foreign Office. With hindsight it is clear that immediate steps should have been taken to inform the US State Department that Maclean and Burgess had gone; that the former had certainly defected and, in all probability, the latter as well. An Anglo-American meeting for damage assessment should then have been proposed and a communiqué drafted against the day when all would be revealed. No doubt a communication along these lines would soon have leaked in Washington, but it would at least have displayed a businesslike approach with no intent to cover up what had occurred. Nothing of this kind had been attempted before 7th June, when the *Daily Express*, exploiting an indiscretion by the Sûreté in Paris, came out with the banner headline: 'Yard Hunts Two Britons'; below it was the speculation that both were from the Foreign Office and were headed for the USSR.

The NKVD must have been watching closely for just such a leakage in Paris, because on the night that it took place two telegrams were despatched from a post office there, constituting the first tenuous evidence that the fugitives were still alive. The telegram to Lady Maclean's London address, which was correctly given, read: 'Am quite all right. Don't worry. Love to all': it was signed with Donald's childhood nickname, 'Teento'. The telegram to Melinda, which incorrectly placed Tatsfield in Surrey, read, after some spelling corrections: 'Had to leave unexpectedly. Terribly sorry. Am quite well now. Don't worry darling. I love you. Please don't stop. Loving me. Donald.'

It would have been difficult to have concocted a more confusing and less informative message. Melinda and Lady Maclean discussed their respective messages on the telephone and concluded tentatively that Donald had quite likely dictated them at some point subsequent to his departure, but this conclusion did not provide much comfort, let alone an explanation.

The *Daily Express* story of 7th June was picked up later on the same day by American press and radio. As luck would have it, the US Secretary of State, Dean Acheson, who was widely regarded within the Republican Party as altogether too anglophile, was giving evidence on that day before the Senate, which was enquiring into the dismissal of General MacArthur, a victim, it was believed, of the Democratic

Party and the conniving British. Acheson was asked about the story from London by the Republican Senator Brewster, to whom he was obliged to admit that he himself had learned of it from a broadcast. On that day the US Embassy in London, which had approached the Foreign Office, reported to the State Department: 'Foreign Office professes have no information re intentions.'[7] If this was less than frank, the Foreign Office statement put out later that day was actually misleading. It read, after giving the names and date of departure: 'It is known that they went to France a few days ago. Mr Maclean had a breakdown a year ago owing to overstrain but was believed to fully have recovered.'

The implication was that Maclean had committed nothing more than an act of indiscipline in a moment of aberration; indeed this explanation continued for some while to be believed by those of his friends in the Service who were not aware of the full story. But the Foreign Office knew better; on 30th May Donald's younger brother, Alan, who was working for Sir Gladwyn Jebb (Lord Gladwyn) at the United Nations, had been summoned back from New York and sworn to silence. On 8th June the State Department, after trying in vain to extract information from the British Embassy in Washington, laconically notified the US Embassy in London: 'British Embassy apparently uninformed.'[8] The US press fared no better with the British Embassy, one of whose staff was quoted as describing Burgess' duties there as 'not particularly exciting or important'. Another spokesman, who was more of a wag, was quoted in the Washington *Evening Star* as having said: 'At worst, this thing is certainly more Hess than Hiss.'[9] He thus conjured up a picture of Maclean as having carried to Moscow the kiss of peace, rather than secret information.

On 15th June, as pressure continued to build, the State Department suggested that they should work out with the Foreign Office a common line for dealing with enquiries, but this found no favour in London. The only section of the Foreign Office that was behaving in an entirely rational and incisive manner was the Finance Department, which had ceased to pay Maclean from 1st June. Morrison had had to make a statement in the Commons on 11th June, but it included no specific comment on the possibility that the fugitives had gone to the USSR. It stressed that neither had been dismissed from the Service: 'The security aspects of the case are under investigation and it is not in the public interest to disclose them.' The security aspects were indeed generating great activity. On the day that Morrison made his statement Sillitoe, clad in sackcloth, flew to America in a desperate bid to

placate Edgar Hoover and the FBI. Hoover waited until Sillitoe had
returned to London and then sent a report to the US Attorney-
General, which came to the conclusion that it was 'highly probable'
that Maclean and Burgess were Soviet agents.[10] He said nothing about
Philby; but General Bedell Smith, Director of the CIA, had already
reached his own conclusion and abruptly informed 'C' in London that
he could no longer do business with his representative in Washington.
Philby was promptly withdrawn and in the following month resigned
from SIS. He still had his adherents, however, and the friction that
this promoted, both within SIS and between SIS and MI5, was a
bonus that must have delighted the NKVD.

The Soviet press remained silent until 15th June, when it contented itself with quoting Morrison's statement. We shall consider
in the next chapter the reasons that may have led the Russians to
delay so long in making known that the two fugitives from the
running dogs of capitalism had at last found refuge in the USSR.
Their initial silence was certainly due to the need to debrief
both men and reassure doubters that they were true defectors
and not double-agents planted by SIS. As time went on and the
NKVD observed the confusion and recrimination on both sides
of the Atlantic, they may well have concluded that silence,
which had begun as a simple precaution, was proving to be the
most effective form of disinformation that could have been
devised.

The London press, deprived of matter with which to inflame their
readers, raised a continuous howl against officialdom; no elabora-
tion is necessary, since the recent case of Peter Wright and his
banned *Spycatcher* has shown that, whilst Fleet Street may be
no more, its long tradition of self-righteousness and the specious
identification of profitable sales with public interest, is still flourish-
ing. As soon as public interest in the disappearance began to slacken,
steps were taken to rekindle it. A *Daily Express* reporter, interviewing
Spender in Italy, managed to secure a copy of a letter from John
Lehmann, warning Spender that he and his sister, Rosamond,
regarded Burgess as a convinced communist. This brought the case
back into the headlines on 16th June. The same enterprising reporter
interviewed Auden on Ischia and came away with the statement that
Maclean

'knew quite a lot about the Atom Bomb, not about the technical
aspects, but about the number of bombs stored by the Americans.'[11]

This shrewd statement was reproduced in American newspapers at a time when the columnists were beginning to link the case to those of the atom spies, Fuchs and Pontecorvo. As we saw in Chapter Seven, American opinion was already critical of what was seen as lack of wholehearted British support for the American war effort in Korea. This criticism meshed into the widespread impression that the British Labour government was 'soft on communism', an impression that gained strength from failure to draw any clear distinction between socialism and communism. If in these circles the defection of two Britons caused more pain than surprise, the pain was intensified by the unquestionable fact that both defectors had been directly involved in Anglo-American relations, despite the evidence that the conduct of Maclean in Cairo and Burgess everywhere should have prevented the Foreign Office from exposing contacts with the US government to this added strain.

Patriotic Americans rallied around the FBI by sending in reported sightings of the two men that owed more to imagination and enthusiasm than to good sense. In June one informant found a hotel register in Barcelona signed 'M. Maclean: W. J. Burgess'. Another insisted upon the 'strong possibility . . . that Donald went to Buenos Aires, disguised in women's clothes, along with Burgess'. In July a woman achieved the feat of recognising Maclean at a Greyhound bus station in New York, despite her observation that he had 'very black hair and protruding front teeth'.[12] Connolly was scarcely exaggerating when he wrote in 1952:

'Meanwhile a myth is slowly transfiguring them. At first they were seen all over Montmartre and Montparnasse, in Brussels and Bayonne, on the high pass to Andorra, in a tiny bar in Cannes and, with brimming tankards, in a garden-restaurant in Prague.'[13]

The whole episode had a peculiar fascination for the neo-Bloomsbury set connected with *Horizon* and *Penguin New Writing*, many of whom had toyed with communism in youth and had known either Maclean or Burgess. Poets who could quote Browning asked:

'What's become of Waring
Since he gave us all the slip . . .?'

It was recalled that Elizabeth Bowen had written about an attractive traitor, whom mutual friends had recognised as having a striking resemblance to Goronwy Rees. Humphrey Slater, who had been a communist at Cambridge and had written a book entitled *The Conspirator*, told John Lehmann that he had been 'almost certain for a long time that Donald had been a secret member of the Communist Party, and had wondered whether he ought to turn him in'.[14] It was as if fiction had left the printed pages and taken flesh and blood. Rosamond Lehmann rang up 'C' at home to tell him what she knew about Burgess and was disappointed that he seemed disinclined to discuss the case with her on the telephone.

Whilst waves of publicity and execration were sweeping back and forth across the Atlantic, Melinda in her backwater in 'Beaconshaw', awaiting her baby, was being tossed to and fro. In response to her appeal, her mother had arrived on 30th May and soon began to bombard the Personnel Department of the Foreign Office with demands for information and complaints that her daughter had been left in the lurch. Melinda, she insisted, had been ostracised by Donald's Service friends, as if she were guilty of some crime. I heard of this complaint from Robin Hooper and offered to go to Tatsfield on the following Saturday, 9th June, when my wife and I were due to visit one of our daughters, who was boarding at a convent in neighbouring Woldingham. Mrs Dunbar warned us that we should find the house under siege by the press with the drive gates padlocked and blinds drawn against the intrusion of photographers. So it proved, and we were only able to gain admittance by seeing the anxious face of Fergus at an upper window and convincing him that we were friends and expected. Fergus, who was recovering from measles, regarded the press as his and his mother's real enemies; later, when he was back at the local school, reporters used to follow him, and a local girl, employed to look after the children, was offered £100 – for any photograph or document that she could smuggle out of the house. These points require emphasis, because they help to explain Melinda's subsequent decision to leave England.

Melinda, as was natural, showed a great deal of distress; there was no sign of reserve in her discussion with my wife of her predicament and no inclination to extenuate Donald's dereliction, by which she had been hurt and bewildered. She was willing to concede his failings as a provider and a husband in ways that made it very difficult to believe that she had been in the plot and knew the desperate risks he had been running and the imperative need for him to go. Nor was there any need for her to have admitted that, when drunk, he showed homosexual tendencies. She could have avoided all discussion simply by pleading that she was not well enough to see us; but we had the impression that she was glad to be able to unburden herself of much that was on her mind. Part of her problem was financial; an instalment of the mortgage on the house was due soon, but no money was coming in from the Foreign Office and the bank was refusing to extend the overdraft. She hated to be dependent on her mother. If she was ·playing a part that had been previously rehearsed, then she was displaying remarkable talent as an actress, of which none of her friends had up to that time observed the smallest sign.

Against the evidence of those of us who saw her in the summer of 1951, including Clare and Geoffrey Hoare, who knew her well, must be placed the opposing verdict delivered in 1955 by the Soviet defector, Vladimir Petrov: 'I am now convinced, though conclusive evidence is lacking, that she knew all about her husband's plan to flee.' Petrov went on to describe her as 'guilty of a staggering piece of duplicity'.[15] In assessing this evidence, one must bear in mind that Petrov, who defected in Australia in April 1954, had never met Melinda and knew nothing of the case at first hand; his information derived from Filip Kislytsin, who was a NKVD colleague in Australia. Moreover some of Kislytsin's statements about Maclean and Burgess are manifestly untrue; thus he told Petrov that, when the fugitives arrived in the USSR, 'he saw them installed in a comfortable house on the outskirts of Moscow.' The fact is, however, that they were relegated to Kuibyshev, over 500 miles from Moscow, and were not allowed in the capital city until after the death of Stalin nearly two years later. Petrov's story was tailored in 1955 for readers of the *People*; it cannot be held to override more reliable testimony.

Three days after our visit, Harriet and Jay Sheers arrived from Paris to help Mrs Dunbar look after the children, whilst Melinda was in hospital. She was still so nervous about photographers that she had hired a car with darkened windows to take her to London, where she was delivered of a baby girl. The baby was christened Melinda, after her mother and grandmother; but to avoid confusion she soon acquired nicknames. At first she was 'Pinkers'; later in Moscow she was called 'Mimsie' in the family. Early on 14th June, before Melinda went under the anaesthetic, she wrote a letter to Donald; he never saw it, since she left it among her papers in Geneva when she went to rejoin him in September 1953. As such was the fate of the letter, it can scarcely have been written as an act of self-dramatisation; one must surely accept it for what it appears to be: a letter of love.

'My dearest Donald,

If you ever receive this letter it will mean that I shan't be here to tell you how much I love you and how really proud of you I am. My only regret is that perhaps you don't know how I feel about you.

I feel I leave behind and have a wonderful gift in your love and the existence of Fergie and Donald. I am so looking forward to the new baby. It seems strangely like the first time and I think I shall really enjoy this baby completely. I never forget, darling, that you love me and am living for the moment when we shall all be together again.

All my deepest love and wishes for a happy life for you and the children.

                                                                Melinda.'[16]

It is not a letter that throws light on Maclean's career as a spy, nor on Melinda's complicity; it comes from a deeper stratum of feeling and could bear the emotional weight of Browning's title: 'Any Wife to any Husband'.

If, as suggested, we ought to take this letter at face value, it does not follow that it reflects what Melinda was feeling at all times during that desperate summer. Inevitably there were days when she was oppressed by the burden of responsibility that she had to bear alone and when she felt bitter about the husband who had deserted her. She was not expressing much affection for him in mid-July, when we next saw her. 'Beaconshaw' was still virtually besieged and she was anxious to escape for a night; we therefore invited her to come to London for a theatre and to stay the night. The play was Peter Ustinov's *The Love of Four Colonels*, which is an attempt to graft a fantasy of an enchanted castle and good and wicked fairies on to the contemporary setting of territory jointly occupied by military contingents of Britain, France, the USA and USSR. Even in such a play there were sure to be one or two lines to disturb Melinda's equanimity. Two of the Colonels have accepted the Wicked Fairy's invitation to enter the mysterious castle, from which there is no return:

'Any message to your wives?' queries the British Colonel, who is staying on.
'That is not permitted,' insists the Wicked Fairy.[17]

It was around this time that Melinda said to the Hoares: 'I can't tell you how glad I am this façade of a marriage is over.'[18] To us, too, she was talking about the possibility of divorce for desertion, which in Britain at that date would have meant waiting three years. An American divorce would have been quicker, but she had set her face against returning there and becoming, with her children, the pensioner of her mother and step-father. She was increasingly distressed about the plight of her fatherless boys. Fergus, in his seventh year, was almost old enough to understand that sons can be deprived of their fathers through death or divorce; but this relatively common fate was not his. No one could tell him where his father was, or whether he would ever see him again. Only his former playmates at school seemed in no doubt: 'Your father's in prison,' some of them shouted, and threw stones at him and his small brother.

By the end of July Mrs Dunbar had had enough and decided to take the family to France for a few weeks. Her second daughter, Mrs Catherine Terrell, had rented a large house at Beauvallon on the Riviera, where the whole family could be accommodated. In the first week of August, before they had left, three communications were received. Two were addressed to Mrs Dunbar, each containing a draft on a Swiss bank for £1,000: this added up to the sum that Melinda herself had raised towards the purchase of 'Beaconshaw'; the sender was never traced. The third communication was a letter from Donald to Melinda, confirming that he had arranged for the money to be sent. It was written in his hand and had been posted in Guildford; it contained no indication where he was, why he had gone, or whether he expected ever to see her again. Apart from omission of these points, which Melinda was chiefly concerned about, it was an affectionate letter, such as might have been written by any husband who had been called away on business just before the birth of a child. Despite this rather bland tone, Melinda ever after carried the letter around in her handbag, until the day came when they were reunited. She told MI5 that she believed Donald had indeed written it, though he seemed to be under some constraint. She could now be reasonably confident that Donald was alive and, even if she was not yet admitting it, she must have thought it almost certain that he was in the USSR.

Departure from England meant consultation with MI5, who this time turned to their most experienced interrogator, Jim Skardon, to cross-examine Melinda. He was inclined to conclude that she had not been privy to any conspiracy; no objection was raised to her proposed journey, but she was requested to report any clandestine attempt to get in touch with her.[19] To MI5 Melinda stoutly maintained that her husband was no traitor; but afterwards she said wistfully to her mother, 'Maybe you can be married to a man for a long time and really never know him at all.'[20] This, too, could have been said by any wife of any husband. Certainly it could have been echoed by the first Mrs George Blake and both the second and third Mrs Kim Philby. Their one-month holiday, ending on 17th September, was only moderately successful. The villa was picketed by the press and by the French police, both hoping to participate in a rendezvous between Melinda and some emissary of her husband. Kislytsin maintained that such a rendezvous was attempted, but was frustrated by the vigilance of the watchers. It may be so; but it is much more likely that Maclean, immured in Kuibyshev, was still uncertain whether to send for her, or was inhibited by the NKVD from doing so.

Melinda and her children were not the only casualties resulting from Donald's departure. His sister, who had recently married, had arrived in England with her American husband on the day after his unheralded departure and missed seeing him; they stayed briefly with Lady Maclean, but were already out of Britain when the news of his defection broke. Nancy's husband lost his job, although his only offence was to have contracted an untimely marriage. Alan Maclean fared little better. His career, after leaving the army, had begun promisingly enough; indeed it owed something to Donald who, learning in 1946 that his brother was with his regiment in West Berlin, suggested that he should call on Christopher Steel (the late Sir Christopher), who was one of the political advisers to the British Commander-in-Chief, and had headed the department of the Foreign Office in which Donald had worked during the war. The encounter was so successful that, when Alan was demobilised, he was offered a temporary appointment and, after serving in the News Department, was sent in 1950 to New York with the prospect of becoming in due course the Information Officer of the British Delegation to the UN. Recalled immediately after Donald's flight he found himself in London without employment and without the allowances that in New York would have kept him above subsistence level. Eventually he resigned, as the Foreign Office, who had nothing against him, had no doubt assumed he would do. Many years later in Moscow Donald hesitantly explained how impossible it would have been for him to have warned his brother that any other profession would have been preferable to his joining the Diplomatic Service.

As the numbness wore off, the Foreign Office began to take

measures designed to avert in future a débâcle such as that which had just occurred. All staff received a warning that no one was to go abroad, even for a weekend, without obtaining permission and leaving his overseas address. The status of the Security Department was raised, in so far as Strang told Carey-Foster that he must feel free to approach him direct, if need be, without going through channels. The system of confidential reporting by Heads of Mission on their staff was also tightened up. Remedial measures of this order, however, were unlikely to satisfy the critics; clearly some general review of security was needed. Strang accordingly turned to one of his predecessors as Permanent Under-Secretary, Sir Alexander Cadogan, who had recently retired, and asked him to chair a small committee 'to consider Foreign Office security arrangements in the light of the disappearance of Maclean and Burgess'.[21] The other members of the committee were the Cabinet Secretary, Sir Norman Brook (the late Lord Normanbrook), and Sir Nevile Bland, an ex-Ambassador. The Committee's secretary was Strang's own private secretary, Alan Campbell (Sir Alan). It was a committee of men of experience; but it was evident that no outsider was to be allowed to peep behind the curtain whilst the Foreign Office washed its dirty linen. Between 20th July and 21st August, five meetings took place and seven witnesses attended; three were from the Foreign Office and one each from the Cabinet Office, MI5 and Scotland Yard's CID. Four years later in the House of Commons Macmillan insisted:

'The committee considered not only political unreliability in itself, but the problem of character defects, which might lay an officer open to blackmail, or otherwise undermine his loyalty and sense of responsibility.'[22]

No doubt it did; but it cannot be said that, in doing so, it ranged very widely. No witness was called from the Civil Service Commission, which actually did the recruitment; no psychologist was asked to testify, nor anyone connected with man management in industry or the armed forces. Cadogan, commenting on his report, confided to his diary, 'I'm afraid it doesn't help very effectively.'[23]

The only major decision taken on the committee's recommendation was to apply positive vetting not only to new entrants into the Service, but also, as Carey-Foster had vainly proposed earlier, to those who had entered it before the war, when this precaution was unknown. Positive vetting, as originally practised, was not very far-reaching; it consisted of little more than asking public servants in sensitive positions to provide the names of two referees, who would be required to answer questions; enquiries were also addressed to the institutions at which those under examination had been educated. It was not, in the early days, a very testing examination. It transpired, for example, that John Vassall, who was blackmailed as a result of homosexual activities whilst serving as an Admiralty clerk in the British Embassy in Moscow, had given as his referees two maiden ladies, who could have known nothing of his sexual tendencies. Nonetheless, a beginning had been made with impressing on members of the Service that they could not rely on caste and connection to compensate for what Crossman termed their 'eccentricity'. Between 1952 and 1955 four officers left the Service on account of undefined 'political activities and associations'.

One year after Maclean's flight, the press did not fail to recall the anniversary. Melinda wrote to Harriet:

'We are badgered again by the Press . . . and they took photos of the boys coming out of school which infuriated me . . . I don't think the bloody Press are ever going to let this story die, do you?'[24]

Aside from the continued persecution, Fergus was nearing the age at which he would have to leave his primary school at Woldingham and a decision about his secondary education would soon have to be taken. Mrs Dunbar would have liked the family to go to the USA, but Melinda would not hear of it. Talking over the position with her mother, she may have recalled her own period of education in Switzerland; there was a well-known international school in Geneva, which had originally been founded for League of Nations employees, and she decided to settle there. In July 1952 she notified MI5 of her intention and she and her mother had a talk with one of the officers, who assured her that this time there would be no surveillance; he was unable to give her any information about her husband. The move was made in stages; first they rented a house at Glanville, near Deauville; then they went on to Paris where Harriet and Jay were still living. There they saw the Hoares, and Melinda told them of her plan to settle in Geneva. She was still talking about divorce and also said that she might try to get back her US passport, when her British passport, which had been issued in Washington in 1948, ran out after five years. They were in Geneva for the start of the school term in September and in the following month moved into a furnished flat in the rue des

Alpes. There they celebrated a sombre Christmas and New Year. Melinda wrote to Harriet: 'Thank God for a new year. I couldn't have been happier to see 1952 go.'[25]

Mrs Dunbar was in the USA from February to mid-May 1953 and it was probably in the latter part of this period that an approach was made to Melinda by the NKVD on Donald's behalf. The approach may have been made at Sanenmöser, near Gstaad, where she had gone with the children for two weeks' ski-ing. Soon after her return to Geneva she wrote to Harriet:

'I am in a dismally unstable state and have the horrid feeling almost anything might push me over the precipice. If I can only hang on for another year.'[26]

She never explained what the precipice was. Since nobody ever heard her speak of suicide, it seems likely that the journey to the USSR was what she had in mind. Enormous pressure was exerted on her when she learnt from the NKVD that Donald, oppressed by the loneliness of life in Kuibyshev, had tried to commit suicide.[27] The NKVD was able to show sympathy with the plight of their former agent because Stalin had died on 5th March 1953 and it was a good moment for Donald to press his claims to have Melinda and the children with him, if she were willing to come. At the end of June, when Mrs Dunbar had returned to Geneva and they had completed arrangements to go for a holiday in Majorca, Melinda suddenly postponed everything and insisted on making another trip to Sanenmöser. She came back to Geneva after only five days, saying there was nothing much to do there out of the ski-ing season. This could have been foreseen and Mrs Dunbar was puzzled, but did not suspect any sinister development.

There is another piece of evidence pointing in the same direction. In May Melinda met by chance Donald's old friend Robert Kee, who was working in Geneva. She confided to him that she had recently been approached by a stranger, who had offered to arrange for her to join Donald.[28] She did not give Kee the impression that she was in a hurry to make up her mind; but it is significant that she said nothing to her mother or Harriet, both of whom would have actively opposed any such move and might indeed have taken measures to prevent it. Nor was word passed to MI5. On the other hand, Melinda's action in telling Kee of the approach was not that of a trained conspirator. All through this interim period she was keeping in touch with friends in the Diplomatic Service. Passing through Paris, she rang up Lees

Mayall and on a short trip to London she got in touch with Michael Maude and had dinner with him at an hotel in Queen's Gate. They did not talk about Donald; but had a good deal to say about continued press persecution. Another friend of Maclean's, who gave her advice on this thorny subject, was John Beith (Sir John), who at that time was head of the British delegation to the UN at Geneva.

The invitation to go to Majorca in the summer of 1953 came from Douglas MacKillop, a friend of Jay and Harriet, who had been security officer at the US Embassy in Paris. On retirement he had settled down in a large house at Cala Ratjada and, after the death of his wife, was looking for congenial company. In late September, after Melinda's disappearance, the *Daily Express* sent Rene MacColl, one of their star reporters, to interview MacKillop, who insisted that he and Melinda had been 'just good friends'. On the return flight, however, MacColl met another friend, who hinted that MacKillop had looked on Melinda as a prospective wife.[29] She was still an attractive woman and her predicament, which would have been an obstacle, as she knew, in the eyes of some men, excited in others their protective instincts. One of those who at first sought out Melinda in order to interview her and stayed because he found her an appealing figure was Teddy Weintal, assistant foreign editor of *Newsweek*.

If MacKillop did make some proposition whilst the family were in Majorca, this would have added to her perplexity. Donald was certainly in her mind, because one day, returning from the beach with the children, she told her mother she had talked with 'a tall, fair man of about fifty', who looked like Donald, and she went on, 'He doesn't believe in war either.'[30] Mrs Dunbar's heart sank, but her suspicions were not aroused. They returned to Geneva on 7th September and Melinda surprised Mrs Dunbar by suggesting to her mother that she needed a change and should make a trip to Paris or London. Melinda seemed restless; on the morning of Friday, 11th September, she returned from the market in an excited state to announce that she had met an old friend from Cairo, a mythical 'Robin Muir', who had invited her to spend the coming weekend with him and his wife at their villa at Territet. She had accepted, promising to be back by Sunday evening, as the boys' school term would begin on the following day. After hurried preparations, they drove off in mid-afternoon, ostensibly in order to meet 'Muir' at an hotel in Montreux; but in fact she went to Lausanne, left the car there and took a train to Zurich, where she caught the Arlberg express going east. They had no sleeper and had to sit up all night, before leaving the train on Saturday morning at Schwarzach St Veit, where a car met them. They were presumably driven into the zone of Austria that was still under Soviet occupation.

On the front seat of the car left at Lausanne was an American edition of a children's book, which Mrs Dunbar had never seen before; it was entitled *Little Lost Lamb*. Was it a message? There was no other for six weeks. Near the end of October Mrs Dunbar at last received a letter in her daughter's hand, which had been posted in Cairo. It was affectionate, but neither very long nor very informative:

'Please believe darling in my heart I could not have done otherwise than I have done.'

The letter ended, 'Goodbye – but not for ever.'[31]

Moscow:
The Broken Partnership

It might be thought that, once Maclean had reached Moscow, his eventful story was virtually over; the hunt had ended, the scent gone dead. It must be stressed at the outset that this was not how he himself regarded the last thirty-one years of his life; his travels might have come to an end, but not his usefulness. On the contrary, he once insisted in conversation with an English visitor and fellow communist that the years in the USSR had greater significance than the earlier and more notorious part of his career. These latter years were more congenial in that, after leaving the West, he was no longer obliged to practise deception on his family and friends. Unlike Blunt and Philby, who enjoyed the duplicities they had to adopt, Maclean never fully overcame his repugnance. His estimate of the importance of his role in Moscow, however, was related not only to his feeling that he had regained his integrity, but also to his dispassionate observation of Soviet realities, which he had never previously experienced, nor closely studied in default of a working knowledge of Russian.

The vicissitudes of his years in the USSR must have filled him with conflicting emotions, as the paranoia of the final period of Stalin's rule gave way to the more promising reformism of Khruschev. After the fall of the latter in 1964, however, there followed the bureaucratic inertia of the Brezhnev period; only at the end of Maclean's life, when Andropov took over, did it seem that a new wind might again begin to blow. In international relations lack of progress was equally discouraging; the brief flowering of détente at Helsinki in 1975 came to grief in ways for which it was impossible even for a Marxist to blame only the West. During his time as a diplomat Maclean had undoubtedly worn ideological blinkers, but his powers of political perception and analysis had not atrophied; he could note the wide and sterile gap between Marxist theory and communism, as practised in the USSR. The term *glasnost* (openness) had not come into use, except among a few dissidents; but Maclean could not fail to observe the stultifying effect of trying to blind the Soviet people to the defects of the system under which they lived. He saw, too, that Soviet rulers' misperception of Western realities hamstrung their policy-making: parallel with the growth of Soviet military might went a decline of the power of Soviet communism to attract adherents in the Western world. Towards the end of his life he must have begun to see that he and his Cambridge contemporaries would be the last of the ideological spies, sucked into the Soviet machine by the idealism of their convictions.

If his diagnosis had had a wholly negative character, Maclean would have lived out his Moscow years much as Burgess did; he would have evaded responsibility, tried to maximise his material comforts and sunk himself in nostalgia for the social and intellectual delights he had once known in the West. Burgess' Marxism had never run very deep; it had not been, as it had for Maclean, a substitute for religious belief. Because Maclean never lost his belief, he did not regard communism as a failed experiment; it might still be at the experimental stage, but this committed him all the more deeply to making some contribution to its eventual success. For this it was necessary that Party hard-liners, instead of regarding the Soviet intelligentsia with uneasy suspicion, should take the latter into partnership. This meant allowing contact across frontiers, since no national intelligentsia could flourish in isolation. This understanding was at the heart of his work in the Institute of World Economics and International Relations (IMEMO), on which he embarked in 1961, and led him into cautious contact with dissidents. It was the final tragedy of his life that he did not live to see the beginning of the Gorbachev era.

When Maclean and Burgess arrived in the USSR in 1951, Gorbachev and his aims were not even a glimmer on the eastern horizon; the permafrost of Stalin prevailed. As soon as the 'Great Patriotic War' was over, Stalin began deporting large ethnic groups, such as Krim Tatars and Volga Germans, from their homelands. As the economic situation failed to improve, he adopted the familiar Hitlerian tactic of blaming the Jews. To tighten the ideological grip of his 'campaign against cosmopolitanism', Stalin orchestrated a vicious attack on Jewish intellectuals, of whom twenty-four were arraigned in July 1952 and all but one were shot. There followed in January 1953 the arrest of the so-called 'poisoner-doctors', who were alleged to have been working under the direction of US Intelligence. Only Stalin's death in

March saved these innocent victims. In 1956 Burgess related to Tom Driberg, who was in Moscow on a visit :

> 'Russians . . . tell me I'm lucky to be alive – at the time of that disgraceful business of the "doctors' plot", I wrote a sharp note to Beria telling him he was wrong . . . .'[1]

Fortunately for Burgess, the head of the NKVD never received the sharp note, which Burgess' Russian friend did not deliver. It was a time when all foreigners were under suspicion. Many years later the Russian historian, Roy Medvedev, wrote: 'Maclean was decorated with the Order of the Red Banner. He could equally well have been shot.'[2] The Order of the Red Banner had not saved Poretsky from being shot in 1937; Stalin had never trusted his foreign agents. His cynical cast of mind made it difficult for him to understand why young Englishmen, enjoying the advantages of the governing class, should put all at risk in the service of an ideology which, for Stalin, was no more than an instrument for the consolidation of his power.

From the early days of Maclean's recruitment by 'Teddy' – himself one of the victims of Stalin – he had never been an admirer of the Soviet dictator. Nonetheless, the pain and peril of his reception, after so many years of working for the USSR, must have been as surprising to him as it was discouraging. Unlike Burgess, he never unburdened himself of complaints on this score, although some twenty years later he made an oblique comment to Robin Denniston, who had come to Moscow bringing a contract for a book. 'Nobody,' said Maclean, 'knew why we were there.'[3] This can be translated to mean that, until Stalin had been told, nobody knew how the defectors should be treated. So long as they were in the small circle of NKVD men, who had been handling their case, all was well. They were taken to an hotel overlooking the Kremlin and, as it was a fine June evening, they all had dinner on the balcony and remained there until 3 a.m., consuming immense quantities of vodka. Twelve years later Maclean told Nigel Burgess, who had come to Moscow for his brother's funeral, 'People were running about all over the place looking for us and there we were on the balcony boozing.'[4]

Within a few days the party was definitely over; they were put under Beria's surveillance and despatched for debriefing to Kuibyshev. This was the city, formerly known as Samara, to which the Soviet government had been evacuated in 1941, when Moscow was threatened by Hitler's Wehrmacht. 'There was an awful time', said Burgess some years later to Stephen Spender, 'when we were sent to Kuibyshev . . . it was a horrible place.'[5] In conversation with Driberg, Burgess described Kuibyshev as 'permanently like Glasgow on a Saturday night in the nineteenth century – you know, drunks in all streets and hotels . . . .'[6] On that occasion, trying as he was to convince Driberg that he had never been a spy and would soon be able to return to England, he maintained that he had only spent six months in Kuibyshev, and his debriefing had involved no more than answering a few written questions about the Korean War. Four years later, talking to Spender, he told a different and more accurate story; Kuibyshev, he said, 'was invaded by gangsters and scoundrels,' who had been released by Beria after the death of Stalin in 1953. 'A thug saw the watch on my wrist and knocked me down.'[7]

One reason for the two-year seclusion in Kuibyshev was that it minimised the risk that the two defectors would be seen by Western diplomats or correspondents, who might well have recognised them. If the debriefing proved unsatisfactory, or the whim of Stalin decreed that they should 'disappear' for good, it would clearly be better not to admit that they had ever arrived. The NKVD may also have feared that it would not be safe for Maclean to be at large in Moscow; they believed that, because of his involvement in atomic espionage, he was an object of special hostility on the part of the Americans. In 1968, when George Blake was in Moscow with Sean Bourke, who had helped him to escape, an officer of the KGB (as the NKVD had become) said to Bourke:

'Be sure to avoid restaurants like the National . . . especially when you are with George. We know for a fact that the Americans at one time planned to shoot Donald Maclean in a Moscow restaurant.'[8]

In Kuibyshev Maclean and Burgess, as instructed, assumed new names. Guy, whose admiration for George Eliot was second only to his love of Jane Austen, called himself Jim Andreyevitch Eliot; Donald became Mark Petrovitch Frazer. Why Frazer? The Russian poet and Nobel prizewinner, Joseph Brodsky, who was expelled from the USSR in 1972, has stated that he chose the name because he had been so much impressed by Sir James Frazer's famous twelve-volume work, *The Golden Bough*.[9] This may be only part of the explanation. It is certainly true that Frazer's great work became, especially after it was condensed in 1922 into one volume, a sacred text for intellectuals, whether or not they knew much about anthropology. The ultimate accolade was bestowed when T. S. Eliot included a mention of 'the Hanged God of Frazer' in the notes appended to *The Waste Land*. There are, however, more personal links between Frazer and Donald's father; both were Scottish Presbyterians and in 1920 both received honorary degrees from Cambridge University. This honour was particularly welcome to Sir Donald, who had not been to a university; three of his sons subsequently went to Cambridge.

Young Donald's interest in Frazer, the recluse of Trinity, may well have taken a very different turn from that of his father. For those who are not anthropologists, Frazer's most familiar thesis is that embodied in his volume, published in 1911, *The Dying God*. The man-god, who in another guise is also priest-king, owes his eminence to his magical powers, which ensure the cycle of fertility and so the survival of the tribe; but he, too, is subject to the cycle of decay and re-birth and, when he begins to lose his powers, he is slain to make way for a younger and more virile successor, who may be his own son. It is tempting to believe that Maclean who, as a boy, had smarted under the stern rule of his father, may have seen him as representative of the declining cycle of capitalism; the son, in that case, would have seen himself as representative of the resurgent force of communism, the rightful heir. In the depressing environment of Kuibyshev, Maclean would have needed, to sustain him, a fantasy of this kind, linking the remote past to an equally remote future.

As we saw in the previous chapter, the waste land of Kuibyshev drove Maclean to the verge of suicide; but in his more robust moments he set about making something of his enforced exile. As Burgess remarked to Driberg, 'Donald took a job in a linguistic institute, but I wouldn't.'[10] Burgess never acquired anything better than what he called 'kitchen Russian'; but Maclean applied himself seriously to the language. To teach English to Russians was a reversion to the project that he had abandoned in 1934 at the behest of his first NKVD control. Now he had higher ambitions; if he could aspire to teach in Russian, he could instil into advanced students a clearer grasp of the realities of international relations. Neither he nor Burgess had any wish to continue working for the NKVD, nor is there evidence that such a proposition was ever made to them; when in 1956 the decision was taken to expose them to public view, they were presented as true believers in Marxism since Cambridge days but, as their statement emphasised, 'Neither of us were communist agents.' Both had entered the service of the British government, hoping 'to put Marxist ideas into practical effect'; but they had come to see that nothing could be achieved, because 'neither the British, nor still more the Americans, were at that time seriously trying to co-operate with the USSR in upholding world peace.' It was in order 'to further understanding between East and West' that they had come to the USSR. This was their 'legend'.

In order to understand why it was decided to present the defectors as political refugees, rather than spies, it is necessary to see the decision in its international context. Ever since the death of Stalin, Churchill and Eden had shown increasing interest in détente and had come to believe that Khruschev shared their hopes. These culminated in an invitation to Khruschev and Bulganin to visit Britain in April 1956 and the Soviet leaders, travelling to the West for the first time, were anxious to make the visit a success. In February Richard Hughes, who was on a visit to Moscow for the *Sunday Times*, had an interview with Molotov, the Soviet Foreign Minister, and left with him a memorandum, in which he referred to the fact that continued Soviet reticence about the fate of Maclean and Burgess was not conducive to better Anglo-Soviet relations. That same evening he was told to go to the National Hotel, where he found the correspondents of Reuters, Tass and *Pravda*; the *Daily Worker* correspondent was conspicuously absent. There the two defectors read their prepared statement and left without answering questions.

Apart from promotion of better relations, two other factors must have been taken into account in Moscow by those who prepared the statement made by Maclean and Burgess. The more important of these was that in the previous November Macmillan, the Foreign Secretary, had felt obliged to announce in the House of Commons that he had no evidence that Philby was 'the so-called Third Man, if indeed there was one'. Open admission of the guilt of the First and Second Men would not have buttressed Philby's defences. The debate in the House had been brought about in large measure on account of the revelations of the Soviet defector, Vladimir Petrov, which had appeared in the *People* in September 1955 and had contained information – not all of it accurate – about the escape of Maclean and Burgess. A secondary factor may therefore have been the reluctance of the KGB to give any added credibility to Petrov. If Maclean and Burgess themselves were consulted, they would certainly have fallen in with the authorities' wishes – Maclean, no doubt, with a shrug of the shoulders; Burgess with more enthusiasm, since he still had hopes of returning one day to England with a well-simulated air of injured innocence.

We should probably be paying too high a tribute to the subtleties of the KGB if we concluded that the delay of nearly five years in disclosing the whereabouts of the two defectors constituted a deliberate attempt to heighten the suspense and keep on the boil a pot that was still generating a great deal of steam on both sides of the Atlantic. This was a period, however, when the KGB was evolving increasingly sophisticated disinformation projects and some officers with insight into the mysteries of interaction in the West between government, media and public opinion may have seen that there could have been no more effective way of generating suspicion, controversy and recrimination. Whilst in the USSR the KGB and its forerunners have always been an elite force, regarded by the population with respect as well as fear, secret services in Britain and the USA have long been looked at, especially in time of peace, with some of the mixed feelings that are commonly accorded to the careers of brothel-keepers – a mixture of revulsion and prurient excitement. The insatiable demands for more details, conflicting with the British government's determination to reveal as little as possible, ensured not only that the file could never be closed, but also that wise heads in London and Washington were constantly diverted from the more useful task of pursuing KGB agents. An added ingredient of the poisonous brew was the acrimony felt in Washington, especially on the part of the FBI.

As we have seen, it was in September 1953, when the first hubbub was dying down, that it was resuscitated by Melinda's departure from Switzerland to join her husband. She had not been under any close surveillance and could certainly have quit the West earlier, if sent for. The timing was clearly determined by events in the USSR; Donald may not have been an ideal husband, but he was a loving father and he would not have wished to bring his family to a country where Stalin ruled. In a letter written in 1957, he referred to

> 'the nightmare of Stalin's and Beria's persecutions. The process of undoing and, as far as anyone could, making good, the evils done, has been going on steadily not just since the 20th Congress last year, but since Stalin died in 1953.'[11]

In the July following Stalin's death his Georgian henchman, Beria, had been killed; the way was now open for Maclean to come to Moscow and make a home for his family. According to Philby, Maclean finally clinched the move by addressing a personal letter to Molotov, whose authority over foreign affairs had survived the disappearance of Stalin and Beria. Although no longer threatened by the terror of Stalinism, the Macleans were still wholly dependent on the goodwill of the KGB for the many privileges that raised them above the drab level of the life of the ordinary Soviet citizen. Good food, housing and education for the three young Macleans all hinged on their parents' standing with higher authority. It is necessary to emphasise this point, because it has a bearing on statements unquestionably made by Melinda after her arrival about her complicity in her husband's espionage. When she began to meet friendly members of the expatriate community, such as Sam Russell, the *Daily Worker* correspondent, she told them she had known what Donald was doing and had co-operated.[12] Presumably she had already said as much to the KGB and Donald would have warned her that apartments occupied by foreigners were normally 'bugged'. Some years later, when the Macleans happened to meet in Leningrad their old friend Mark Culme-Seymour, Melinda spoke to him in the same sense.[13]

Melinda went to the USA in 1979 and there she remains, refusing to speak of the past. We are therefore left to make up our own minds whether, on arrival in the USSR, she was at last telling the truth or whether, in her first uncertainty about how she would be received and what the future held for the children and herself, she decided to play it safe and encourage the KGB to believe that she had all along been one of their loyal supporters. Having once made such a claim, she would, of course, have had to stick to it; but it does not follow that it was true. She had long been aware that Donald and his more intellectual friends had never thought very highly of her intelligence; pride may well have inhibited her from allowing it to be supposed that she had spent eleven years married to a spy without knowing it. If such had been her experience, she would not have been the first. No charges were brought against her, when she finally settled in the USA; the verdict must remain open.

It was not until 1955 that the Macleans were able to move into the large, sixth-floor apartment in the Bolshaya Dorogomilovskya, where Maclean remained till his death in 1983. The district was one of the best in Moscow, where many high-rise blocks had been built after the slum clearances of the 1940s and early 1950s. The local landmark, which he could see from his bay window, was the Ukraina Hotel, a rococo monstrosity, topped with a spire, which he once described as 'the last of those terrible Stalin buildings'.[14] There were redeeming features, however, quite apart from the fact that, by Moscow standards,

there was ample room. The Moscow River was not far off and was
flanked by a boulevard, lined with poplar trees, where in summer
fishermen put out their lines. There was an old-fashioned, segregated
bath-house, 'all chipped ceramic tiles and down-at-heel furnishings'.[15]
To supplement the produce of the special shops, to which the
Macleans, like the elite of Soviet bureaucracy, had access, there was a
local peasant market; it was muddy in wet weather and crowded in all
weathers, but at a price flowers and fresh vegetables could be got there.

The Macleans settled in. In January 1956 Donald described in one
of his letters a happy family Christmas. Christmas Day is not a holiday
in the USSR, but this does not deter Russians from a celebration of
'Grandfather Frost'. There were presents for the Maclean children,
including an accordion for Fergus. 'We had (and have)', wrote
Donald, 'a giant Christmas tree in our sitting room, with lights and all
the trimmings (Russian ones are better than any I know).' Prospects
for the summer were also improving; in August 1957 he wrote,

> 'About my life, the best thing in it recently is that I have got a
> *dacha* and can go and root about there when I have time. It is
> wonderful for the children, since there is swimming, fishing,
> bicycling, mushrooming, television and cinema all at hand.'[16]

The *dacha* was in a birch forest about two hours' drive from Moscow
in an area from which the unprivileged were rigorously excluded.

One major gain resulting from emergence in 1956 into the light of
day was permission to communicate with the outside world. Alan
Maclean was startled to receive a telegram: 'You can write *poste
restante*, Moscow;' he promptly complied. Donald Maclean's bank
account with Barclays had never been closed and he was now able to
reactivate it; in due course it was replenished by a legacy from one of
his Devitt grandparents. He arranged for furnishings, including glass,
china and pictures, which had been in the keeping of the Army and
Navy Stores, to be shipped out to him. In 1963 Eleanor Philby
described the Macleans' apartment as 'crammed with furniture'.[17]
Another high priority was to reopen his account with Bowes and
Bowes in Cambridge, who sent him a large quantity of books and
periodicals; he had always been a great reader and had passed on the
habit to Fergus. At this time he was, like Burgess, advising the
Foreign Literature Publishing House and sometimes he asked friends
in England to make recommendations. To one he wrote, 'I have
Wained, Brained, Amised, Murdoched and Sillitoed.'

Burgess, who was leading a separate life in another block, had exploited his freedom of communication to enlist Driberg's co-operation in securing the despatch of a selection of his books and furniture from Britain. Driberg took the opportunity to project a biography of Burgess, who was glad to co-operate as a means of propagating his version of his innocent involvement in Maclean's flight. In the autumn of 1956 Driberg visited Moscow and in November published in the *Daily Mail* a series of interviews with Burgess. He did not see Maclean who, as Driberg later recorded, 'strongly disapproved of Guy's arrangement with me'. He did, however, come across the trail of Donald in one of his 'wild boar' moods. Visiting Burgess' *dacha*, he suggested that they go to the local bar. Guy shook his head:

'I can't go there now. Donald was staying here, and he had one of his drunken fits and wrecked the bar. There was a hell of a row about it. That was before he had his last cure.'[18]

Maclean's drinking habits may have been aggravated by the tensions of his life as a spy, but it was too late, even on a more even keel in Moscow, to eradicate them. Much of the time the 'wild boar' could be kept on a leash, but there were evenings when Melinda and the children had to take refuge on the staircase and be rescued by a friendly English family whilst Donald rampaged about the apartment. Whenever all seemed lost, however, something of the resolution and tenacity of Sir Donald reasserted itself and he began once more to struggle with his weaknesses. In a letter of self-examination he listed these as 'unreasonable irritation, refusal or attempted refusal to do one's obvious duty, brooding, slacking ...'[19] Inevitably his excesses undermined his marriage and Melinda began to look elsewhere for affection. The slow disintegration of family life was all the sadder, because Donald was happy to have his children around him again; he was proud of their good looks and aptitude with the language. If Maclean himself was becoming 'completely Russianised' (to use Burgess' phrase), this was even truer of the children, who were working their way through the Soviet educational system. In June 1957 Donald wrote that, whilst he and Melinda were about to go south for their holiday, Fergus would be doing vacation work on a collective farm and young Donald ('Beany') and Mimsie would go to their segregated boy and girl 'pioneer' camps.

Maclean's efforts to integrate himself in the community were stimulated by his hope that a new era was beginning in the USSR. In the spring of 1956 Khruschev had dissolved the Cominform (the successor organ to the earlier Comintern) and enunciated the doctrine of peaceful co-existence with the West. Word was leaking out of the anti-Stalin speech delivered at the Twentieth Congress of the Party, in the course of which he had denounced the 'cult of personality', and asserted its replacement by collective leadership. In one of Maclean's letters he described the changes as

> 'excellent . . . a major clearing away of obstacles in the long march along the right road. I don't believe there was a real danger of going back to the old horrors, but there certainly was of heavy brakes having to be dragged along.'[20]

Yet, even as he was writing, Khruschev was consolidating his personal ascendancy by ousting the 'anti-Party group' and in November the Red Army marched into Hungary and violently suppressed the short-lived government of Imre Nagy.

We know how Maclean reacted to this event, since he discussed it in correspondence with his old friend Philip Toynbee, who had been equally opposed to the Soviet incursion into Hungary and to the Anglo-French invasion of Egypt. In attempting to convert Toynbee to his view of Hungary, Maclean tried to recapture the enthusiasm both of them had felt twenty years earlier for Soviet intervention in Spain. For him, the threat then posed by Franco was paralleled by the US threat to 'impose a Luce-McCarthy civilisation in other people's countries'. If the Red Army had not marched into Budapest, that country would have been

> 'ruled in effect by capitalists, the Church and the landlords with some sort of fascist front and permanent witch-hunts to keep down the enemies of such people – in short a sort of Franco Spain.'[21]

Toynbee was unimpressed by this tortuous reasoning and the correspondence lapsed. Maclean understood why this happened; one of his final letters, containing a long diatribe about unilateral disarmament, ended with the querulous enquiry: 'Why didn't Mary Campbell answer my letter? Disgusted about Hungary?' As correspondence with friends in Britain declined, Maclean became isolated from Western contacts. Unlike Burgess, who would exchange gossip with any visitor to Moscow, Maclean shut himself off from them and would not even

see resident correspondents, apart from the *Daily Worker* representatives, Sam Russell, and his successor, Dennis Ogden. In 1958
Driberg wrote to a friend, who hoped to meet Maclean in Moscow:

> 'I do not think that you will find it very easy to meet the Macleans.
> They see very few people from the West and do not like being
> interviewed.'[22]

Because this was his attitude, he was irritated by the flurry of publicity
that blew up in the spring of 1962. Indeed it was doubly irritating,
because in the previous year he had at last secured an appointment at
IMEMO, looking after research students in international relations. It
was annoying to be distracted from work in which he felt that he could
at last fulfil his aims in Moscow. The cause of the trouble was Burgess,
who was suffering from angina and, although he had had a visit from
his mother, could not rid himself of the yearning to see for the last
time old friends and old haunts in England. Burgess' passport had
expired in 1954 and, as he had never become a Soviet citizen, there
was a problem of travel documents. More serious was the question
whether his protestations of innocence would be taken at face value
and he would be allowed to revisit the playing fields, and perhaps
dormitories, of Eton unmolested. Problems that were on Burgess'
mind soon became problems for all who encountered him and it was
not long before rumours reached the London press that a visit from
him was on the cards. As Lady Maclean, who had not visited her son,
was thought to be failing, the press assumed that he, too, would be
likely to accompany Burgess, although nothing to suggest this had
been said in Moscow.

It was this assumption that led to my final involvement in the long
saga. Because I was serving in London and was known to have been
assistant in the American Department at the time of Maclean's flight, I
was approached by Detective-Inspector George Smith, who was
preparing the case against the two defectors in anticipation of their
arrival in this country. In the course of conversation it became clear
that Scotland Yard were in a quandary; the public regarded Maclean
and Burgess as traitors, who should be subjected to exemplary
punishment; on the other hand, the evidence against them was
scarcely better than it had been when they left our shores for good
eleven years before. It had then been the hope that Maclean, who had
for some time been on the run, could be brought to admit guilt; if he
were now to reappear, it would be, presumably, with the intention of

brazening it out, as was certainly thought to be Burgess' intention. The Inspector would not, of course, have known about the cryptanalytic evidence against Maclean; even if he had done, he would have had grave doubts whether it would be disclosed in court. Even if the case were tried *in camera*, the concurrence of the US, as well as the British, security authorities would have been required.

Knowing something of their dilemma, I watched with admiration how the Inspector and his colleagues played their hand. They chose a morning in April when a case, in which there was a keen press interest, was due to be heard at Bow Street and there applied to the Chief Metropolitan Magistrate for a warrant for the arrest of Maclean and Burgess under Section One of the Official Secrets Act. Soon Smith, who was accompanied by a representative of the Director of Public Prosecutions, was busy telling assembled journalists about the warrant; to make doubly sure, a release was made to the press in the afternoon. On 19th April the *Daily Mirror* blazoned the headlines: 'Burgess and Maclean Arrest Riddle: Are They Flying from Moscow?' Reuters flashed the story to John Miller, their man in Moscow and, as Burgess had gone south on holiday, the hunt for Maclean was on. When Miller finally tracked him down and asked for 'Mr Frazer', the door was opened by 'a crew-cut youth with black horn-rimmed spectacles, wearing a red shirt'. Fergus, who was eighteen, was renewing his painful acquaintance with the British press. When Donald came to the door, he said, 'I've nothing, absolutely nothing to say to you ... I've asked you not to come here ... Please go away.' Despite this reception, Miller tried again later. This time the door was opened by 'a middle-aged, bespectacled woman with a slight Cockney accent'. Maclean's voice was heard shouting, 'Shut the door,' and it was slammed to.[23] As far as he was concerned, it was a non-event; but in England it was not yet over. When in July Lady Maclean died and was laid beside her husband in Penn churchyard, no less than six policemen, uniformed and in plain clothes, attended the funeral in the expectation that Donald might put in an appearance.

What had been a non-event for Maclean proved to be the last fling of 'Brigadier Brilliant'. In addition to angina, Burgess was suffering from a liver disorder and hardening of the arteries. He was taken to Bodkin Hospital and died there on 19th August 1963. According to Eleanor Philby, he had a final meeting with Kim, who had defected in Beirut in the previous January and was still undergoing a prolonged debriefing. Many years later, however, Philby denied that any such deathbed reunion had taken place.[24] In any case he was not allowed to attend the funeral and it was Maclean who made the farewell oration. A brass band played the 'Internationale', which can hardly have been what Burgess would have wished. He liked to pick out hymn tunes on the piano and would undoubtedly have preferred 'Rock of Ages' or even 'Abide with Me'. Best of all would have been the 'Eton Boating Song', if anyone had been able to induce a Soviet brass band to play it. His ashes were collected by his brother, Nigel, and interred in the church-yard at West Meon in Hampshire; it was a precedent that Maclean later decided to follow.

It cannot be supposed that Maclean experienced much grief over the severance of the long partnership; in the preceding ten years he and Burgess had seen little of one another. In one of Maclean's letters to Toynbee he wrote that 'he seldom saw Guy, and it gave him a very odd feeling that the names Burgess and Maclean had become as indissolubly linked as Swan's with Edgar's and Debenham's with Freebody's.'[25] He had disapproved of the feckless and irresponsible side of Burgess' nature and in this comment some of his old arrogance emerges. Nevertheless he showed typical kindness in shepherding Nigel Burgess, who had the task of disposing of Guy's effects. It was due to Maclean's intervention with the Muscovite bureaucracy that Nigel was able to get away after one week.[26] Whatever Guy Burgess' shortcomings as a fellow member of the renegade group in Moscow, his company was greatly preferable to that of Kim Philby, who had accepted Soviet citizenship and the full confidence of the KGB.

Exile's End

In the years following Guy Burgess' death Donald Maclean must often have wished that it had been Kim Philby's body that had been cremated. Shortly before his own death Maclean remarked to an English visitor, 'Kim is a real shit!' It was an Englishman's understatement. Philby's third wife, Eleanor, who like Melinda was American, had joined him in Moscow in September 1963 and from the start found it hard to settle down. Whilst Philby struggled to master the language, she found the effort beyond her and she never got used to queuing for almost everything. Inevitably Kim and Eleanor were thrown together with the Macleans and there were endless sessions of gossip, in which Melinda, but not Eleanor, could join. This ill-assorted quartet made regular visits with their privileged tickets to the Bolshoi and the Conservatoire: but even with the help of vodka the nights of winter must have seemed interminable. At least Maclean, who was a proud and affectionate father, was able to take pleasure in his children as they grew up.

In the light of Melinda's *affaire* with Philby, it is hardly to be expected that Eleanor, in retrospect, would have had anything good to say about her. She described Melinda as 'a short, plumpish brunette, not unattractive, extremely nervous and highly strung'. Mimsie, her daughter, then aged twelve, was 'unusually spoiled and terribly rude to her mother'. On the indifferent relations between Donald and Melinda, she wrote:

'I sometimes wondered why Melinda, who had clearly been close to divorcing Donald a number of times, had chosen to join him . . . she seemed to yearn for the luxuries of Western capitalism.'[1]

Eleanor's big mistake was to visit the USA in June 1964. Up to that time she had no suspicions about Kim and Melinda; indeed she exhorted the latter, 'Look after my husband.'[2] Melinda complied all too willingly. In July and August the Macleans toured the Baltic States, taking with them Mimsie, whose Russian was much more fluent than Donald's, and for part of the journey Kim accompanied them. At this stage he was still a frequent weekend visitor to the Macleans' *dacha* and, as winter came on, he persuaded Maclean to keep it open for ski-ing. With a choice of three places to go to, Kim and Melinda must have found it easy to evade the eye of the injured husband.

When Eleanor Philby returned to Moscow towards the end of 1964, Kim greeted her with the news that he and Donald were no longer on speaking terms. She was besieged with Melinda's demands for sympathy: 'Donald has become quite impossible and I can't live with him any more.'[3] Melinda's spirits improved in January 1965, when she moved into Philby's spare room, and in February Harriet arrived on a visit. Philby evaded the issue as long as he could, but eventually made it clear where his real sympathies lay: 'Melinda is so unhappy. Donald is impotent. She's had a miserable time for fifteen years.'[4] Eleanor had only six years of marriage to be miserable with Kim. In May she left Moscow for good, dying three years later in California. By that date Philby's feelings for Melinda had waned and he rejected her in favour of Rufa, a Russian woman twenty years younger, whom he married. The Maclean-Philby expatriate quartet was replaced by a new one: at the end of 1966 George Blake arrived in Moscow, having escaped from Wormwood Scrubs with the help of two members of CND and an Irish ex-convict named Sean Bourke.

Blake's cynical and opportunist attitude to life was much more congenial to Philby than Maclean's had been. Blake had already divorced his English wife, who had been an employee of SIS, and soon married a Russian woman named Ida. When Melinda moved out of Philby's apartment, she had nowhere to go and, but for Donald's forgiving nature, she might well have found herself a victim of the perennial housing crisis in Moscow. Instead she was able to move in again with him, whilst awaiting allocation of an apartment of her own. This period of uneasy cohabitation lasted about eighteen months. When in 1969 Robin Denniston visited Moscow in connection with publication in England of Maclean's book, he found Melinda in the apartment doing the cooking and shopping.[5] She also did duty as grandmother; in the years 1969 to 1971 all three Maclean children married and had children of their own, but neither marriages nor births were synchronised with housing allocations. Young Donald

('Beany') and his wife Lucy, who had been the first to wed, finally moved in February 1971 with their four-month-old baby into a one-room flat, in the hope of getting a two-room flat later.

The split between Maclean and Philby did not take place without hard words and recriminations. Philby seems at one moment, after one of Maclean's drinking bouts, to have had what, as applied to anyone else, might have been called a twinge of conscience: 'Poor Donald, I'm partly responsible for his crack-up.'[6] Philby told his wife that Maclean had accused him of being a double-agent; to anyone as loyal as Philby to the KGB this was as gross an insult as could have been framed. It is probable that the personal friction between the two men also had political undertones. Philby had never had misgivings about the Soviet system and had only arrived in the USSR some ten years after the death of Stalin and Beria, when the worst abuses of their tyrannical rule had been mitigated. By contrast, Maclean had shown disquiet about aspects of Stalinism long before he had come to Kuibyshev and experienced at first hand the vicious character of the regime. After his arrival in Moscow, as his mastery of the language grew, he began to make contacts in those circles of the intelligentsia that were critical of the rigidities of Soviet bureaucratic control and had suffered for it. Eleanor Philby recalled that one of his friends, with whom he made a trip to Samarkand, was 'a writer and scholar . . . who had spent some years in gaol'.[7] Another of Stalin's victims, whom Maclean got to know in Moscow, was Len Wincott of Invergordon, who had been hailed by the Kremlin in 1931 as 'Symbol of the British Working Class'. This had not saved him from imprisonment in 1936 as a British spy and twenty years passed before he gained his release.

Maclean had a similar contact nearer home in the person of the American communist, George Hanna, who had worked for the Comintern and so incurred Stalin's hostility; he was the father of 'Beany's' first wife, Lucy.[8] He had spent many years in a labour camp before being released in the course of the modest measures of rehabilitation introduced in the wake of Khruschev's de-Stalinisation programme of 1956. Another friend with earlier Comintern associations was Semyon Rostovsky, who had been active in the West as a journalist under the name Ernst Henry. There is no evidence that Maclean's basic loyalty to Marxism was seriously shaken; but he moved gradually and cautiously into a critical stance towards the Leninist version that had merged so lethally with Russian traditions of autocracy. When in 1968 the Red Army entered Czechoslovakia and extinguished the 'Prague Spring', there were no letters from Maclean to friends in the West, justifying the invasion, such as he had written twelve years earlier to Toynbee, backing Soviet aggression against Hungary. On the contrary, English visitors were left in no doubt that Maclean disapproved of the 'Brezhnev doctrine', licensing Soviet intervention in the internal affairs of all Warsaw Pact countries. In 1970, he visited Poland with Mimsie and in the following year toured Hungary with Fergus. He was an experienced observer and could not have failed to see how the dead hand of Moscow was stifling initiative and enterprise throughout the Soviet Bloc.

Another friend of these years was the historian Roy Medvedev, who with his brother, Zhores, attacked in a book, *A Question of Madness*, the practice of confining dissidents in psychiatric hospitals. This inhuman innovation was one of those introduced by Andropov, when he took over the KGB in 1967. Zhores, after himself suffering confinement, was allowed to settle in Britain in 1973, when his Soviet citizenship was cancelled. Roy Medvedev has confirmed that in the 1960s Maclean belonged to a group of Moscow intellectuals meeting in homes 'where those united by similar opposition views could gather to discuss the kind of political and literary news you did not find in newspapers'.[9] He and Medvedev first met at such a gathering, where there was a reading by the dissident poet Natalya Gorbanevskaya, who later emigrated. The brief thaw under Khruschev had ended in 1958, when he banned *Doctor Zhivago* and refused to allow Pasternak to travel to Stockholm to receive the Nobel Prize. Another dissident writer was Viktor Nekrasov, who was expelled from the Party and Union of Writers and in 1968 denounced the invasion of Czechoslovakia. Medvedev used to discuss with Maclean the manuscript of his study of Stalin, *On Stalin and Stalinism* (Oxford University Press 1979). The historian knew no English and Maclean was able to help him by translating English texts; in return Maclean was supplied with *Samizdat* literature, which circulated illegally among the dissidents.

One interesting episode related by Medvedev concerns two schoolgirls, who were arrested in 1970 for distributing leaflets; one of the girls, Olga Ioffe, was put in a psychiatric hospital. Medvedev writes:

'Maclean knew the girl's family. That summer there were elections to the Supreme Soviet, in which Maclean was entitled to vote as a Soviet citizen. He went to the polling station, took the voting slip and wrote on it: "As long as girls like Olga Ioffe are put in psychiatric hospitals, I cannot take part in the voting."'[10]

It was not an heroic act, but it required a certain degree of resolution and integrity, especially in the light of the privileged status that he was putting at risk. It is perhaps most eloquently described in a poem written a few years earlier by another of his friends, Yevgeny Yevtushenko:

> 'You're a brave man they tell me. I'm not.
> Courage has never been my quality.
> Only I thought it disproportionate
> so to degrade myself as others did.
> No foundations trembled. My voice
> no more than laughed at pompous falsity;
> I did no more than write, never denounced . . . .
>
> And now they press me to tell them that I'm brave.
> How sharply our children will be ashamed
> taking at last their vengeance for these horrors
> remembering how in so strange a time
> common integrity could look like courage.'[11]

One reason why Maclean had to brace himself in order to make a stand of any kind was that his children's demands were making him increasingly a suppliant at the feet of the Soviet bureaucracy. When his children asserted their wish to visit Britain, Maclean could have vetoed their plans and that would have been the end of it; but he did not feel entitled to act in so authoritarian a manner. Although only Mimsie had actually been born in England, and she had been removed when only one year old, it seemed natural to Donald that they should all regard England as their homeland. As he conscientiously explained to relatives in England, his children were not in the USSR through any choice of theirs: he felt under a moral obligation to enable them, if he could, to go to England and make contact with relations there, despite the risk that they might wish to remain in the West, where he could not join them. Lady Maclean had never visited him in the USSR, but her unmarried sister, Miss Mary Devitt, had come to Moscow in 1966, although then over seventy. Her visit had been especially welcome at a time when Melinda had moved in with Kim Philby; she had made friends with the children and encouraged their hopes of visiting England, where Donald's younger brother, Alan, was also prepared to make them welcome.

These plans involved Maclean in interminable negotiations with officialdom; as he observed in a cautious understatement, 'A lot of things here take twice or three times as long as one thinks they will.' He had also to meet the cost of the journeys and money to support his children's stay in Britain. The first to go in April 1972 were 'Beany' and Lucy, who had an aunt living in Essex; his passport, as a Soviet citizen, was issued in the name Maclean and the British Embassy affixed a visitor's visa. Fergus and his wife Olga made their first visit in 1973 and Mimsie and her husband Dimitri soon followed. These trips to the West were to prove decisive; eventually all three children settled either in Britain or in the USA. Fergus enrolled at University College, London, and in 1976 graduated with a degree in history.[12]

One wonders whether Maclean ever reflected on his privileged status, which permitted freedom of movement to his children at a time when Russian wives were often debarred from joining non-Russian husbands abroad and Jewish citizens were denied exit visas to go to Israel. By the end of 1969 some 34,000 Jews had applied to go; but in the following year, when Maclean first began corresponding with relations in England about his children's visits, only 1,044 Jews were allowed to emigrate. In 1974 Avital, wife of Anatoli Sharansky, was given an exit visa, but her husband was prevented from joining her in Israel and in 1978 was imprisoned after a show trial.[13] During these years, when Andropov and the KGB were making a calculated effort to break the will of the 'refuseniks' by mounting an anti-Semitic campaign in press and film, Maclean must certainly have been aware of what was going on. It has been reported by some familiar with the covert sign language of Moscow that his apartment had a sign indicating that anti-Semites were not welcome.

During the period when his children's first visits were being planned, Maclean was preoccupied with his book, *British Foreign Policy Since Suez*, which was originally published in England and later in the USSR. Donald was encouraged by his brother Alan, who was a publisher, to embark on authorship and he was fortunate to have Robin Denniston as his editor at the London firm to which he referred in correspondence as 'Hodderski and Stoughtonov'. Much of the material for the book existed already, either in the form of lectures delivered at the Institute or as articles on British foreign policy written for Soviet publications under his pen-name, Madzoevsky.[14] His book served as a doctoral thesis and so enhanced both his salary and status in Moscow. He supervised the translation into Russian and the expanded edition appeared in 1972 in a print of 15,000 copies.

Much of his satisfaction in the London publication was psychological:

he had long wished to demonstrate to former colleagues, whom he had
betrayed, that these activities, by which they remembered him, had
represented only a part of his life and, in his own estimation, the less
significant part. The underground stream, which they condemned,
had been unimportant, in his view, compared with the broad ocean of
international understanding, to which he believed he was contribu-
ting. He was hurt and puzzled that so much hostility to him persisted
in England: he saw himself as a man of principle, who to his own
detriment had acted throughout his career in conformity with his
principles. As Eleanor Philby recorded:

> 'Donald had a vision of himself as a statesman and a diplomat,
> whose life had been dictated by his convictions. He possessed a
> highly inflated ego. He had been deeply wounded by his treatment
> in the Western press ....'[15]

If it was his aim by implication to put the record straight, it was no
part of his intention to glamorise the life of a spy, as Philby had done
in his book, *My Silent War*. If Maclean had wished to follow this
profitable course, he would not have taken the year 1956 as his starting
point, but would have begun his narrative ten, or even twenty years
earlier, so that he could have introduced allusions to his own role. In
conversation he showed no reluctance to do this; indeed he sometimes
exaggerated his own importance. For example, he left Roy Medvedev
with the impression that in December 1950 he had accompanied
Attlee to Washington on his visit to Truman: this was not the case.
One of the last comments about British policy attributed to Maclean
was made shortly before his death, during the Argentine invasion of
the Falkland Islands: 'I told them in 1951 to get rid of them!' he is
reported to have said.[16] It was certainly his opinion that Britain
should hand over the Islands; but he never made any formal proposal
to that effect, since he knew that it would have had no chance of
acceptance.

His purpose in his book, however, was to raise debate above the
personal level and to show where British policies, of which he had
disapproved, had all the while been leading. In this way his judgment
of the present could be read as vindicating the silent criticisms of the
past. This treatment also served to uphold the statement first made by
Burgess and himself, when they came out of seclusion in 1956, that
they had not been spies, but had come to the USSR 'to further
understanding between East and West'. At the same time the book

undoubtedly had for him a cathartic function: during the years of his servitude to the British government he had been obliged, in order to sustain his cover, to share in the execution of policies which he deplored. From the security of his desk in Moscow he could now castigate the failures of his former employers and point to future calamities. The sub-heading of his first chapter reads: 'Twilight of Western Unity'. Here and in later chapters he predicts that the 'Anglo-American common front may ... before long begin to crumble;'[17] 'NATO is beginning to disintegrate ...;'[18] 'the Commonwealth in its present form will begin to break up.'[19] None of these prophecies has been fulfilled.

In all this tale of woe Maclean traces only one major trend in British policy that merits respect and even commendation:

'The relative weight of anti-communist considerations in British foreign policy was far greater in, say, 1950, at the height of the Cold War, than it is now at the beginning of the 'seventies.'[20]

What is more, he noted, is that since 1955 Britain has exerted such influence with the USA as she still possesses with the aim of guiding Washington 'to seek a *modus vivendi* with the Soviet Union'. Did he, as he wrote these passages, have any realisation of their ironical relationship to his own career in espionage? There can be no doubt that his anti-American reports, instead of promoting better American-Soviet relations, must have fed Stalin's paranoia. If indeed Britain's vital role in the 1960s had been to lay a restraining hand on the sleeve of her over-mighty ally, Maclean could himself have been part of the conciliatory process. The fatal decision made in Cambridge in 1934 had come between him and the very real possibility of becoming Ambassador in Washington and helping to create a measure of mutual trust between the two superpowers. In this lies the tragic irony of his career.

Robin Denniston in his foreword to the book wrote:

'We have the author's word that the book is his own, that it was at no point revised or redrafted by any higher authority in the Soviet Union ...'[21]

This verdict is probably correct: there is no internal evidence of an alien hand, nor does the book read, as Philby's does, as containing deliberate disinformation. If it had been primarily designed to serve the Kremlin's purpose, it would surely have exhibited at various points more pro-Soviet bias. For example, Soviet intervention to terminate the Anglo-French adventure at Suez is barely mentioned. Formation of the EEC is not presented as an anti-Soviet move fostered by the USA, but is correctly treated as a development inherent in Western capitalism. None of this means, of course, that the KGB would not have intervened if they had seen any need to do so; but Maclean was an old hand at self-censorship and was unlikely to have given them any trouble. In 1972 he contemplated writing another book, which he insisted would be 'strictly non-personal', about British foreign policy in the 1970s; but his first venture had not been profitable enough for a British publisher to make an offer. It would have been otherwise if he had taken as his model Philby's book, of which he deeply disapproved.

One side-effect of publication under his own name was that Maclean acceded to his children's wish that he abandon the assumed name 'Mark Frazer'; instead he began to call himself Donald Donald-ovitch, or son of Donald. He allowed his name to appear in the Moscow telephone directory and, as a result, had a pleasant meeting a few years later with one of his oldest friends. In October 1970 a rumour had reached him that Tony Rumbold, who had become Sir Anthony, might be coming to Moscow as Ambassador with his wife, Felicity, who had been a friend of his youth. It is interesting to speculate how this appointment might have affected his reclusive existence, but it was not to be; either the Foreign Office, or Rumbold himself, decided that it would be wiser not to put matters to the test. Some years later, however, when Rumbold had retired from the Service and was divorced from his wife, Felicity went to Moscow on a group visit organised through Intourist. She rang up Donald and asked if he would come to her hotel. He declined to do so, on the ground that it was an hotel frequented by foreign journalists and tourists, one of whom might recognise him and subject him to insulting remarks. He suggested instead a café in the vicinity. There they met and for an hour or more talked about the old days; it was one of Maclean's rare indulgences in nostalgia about the past and what might have been. In the course of conversation she asked whether there were any of his former colleagues in the Service whom he would have liked to see again; the three whom he named were Con O'Neill (see Chapter Four), Lees Mayall (see Chapter Six) and Rumbold himself.[22]

The strains of his life, recently aggravated by the defection of

Melinda, had had their effect upon his health. He had always been a heavy smoker and persisted in the habit despite recurrent bronchitis. More serious was the discovery of bladder tumours (papilloma), some of which proved to be malignant. In November 1971 he went into hospital for an operation, which was followed by radiation treatment in the hope of preventing recurrence. It was before this operation that, in addition to making a new will, he expressed the wish that, after his cremation in Moscow, his ashes should be laid to rest in Penn churchyard, where his father and mother were buried. It was the strongest intimation he ever gave that he regarded as indissoluble the links that still bound him to England. Did it also indicate a weakening of his strong antipathy to religion? Probably not: on the other hand there is a passage in a letter, written shortly before he went into hospital, which strikes a wistful note barely compatible with dogmatic materialism. He had been informed of an accident suffered by the favourite aunt, who had visited him in Moscow, and wrote in reply:

'I am hoping for her, feeling for her, just as she, I know, prays for us and others when they are in distress, danger or anxiety. I know hoping doesn't do any good, but it would be sad indeed if that light went out before it has to in the normal course.'[23]

In the spring of 1978 he was back in hospital and this time the operation was followed by pleurisy and four months elapsed before he was allowed home. He was now sixty-five but had no thought of retirement; as soon as he was well enough, he returned to his desk in the Institute. In addition to his contacts with Russian intellectuals, he saw old friends, who had remained communists, such as Sam Russell and Brian Simon; to them he confided his misgivings about the failure of the Brezhnev era to build on the hesitant reforms that Khruschev had introduced. He believed, as did the Eurocommunist wing of the CPGB, that the record of the past required to be set right, if a straighter course was to be followed in the future. For this reason he warmly welcomed an article that appeared in the *Morning Star* on the fortieth anniversary of the Hitler-Stalin pact. In this article Dennis Ogden, who had been the *Daily Worker* correspondent in Moscow in 1959, reminded his readers of 'the feelings of shock and bewilderment with which the pact had been greeted . . . the CPGB at first called for military victory over fascism,' before reluctantly accepting the Soviet verdict that it was an 'imperialist war'.[24] Stalin's aberration had been a special case; but in Maclean's view there was always a risk of going astray, so long as the Kremlin was dominated by men 'who had grown up with little knowledge of the outside world'.

It was this pervasive ignorance that his work at the Institute aimed to correct, substituting reasoned argument for vilification. He was also a stickler for accuracy; on one occasion when a Russian colleague blamed the USA for having forged NATO as an instrument of aggression, Maclean insisted that the originator of the alliance had been Ernie Bevin. On Russell's last visit in 1981 they had a detailed discussion of the defects of Brezhnev-Gromyko foreign policy, much of which was reproduced in an article in *Marxism Today*, entitled 'Goodbye to Detente?' Russell pointed out in this article that in the years following the Helsinki conference of 1975 'the situation, looked at from the point of view of the interests of the Soviet Union, has changed for the worse.' This deterioration was partly ascribed to the preponderant influence of the military upon Soviet policy, which meant that the USSR 'is continually adding to its own over-kill capacity ... with seriously harmful consequences'.[25] Such opinions, even if not widely shared in the USSR in 1981, clearly foreshadow the negotiating position later adopted by Gorbachov in US–Soviet discussions of arms control.

In July 1979 Mimsie married again; her second husband was a painter named Sanya Druchin, and both set their hearts on emigrating to the USA, taking with them Mimsie's daughter by her first marriage. Donald was especially devoted to this little granddaughter, the fourth in the line of Melindas, and affectionately known as Melindushka; their departure left him more lonely than ever. He now had two home-helps, one at his *dacha* and one of long-standing in Moscow, named Nadezhda. In the late summer of 1981 he had another three weeks in hospital, but at the turn of the year was still hoping to get some ski-ing at his *dacha*, finding that gentle movement on the level relieved his asthma. On 4th December 1982 there was a blaze of publicity, as Nadezhda took the unprecedented step of telephoning to British correspondents in Moscow to tell them that Maclean was dying and had been taken to hospital. Only the second part of this statement was true; it is probable that his illness was deliberately exaggerated to suit the needs of the GRU. One of their agents in London, Captain Anatoli Zotov, the Naval Attaché, had been expelled by the Foreign Office and was due to leave that weekend. Maclean's impending demise duly pushed Zotov's departure off the front pages of the English Sunday papers, as was presumably the intention.[26] Maclean, without knowing it, had performed his last service to the cause. That Christmas Fergus, now settled in Britain, came to Moscow to see his father for the last time. Early in 1983, Alan Maclean also paid a visit; he was seeing his elder brother for the first time since 1950; it was to be the last time.

Donald kept his wits and his composure and continued almost to the end to see students from IMEMO. Five days before his death on 6th March 1983 he agreed to see Mark Frankland, the *Observer* correspondent in Moscow, on the understanding that nothing said should be published whilst he was alive. It might have been thought that with death so near and all his family outside the USSR, he might make a last bid for rehabilitation in Britain by making sour comments on the country where he had spent his years of exile. If he was indeed tempted to dirty his nest before leaving it for good, it was a temptation that he resisted; he was determined to preserve to the end what he regarded as the consistent course of his life. All that he allowed himself was a wistful reference to Khruschev's famous speech of 1956 (still unpublished in the USSR) and an expression of hope that the judiciary would abandon the pending trial of six young Euro-communists, two of them connected with IMEMO. But this hope was balanced by insistence that he had no fear 'that Stalinism could return ... it wasn't offered as an admission of defeat. The unapologetic eyes warned against that ... Not once did he mention his past as a spy.'

It was, for a dying man, a display of great dignity, recalling better days; he had given his last press conference. 'He walked me to the lift on the landing as an ambassador might show a guest out of his office. He was crouched and walked very slowly, but his size was still impressive. He was wearing old man's slippers, the sides worn flat.'[27]

Maclean was cremated on 11th March in the grounds of the deconsecrated Donskoi monastery. His coffin was covered with red crepe. For most Russian funerals, the coffin would have remained open during the ceremony, exposing the face and folded hands. Donald's coffin was closed; to the end he was a very private man. The funeral was organised by his colleagues in IMEMO and they and the students made up most of the attendance of about one hundred and fifty. He was spared in death the presence of Philby and Blake, the best known of the remaining British spies in Moscow. Fergus, who was coming from England to collect the ashes, arrived too late, so his family was unrepresented. Solemn music was played by an organist and wreaths were laid, one of them with the message, 'Farewell, dear Donald Donaldovitch'. There was one minute's silence, as light snow fell. Richard Owen, the London *Times* correspondent, approached a Russian woman, who had tears in her eyes, and asked if she was aware that the dead man had betrayed his country. She refused to be drawn, saying only, 'He was a fine colleague and a good communist.'[28] *Isvestia* described him as 'a sensitive and sympathetic comrade' who had 'devoted all his conscious life to the high ideals of social progress and humanism, peace and international co-operation ...'

Donald Maclean left little behind him, except for his unpublished writings, some of which are in the hands of members of the CPGB. The furniture of his apartment was depicted by Mark Frankland:

'Apart from two small and possibly antique tables, the furniture was worn and utilitarian, brightened by woven rugs and blankets ... It was the sort of room an elderly Oxbridge don would feel at home in.'[29]

The pictures on the walls were reproductions of Van Gogh and Seurat. It was a different legacy from that of Anthony Blunt, who died two weeks later in London, leaving a genuine Poussin, valued at several hundred thousand pounds. Maclean's estate in Britain amounted to less than £5,000; either through inadvertence or unexampled generosity, he left it to Melinda.

There remained the question of disposal of Maclean's ashes in accordance with his wishes. From Fergus' earliest years his life had comprised episodes of battling with the British press. On this occasion he stole a march on them and arrived in England with the urn before they could catch up with him. He at once went to see the Vicar of Penn, the Reverend Oscar Muspratt, who at that date had already been vicar for over forty years and taken a keen interest in all members of the Maclean family. He carefully inspected the urn to assure himself that it bore no mark identifying it with the impious Soviet system; meanwhile he was also making up his mind about Fergus and came to the conclusion that the son had come to him as much from a sense of Christian commitment as from a sense of duty to his father's request.[30]

The vicar decided that he would hold a short burial service and read the lesson from *Corinthians*, chapter XIII, which includes the verses (in the New English Bible):

'Love keeps no score of wrongs, does not gloat over other men's sins, but delights in the truth.
There is nothing love cannot face, there is no limit to its faith, its hope and its endurance.'

Not all the vicar's parishioners approved his decision; but happily the days have passed when Englishmen in contention would dig up the remains of regicides or traitors.

It was no part of the original plan to carry out the ceremony after dark; this came about because heavy traffic in the late afternoon of 16th March, the day of the interment, delayed the arrival of Alan Maclean from London. All agreed that it was necessary to act before the media got wind of the event and turned it into black comedy. By the time the service had been completed it was dark outside and the little procession, consisting of the vicar, a sexton and the Macleans, was equipped with a lantern and electric torch, as it made its way round the west end of the church to reach the cemetery extension, which in mediaeval times had been a vineyard. Against an overgrown hedge stood the Celtic cross of granite, marking the grave of Sir Donald and Lady Maclean:

'We buried him darkly at dead of night . . .'

Sir John Moore would not have relished the distant echo.

Trinity Church, Penn, stands on high ground and its squat fifteenth-century tower looks out across a well-wooded landscape. A little way along the road is the ivy-clad 'Crown Inn'. The rural scene offers a striking contrast with that on which Donald had closed his eyes for the last time – the bustling city of Moscow, the self-assertive spikes of the Ukraina Hotel, which he had associated with Stalin, Lenin's tomb in Red Square . . . Had he in the final days remembered the undergraduate quip: 'The tomb of Donald Maclenin in red bakelite'? In Penn church, to show how far his ashes had come, there were the aristocratic brasses and hatchments of the Howe and Curzon families. Instead of the Asiatic features of Lenin, embalmed under glass,

'Side by side, their faces blurred,
The earl and countess lie in stone,
Their proper habits vaguely shown
As jointed armour, stiffened pleat . . .'[31]

Maclean had turned back at last from the long eastward journey that had begun half a century before; all those years he had pursued the ideological will-o'-the-wisp and it had led him a strange dance. In youth he had had a vision of a better world; what he had found in middle-life had been a worse one. Now he had come back from exile to the tranquility and tradition of the English countryside. In the end the aberrations of Marxism-Leninism had faded away; what remained were the ties of family and the kindly tolerance of the Church he had so long despised. Donald had come home.

Epilogue

Nobody who worked for any length of time alongside Donald Maclean (or indeed any other spy) can be free of the uneasy feeling that, if he had been more vigilant, he could have contributed to putting a stop to activities that were damaging to his country. It is true, of course, that a vital part of the art of seeing consists in prior knowledge of what we expect to see and this governs the way in which we interpret what passes before our eyes. Because we cannot think the unthinkable, certain things remain outside our field of vision. Those whom we have learned to trust continue to appear trustworthy. Despite such rationalisation, however, the uneasy feeling remains. When I find myself affected in this way, I sometimes recall two episodes, contrasting strongly one with the other, that bear on the vexed question of how the security of the state can be reconciled with harmonious co-operation among individuals serving the state, in such a way that the latter are not constantly looking over their shoulders, or wondering if their telephones are being tapped.

In the summer of 1948, some weeks before Maclean finally left the USA, there sailed from New York, *en route* to London, a deeply divided and unhappy group comprising three Soviet scientists, who had been sent to the USA to acquire technical data and equipment for the construction in the USSR of a penicillin factory.

The group, which was temporarily attached to AMTORG, the Soviet Trade Mission in New York, was headed by Dr N. M. Borodin and included two other scientists, named Utkin and Zeifman, of whom only the latter was a party member. Antagonism soon developed between Utkin and Zeifman and it was not long before the latter denounced the former to Borodin, accusing his colleague of having slandered the Soviet state. When Borodin showed himself reluctant to take this charge seriously and urged both men to get on with their real work, Zeifman went behind his back to the AMTORG political commissar. At this point Borodin himself began to come under suspicion, because he had failed to report the original denunciation. Soon all three were sent to London, from where Utkin was despatched to Moscow to be dealt with by the KGB. When orders came for Borodin to follow him, he decided to defect, having come to the conclusion that he could no longer support a system which not only permitted no criticism, but in the supposed interest of its security promoted delation and injustice.[1]

It would be simplistic to dismiss this story as just another example of the inefficiency and inhumanity of the Soviet system. The fact is that most state servants dealing with confidential matters have at some point found themselves at the unguarded level-crossing where national security can come in collision with what are normally regarded as the decencies of civilised behaviour. Any state system can become infected by suspicion in such a way that its security seems to some to require to be upheld at the cost of the personal insecurity of those operating the system. There is no call to elaborate here, since everyone is familiar with the confusion and distress (to use no stronger words) that followed upon the disclosures, whether true or invented, of the Soviet defector, Golitsyn, which in this country culminated in the inquisitorial methods adopted by Peter Wright with some encouragement from others. It is the business of security services to collect information, piece it together and draw whatever conclusions the proven facts may justify. The trouble is that pieces of information can form strange patterns and men's minds, even if free from the taint of ideology, are prone to interpret these patterns in the light of preconceived ideas and personal motivations that are even less defensible. It is not only in Soviet Missions that personal ambition or private vendetta can don the mantle of security. These considerations place a heavy responsibility on him who makes up his mind to cast the first stone.

I do not propose to cite an exact instance of the agonising confrontation at the level-crossing; but I can offer from my own experience a relatively minor example of the difficulty of balancing the demands of security against the human obligations that everyone owes to his or her colleagues. One of the lessons learnt by the Diplomatic Service from the disaster of Maclean and Burgess was that increased notice must be taken of irregularities in colleagues' behaviour and, in particular, homosexual tendencies. In 1962 this lesson was rammed home with the arrest for espionage of the homosexual, John Vassall, who had been the victim of blackmail in Moscow. A few years earlier, when I was serving in a European city, I became aware that a colleague who had previously been *en poste* there, was continuing to visit the city from time to time. His visits were not exactly furtive, but he did not advertise his presence and, although I knew him fairly well, he never seemed pleased to see me or willing to accept my hospitality. I gave this very little thought until one day I happened to see him (let us designate him X) in the company of a pretty, blonde telephone operator, who was one of the locally engaged staff of the British Mission in question. On the next occasion that I saw her I could not resist gently teasing her about the visits of X. She replied, 'Oh, it's not me he comes to see! It's my young brother.'

I now had to decide whether to take the matter further. I could not consult anyone else, because to do so would at once remove the decision from my hands. X's post was an important one located at one of the points of contact between East and West; he could become a valuable scalp for the KGB. On the other hand, he was level-headed and, as far as I knew, was fulfilling his duties to the satisfaction of his superiors. But I could not see the whole picture; for all I knew my report, if I were to make one, might fall into place in a pattern that would spell danger in the eyes of someone more centrally placed than I. Supposing my report were to be the first, however, its reception would depend in large measure on the subjectivity of those at the receiving end. My decision, therefore, could not turn upon my appraisal of one man's personality, but involved others, some of whom I scarcely knew. In the end I did nothing. I am glad to be able to add that X progressed in his career and in due course rose to the rank of Ambassador. It so happened that, before his death a few years ago, our paths very rarely crossed.

I do not draw any moral from this story; to this day I cannot be entirely sure that I made the right decision. I have related it in order to illustrate the point that the demands of security, if rigidly interpreted, can conflict with another imperative, namely that of maintaining the *esprit de corps* of a body of men and women who need to operate as a team. If they are to get the best results from their combined activity, they must trust one another. In doing so, they may from time to time make mistakes; their trust may be betrayed; but at least the team will not disintegrate in the way depicted in the cautionary tale of Dr Borodin and his colleagues. All who have worked in the Diplomatic Service know that there are happy and unhappy Embassies; the distinction has much more to do with mutual trust than with climate or scale of allowances.

It is this aspect that tends to be overlooked when there is a security failure and the media and their investigative journalists are out hunting for scapegoats. The press were right to take up the case of Maclean and Burgess, because complacency in the Foreign Office and toleration of what Crossman termed 'eccentricity' had gone too far. There was also 'unfinished business' in the half-hidden careers of Philby and Blunt that had to be brought into the light of day. The Diplomatic Service, which had withstood the brute impact of war, had not yet adjusted itself to the more insidious pressures of the Cold War. The virtues of sportsmanship, plain speaking and fair play, for which Englishmen had been famous in an earlier and happier epoch, did not equip them to meet the subtler challenges of ideology and deception. It was the case of Maclean and Burgess that taught the necessary lesson and, for this reason, deserves to be remembered.

Notes

Abbreviations: The following are used below:

BFPSS *British Foreign Policy Since Suez*: D. D. Maclean
       (Hodder & Stoughton 1970)
DBFP   Documents of British Foreign Policy
FBI   Federal Bureau of Investigation (Burgess & Maclean
       files)
FRUS   Foreign Relations of United States
HMSO   Her Majesty's Stationery Office
MPB   Maclean (Sir D.) Papers, Bodleian
MLP   Maclean (D. D.) Letters, Private
PRO   Public Record Office
USNA   United States National Archive

Prologue:

1 Trepper, L., *The Great Game* (Michael Joseph 1977), p. 409
2 Besançon, A. & Urban, G. in *Encounter*, May 1987
3 Hoare, G., *The Missing Macleans* (Cassell 1955)

Chapter 1

1 Connolly, C., *The Missing Diplomats* (Queen Anne Press 1952),
  p. 15
2 Cited by Winn, D. in *The Manipulated Mind* (Octagon Press
  1983), p. 40
3 *Ibid.*, p. 41
4 Straight, M., *After Long Silence* (Collins 1983), p. 71
5 MPB

6 Asquith, H., *Letters to a Friend* (First series), (G. Bless 1933), p. 122
7 MPB
8 Riddell, Lord, *Intimate Diary* (Gollancz 1933), p. 51
9 Eccles, J. R., *Cooperation in School Life* (privately printed in 1928). I owe this reference to Professor Brian Simon.
10 Greene, G., (ed.), *The Old School* (Cape 1934), ch. 1
11 Howarth, T. E., *Cambridge Between Two Wars*, (Collins 1978), p. 142
12 Auden, W. H., *Collected Shorter Poems*, '1929', (Faber 1950)
13 Interview with Lady Mary Dunn
14 Private information
15 Letter from Mr J. O. Roach

Chapter 2

1 Interview with Mr Nigel Clive
2 MPB
3 Spender, Sir S., *Journals: 1939–83* (Faber 1985), p. 24
4 Lawford, V. G., *Bound for Diplomacy* (John Murray 1963), pp. 141–2
5 Annan, Lord, review in *The Times Literary Supplement* of 11.2.72
6 Letter from Professor L. Elvin
7 Review in *Cambridge Left*, Winter 1933–4
8 Koestler, A., *The Invisible Writing* (Hutchinson 1969), p. 39
9 *Granta*, Cambridge, 8.11.33
10 *Ibid.*, 15.11.33
11 *The Silver Crescent*, Lent 1934
12 Nietzsche, F., 'Use and Abuse of History' in *Complete Works*, ed. O. Levy (1909–13)
13 *Granta*, Cambridge, 9.3.34
14 Ewart, G., *Poems and Songs* 'Election Song 1935', (Fortune Press, n.d.)
15 Poretsky, Elisabeth, *Our Own People* (Oxford Univ. Press 1969), p. 128
16 Straight, *op. cit.*, p. 102
17 Private information

Chapter 3

1 BFPSS, pp. 286–7
2 Wells, H. G., *Tono-Bungay* (Macmillan 1909), pp. 11–12

3 Lawford, *op. cit.*, p. 227
4 *Hansard*, 7.11.55 (HMSO)
5 Letter from Lady Grimond
6 Connolly, *op. cit.*, p. 19
7 Toynbee, P., in *The Observer* of 15.10.67
8 *Ibid.*
9 Spender, *op. cit.*, p. 215
10 Lawford, *op. cit.*, p. 268
11 Gladwyn, Lord, *Memoirs* (Weidenfeld & Nicolson 1972), p. 57
12 DBFP, 2nd series, vol. XVII, doc.84
13 *Ibid.*, doc.369
14 Cornford, John, in *Penguin New Writing*, (Penguin 1937)
15 Auden, *op. cit.*, 'Spain 1937'
16 BFPSS, p. 109
17 Poretsky, *op. cit.*, pp. 213–14
18 Moss, N., *The Man Who stole the Atom Bomb* (Grafton 1987), App. F
19 Maclean, Sir Fitzroy, *Take Nine Spies*, (Weidenfeld & Nicolson 1978), p. 237
20 Koestler, *op. cit.*, p. 22

Chapter 4

1 Shah, Idries, *Wisdom of the Idiots* (Octagon 1970), pp. 47–8
2 Maclean, Sir F., *op. cit.*, p. 237
3 Harvey, Lord, *Diplomatic Diaries, 1937–40* (Collins 1970), entry 24.9.38
4 BFPSS, p. 76
5 Letter from Mr V. G. Lawford
6 Interview with Sir Lees Mayall
7 Letter from Mr V. G. Lawford
8 I owe this insight to Professor D. Cameron Watt
9 Brook-Shepherd, G., *Stormy Petrels* (Collins 1977), p. 238
10 Koestler, *op. cit.*, p. 255
11 Hoare, *op. cit.*, p. 35
12 *Ibid.*, pp. 47–9
13 *Ibid.*, p. 59
14 Harvey, *op. cit.*, entry 23.5.40
15 Hoare, *op. cit.*, p. 48
16 Harvey, *op. cit.*, entry 9.6.40
17 Interview with Sir Roderick Barclay

18 Harvey, *op. cit.*, entry 22.6.40
19 Knightley, P., Interviews with Philby in *The Sunday Times* of 27.3.88
20 Brook-Shepherd, *op. cit.*, p. 185
21 FBI
22 Letter from Mr A. T. Wolton
23 Interview with Professor Anthony Blunt (1982)
24 Lamphere, R., *The FBI-KGB War* (Random House 1986), p. 234
25 Harvey, Lord, *Diplomatic Diaries, 1941–5* (Collins 1978), entry 13.10.42

Chapter 5

1 Letter from Mr G. Carey-Foster
2 Herken, G., *The Winning Weapon* (New York 1980), pp. 101–2
3 Truman, H. S., *Memoirs*, vol. I (New York 1955), p. 416
4 Report of Royal Commission, Ottawa
5 Balfour, Sir J., *Not Too Correct an Aureole* (M. Russell 1983), p. 113
6 Interview with Col. George Judd
7 Barclay, Sir R., *Bevin and the Foreign Office* (privately printed, 1975), p. 101
8 FRUS (1946) vol.I, pp. 960–3
9 *Ibid.*, p. 978
10 Dallin, D. J., *Soviet Espionage* (Oxford Univ. Press 1955), pp. 443–4. See also Wright, P., *Spycatcher* (New York 1987), p. 228
11 Letter from Sir Thomas Bromley
12 Report of Royal Commission, Ottawa
13 Interview with Mr Robin Denniston
14 Dallin, *op. cit.*, pp. 462–7
15 Interviews with Sir Patrick Reilly and others
16 Interview with Mr Walter Bell
17 Giles, F., in *The Sunday Times* of 6.1.80
18 PRO: FO 115 4258
19 PRO: FO 115 4313. See also FBI
20 FRUS: 1948, vol.I, p. 679
21 Cited in Page, B., Leitch, D. & Knightley, P., *Philby* (Sphere Books 1977), p. 226
22 Rosenberg, D. A., in *Journal of American History*, May 1979
23 FBI

24 Rosenberg, *op. cit.*
25 Gladwyn, Lord, in *The Sunday Times* of 11.11.79
26 Wiebes, C. & Zeeman, B., in *International Affairs*, vol.59, no.3 (1983)
27 *Ibid.*
28 FBI
29 Letter from Mr V. G. Lawford

Chapter 6

1 Hoare, *op. cit.*, p. 55
2 Muggeridge, M., *Like It Was* (Collins 1981), p. 299
3 PRO:FO 141 1339
4 Interview with Lady Luce and letter from Lady Robertson
5 Hayter, Sir W., *A Double Life* (Hamish Hamilton 1974), p. 83
6 Balfour, *op. cit.*, p. 114
7 Hoare, *op. cit.*, p. 56
8 Interviews with Sir Lees Mayall and the late Sir David Scott-Fox
9 USNA:811.2383/II–2248
10 USNA:811.2382/I–2149
11 Interview with Sir George Middleton
12 Philby, H. A. R., *My Silent War* (MacGibbon & Kee 1968), pp. 134–6
13 Toynbee, P., in *The Observer* of 15.10.67
14 Toynbee, P., this and subsequent quotes from his unpublished diary
15 Toynbee, P., in *The Observer* of 15.10.67
16 This and subsequent quotes from Toynbee's diary
17 Toynbee, P., in *The Observer* of 15.10.67
18 This and subsequent quote from Toynbee's diary
19 Interview with Mr Michael Maude (Hammond-Maude)
20 FBI
21 Hoare, *op. cit.*, p. 63
22 Toynbee, P., diary
23 *Ibid.*

Chapter 7

1 Hoare, *op. cit.*, p. 64
2 Jung, C. G., *Memories, Dreams, Reflections* (New York 1965), p. 124
3 *Ibid.*, p. 329

4 Interview with Sir G. Middleton and letter from Mr G. Carey-Foster
5 Letter from Lady Grimond
6 Connolly, *op. cit.*, p. 29
7 Interview with Lady Mary Dunn
8 Cited in Page, Leitch & Knightley, *op. cit.*, pp. 251
9 *Ibid.*, p. 252
10 *Ibid.*, p. 253
11 Rees, Goronwy, *A Chapter of Accidents* (Chatto & Windus 1972), p. 191
12 Interview with Sir G. Middleton
13 Hoare, *op. cit.*, p. 71
14 Letter from Mr G. Carey-Foster
15 *Hansard*, 7.11.55 (HMSO)
16 Letter from Sir John Curle
17 Letter from the late Sir Geoffrey Jackson
18 Hoare, *op. cit.*, p. 71
19 Interview with Mr Robert Kee
20 Interview with Mrs Philip Toynbee
21 Toynbee, P., in *The Observer* of 15.10.67
22 *Daily Worker* of 3. and 5.3.51
23 Muggeridge, *op. cit.*, p. 398
24 PRO:FO 371 92063
25 Henderson, Sir Nicholas, in BBC interview: 'The Twentieth Century Remembered'
26 Truman, H. S., *Memoirs*, vol.II (New York 1956), pp. 395–6
27 PRO:FO 371 90931
28 *Ibid.*
29 PRO:FO 371 90907

Chapter 8

1 Glees, A., *Secrets of the Service* (Cape 1987), p. 365
2 Lamphere, *op. cit.*, p. 228
3 Philby, H. A. R., *op. cit.*, p. 165
4 Boyle, A., *Climate of Treason* (Coronet 1980), pp. 317–18, 333–4
5 Philby, H. A. R., *op. cit.*, p. XIX
6 Interview with Lady Mary Dunn
7 Philby, H. A. R., *op. cit.*, p. 151
8 Newton, Verne, 'The Spy Who Came to Dinner', in *The Washingtonian* (Oct.1984)

9 Philby, H. A. R., *op. cit.*, p. 127
10 *Ibid.*, p. 155
11 Straight, *op. cit.*, p. 251
12 Interview with Prof. A. Blunt (1982)
13 Report of Royal Commission, Sydney
14 Petrov, V., article in *The People* of 18.9.55
15 Philby, H. A. R., *op. cit.*, p. 165
16 Toynbee, P., in *The Observer* of 15.10.67
17 Interview with Prof. A. Blunt (1982)
18 Private information
19 Interview with Prof. A. Blunt (1982)
20 FBI
21 Rees, *op. cit.*, p. 207
22 Private information
23 Letter from Sir Frederick Everson
24 Interview with Mr M. Maude
25 Interview with Sir Frederick Mason
26 Interview with Lady Mary Dunn
27 Connolly, *op. cit.*, p. 39
28 Letter from Sir G. Jackson
29 Letter from Sir J. Curle
30 Glees, *op. cit.*, pp. 362–3
31 Papers of Mr T. Driberg (Lord Bradwell), Christ Church, Oxford
32 Auden, *op. cit.*, 'The Voyage'
33 Private information

Chapter 9

1 Letter from Sir G. Jackson
2 Interview with the late Mr D. Footman (1980). See also Rees, *op. cit.*, p. 207
3 Letter from Mr G. Carey-Foster
4 PRO:FO 371 90931
5 *Hansard*, 7.11.55 (HMSO)
6 *Ibid.*
7 USNA:Embassy, London, box 238/350
8 *Ibid.*
9 FBI
10 *Ibid.*
11 *Ibid.*, quoting *The Jerusalem Post*
12 *Ibid.*

13 Connolly, *op. cit.*, pp. 49–50
14 Lehmann, J., *The Ample Proportion* (Eyre & Spottiswoode 1966), pp. 127–8
15 Petrov, V., in *The People* of 25.9.55; but not mentioned in his statutory declaration of 29.3.56
16 Hoare, *op. cit.*, pp. 16–17
17 Ustinov, P., *Five Plays* (Heinemann 1965), Act III
18 Hoare, *op. cit.*, p. 81
19 Private information
20 Hoare, *op. cit.*, p. 27
21 Cadogan, Sir Alexander, unpublished diaries, Churchill College: ACAD I/22
22 *Hansard*, 7.11.55 (HMSO)
23 Cadogan diaries, *op. cit*
24 Hoare, *op. cit.*, p. 80
25 Hoare, *op. cit.*, p. 89
26 *Ibid.*
27 Private information
28 Interview with Mr R. Kee
29 MacColl, R., in *The Daily Express* of 25.9.53
30 Hoare, *op. cit.*, p. 103
31 *Ibid.*, *op. cit.*, p. 130

Chapter 10

1 Driberg, T., in *The Daily Mail* of 2.3.58
2 Medvedev, R. in *The Times* of 31.5.83
3 Interview with Mr R. Denniston
4 Letter from Mr Nigel Burgess
5 Spender, *op. cit.*, p. 212
6 Driberg papers, Christ Church, Oxford
7 Spender, *op. cit.*, p. 212
8 Hyde, H. M., *George Blake Superspy* (Constable 1987), p. 145
9 Brodsky, J. in *The Times Literary Supplement* of 30.1.87
10 Driberg papers, Christ Church, Oxford
11 MPL
12 Interview with Mr S. Russell
13 Page, Leitch & Knightley, *op. cit.*, p. 324
14 Frankland, M., in *The Observer* of 13.3.83
15 Owen, R., *Letters from Moscow* (Gollancz 1985), p. 14
16 MPL

17 Philby, Eleanor, *The Spy I Loved* (Hamish Hamilton 1968), p. 75
18 Driberg, T., *Ruling Passions* (Cape 1977), pp. 229–30
19 MPL
20 *Ibid.*
21 *Ibid.*
22 Driberg papers, Christ Church, Oxford
23 Sutherland, D., *The Fourth Man* (Secker and Hamburg 1980), pp. 131–3
24 Knightley, P., Interview in *The Sunday Times* of 3.4.88
25 Toynbee, P., in *The Observer* of 15.10.67
26 Letter from Mr N. Burgess

Chapter 11

1 Philby, E., *op. cit.*, pp. 81–2
2 *Ibid.*, p. 119
3 *Ibid.*, p. 162
4 *Ibid.*, p. 169
5 Interview with Mr R. Denniston
6 Page, Leitch & Knightley, *op. cit.*, p. 269n
7 Philby, E., *op. cit.*, p. 158
8 Interview with Mr S. Russell
9 Medvedev, R., in *The Times* of 31.5.83
10 *Ibid.*
11 Yevtushenko, Y., *Selected Poems* (Penguin 1962), 'Talk'
12 Letter from Registrar, University College, London
13 Gilbert, M., *Sharansky* (Macmillan 1986) pp. 17–19
14 Interview with Dr Vasily Istratov of Moscow University
15 Philby, E., *op. cit.*, p. 116
16 Interview with Dr V. Istratov
17 BFPSS, p. 72
18 *Ibid.*, p. 22
19 *Ibid.*, p. 156
20 *Ibid.*, p. 254
21 *Ibid.*, Foreword
22 Interview with Sir L. Mayall
23 MLP
24 Ogden, D., in *The Morning Star* of 23.8.79
25 Russell, S., in *Marxism Today* of 24.6.81
26 *The Observer* of 5.12.82
27 Frankland, M., in *The Observer* of 13.3.83

28 Owen, *op. cit.*, pp. 73–4
29 Frankland, M., in *The Observer* of 13.3.83
30 Interview with the Rev. Oscar Muspratt
31 Larkin, Philip, *The Whitsun Weddings* (Faber 1964), 'An Arundel Tomb'

Epilogue:

1 Borodin, N. M., *One Man in His Time* (Constable 1955), ch. XX

Index

Acheson, Dean, 124, 148–9
Alexandria, 97, 111
Allen, Sir Denis, 74, 80
Andropov, Yuri, 6, 162, 179, 181
Angell, Sir Norman, 56
Angleton, James, 129
Anglican Church, 9, 18, 23, 190
Annan, Lord, 25
Anti-Semitism, 163, 181
Asquith, H. H., 10, 11, 18
Asquith, Margot, 11, 40
Astor, Hon. David, 101
Attlee, Clement, 72, 74, 123–4, 182
Auden, W. H., 14, 17, 26, 47, 138, 143, 150
Austen, Jane, 143, 165
Austria, 74–5, 86, 144, 160

Bailey, Felicity, *see* Rumbold
Baldwin, Stanley, 5, 9, 23, 45
Balfour, Sir John, 3, 72
Barclay, Sir Colville, 52
Barclay, Sir Roderick, 60, 62, 70, 74
Barrie, Sir James, 23, 27
Beaverbrook, Lord, 145
Beirut, 96, 174
Beith, Sir John, 160
Bell, Julian, 29
Bell, Katherine, 102
Bell, Walter, 79, 102
Bentley, Elizabeth, 76
Beria, Laurenti, 83, 164, 168–9, 178
Berlin, 38, 40, 51, 63, 83, 86–7, 89, 93, 131
Bernadotte, Folke, 92

Bernal, J. D., 25
Besançon, Alain, 4
Beveridge, Sir William, 39
Bevin, Ernest, 80, 85, 91, 124, 135, 186
Blake, George, 5, 35, 156, 165, 177, 187
Blake, Ida, 177
Blake, William, 32
Bland, Sir Nevile, 157
Blum, Léon, 45
Blunt, Anthony, 24–5, 33, 36, 43, 66–7, 90, 114, 130, 132–4, 137–8, 162, 188, 194
B-29 bomber, 75, 83
Bonham-Carter, Cressida, *see* Ridley
Bonham-Carter, Laura, *see* Grimond
Bonham-Carter, Violet, 40–1
Borodin, Dr N. M., 191–3
Bourke, Sean, 165, 177
Bowen, Elizabeth, 151
Boyle, Andrew, 128
Bradley, Gen. Omar, 122
Brewster, Senator, 149
Brezhnev, Leonid, 6, 162, 179, 185–6
Britain, 3, 19, 33, 36, 43, 48–9, 52, 55–6, 71–2, 75, 80–1, 92, 94, 98–9, 115–6, 123–4, 130, 154–5, 168, 171, 179, 180, 183, 187–8
British Admiralty, 43, 111, 158
British Commonwealth, 74, 116, 123–4, 183
British Communist Party (CPGB), 17, 25, 35, 67, 152, 185, 188
British Consular Service, 53, 99, 100
British Diplomatic Service, 1, 3, 15, 36, 39, 40, 42–3, 53, 69, 74, 99, 106, 112,